ABANDON SHIP

THE REAL STORY OF THE SINKINGS
IN THE FALKLANDS WAR

ABANDON
SHIP

PAUL BROWN

OSPREY PUBLISHING
Bloomsbury Publishing Plc
Kemp House, Chawley Park, Cumnor Hill, Oxford OX2 9PH, UK
29 Earlsfort Terrace, Dublin 2, Ireland
1385 Broadway, 5th Floor, New York, NY 10018, USA
E-mail: info@ospreypublishing.com
www.ospreypublishing.com

OSPREY is a trademark of Osprey Publishing Ltd

First published in Great Britain in 2021

© Paul Brown, 2021

ISBN: HB 978 1 4728 4643 3; PB 978 1 4728 4644 0; eBook 978 1 4728 4642 6; ePDF 978 1 4728 4640 2; XML 978 1 4728 4641 9

21 22 23 24 25   10 9 8 7 6 5 4 3 2 1

Maps by www.bounford.com
Index by Angela Hall

Typeset by Deanta Global Publishing Services, Chennai, India
Printed and bound in Great Britain by CPI (Group) UK Ltd, Croydon, CR0 4YY

Imperial War Museums Collections
Many of the photos in this book come from the huge collections of IWM (Imperial War Museums) which cover all aspects of conflict involving Britain and the Commonwealth since the start of the twentieth century. These rich resources are available online to search, browse and buy at www.iwm.org.uk/collections. Imperial War Museums www.iwm.org.uk

Osprey Publishing supports the Woodland Trust, the UK's leading woodland conservation charity.

MIX
Paper from
responsible sources
FSC® C020471

To find out more about our authors and books visit www.ospreypublishing.com. Here you will find extracts, author interviews, details of forthcoming events and the option to sign up for our newsletter.

Contents

List of Maps

List of Illustrations

The Argentinian cruiser ARA *General Belgrano*. (Wikipedia, public domain)

The death throes of *General Belgrano* after being torpedoed by HMS *Conqueror*. (*La Nación*/Wikipedia, public domain)

The memorial at Ushuaia to those lost in *General Belgrano*. (Paul Brown)

The nuclear-powered submarine HMS *Conqueror*. (© Michael Lennon)

HMS *Sheffield* was a Type 42 destroyer, completed in 1975. (Crown Copyright – Open Government Licence)

On 4 May *Sheffield* was struck by an Exocet missile fired by an Argentinian Super Étendard jet. (The National Archives, ref. DEFE25/555)

An Argentine Navy Super Étendard, two of which attacked *Sheffield*. (Don Montgomery/US Defense Imagery DN-SC-91-02304)

The abandoned *Sheffield*, seen here, was eventually taken in tow by the frigate HMS *Yarmouth*. (The National Archives, ref. DEFE25/555)

The frigate HMS *Arrow* providing boundary cooling to *Sheffield*. (The National Archives, ref. DEFE25/555)

Two Sea Harriers of the Royal Navy, in the low-visibility paint livery used during the Falklands conflict. (US Defense Imagery, DN-SC-87-05770)

A Douglas A4 Skyhawk of the Argentine Navy, on display at the Argentine Naval Headquarters in Buenos Aires. (aeroprints. com/Wikimedia Commons, public domain)

HMS *Ardent* was a Type 21 frigate, completed in 1977. (Crown Copyright – Open Government Licence)

The abandoned HMS *Ardent* in San Carlos Water after the final two Argentine air attacks. (© IWM FKD 144)

The fire rages aft in *Ardent*. (© IWM FKD 146)

HMS *Antelope* was a Type 21 frigate, completed in 1975. (Crown Copyright – Open Government Licence)

The explosion of one of the two 1,000lb bombs lodged in the hull of *Antelope*. (Photo by Martin Cleaver/Pool/Central Press/Stringer/Getty Images)

HMS *Antelope* afloat at dawn on 24 May 1982. (© IWM FKD 71)

SS *Atlantic Conveyor* in dry dock at Devonport dockyard. (The National Archives, ref. DEFE69/1338)

The wreck of *Antelope* in Ajax Bay. (© IWM FKD 192)

The abandoned hulk of *Atlantic Conveyor* after the Exocet attack. (The National Archives, ref. DEFE69/1338)

HMS *Coventry* was a Type 42 destroyer, completed in 1978. (US Defense Imagery DN-SC-87-0584)

Coventry listing to port after being hit by three 1,000lb bombs. (© IWM FKD 1265)

Two Sea King helicopters hover over the upturned hull of *Coventry*. (© IWM FKD 1274)

The landing ship RFA *Sir Galahad* leaving Devonport for the Falklands on 6 April. (Author's Collection)

Ships' boats bring ashore the survivors from *Sir Galahad*. (© IWM FKD 2126)

Sir Galahad on fire after being bombed by Argentine Air Force Skyhawks. (© IWM FKD 359)

The stern of Sir *Galahad* after the attack. (The National Archives, ref. DEFE69/920)

RFA *Sir Tristram* aboard the heavy lift ship MV *Dan Lifter*. (Wikimedia Commons, public domain)

HMS *Broadsword* returns to Plymouth after the Falklands campaign. (Author's Collection)

The monument to the Malvinas conflict at Ushuaia. (Paul Brown)

The Liberation Memorial at Stanley. (Alex Petrenko, panoramio/Wikipedia, CC BY-SA 3.0)

Preface

After the Falklands conflict a tranche of official documents was released, giving more insight into the actions and events of that brief period in 1982 when the nation was at war. Many of the documents were heavily censored through redactions, and others were kept under wraps as top secret, so that a full understanding of those events could not be gained. Journalists and MPs pursued the facts behind the controversial sinking of the Argentinian cruiser *General Belgrano*, helped by a senior civil servant who was subsequently arrested, and gradually the full story emerged. Senior officers who had been engaged in the conflict published their memoirs, but official secrets restrictions meant that little new information emerged on vital questions about the sinkings, either because some relevant documents were still classified as top secret or because sensitive knowledge held by individuals who had signed the Official Secrets Act could not be disclosed if it was deemed to be damaging to the national interest. More recently, especially after the passing of the Freedom of Information Act in 2000, some documents have been declassified and others have had many of the redactions lifted. In the case of HMS *Sheffield*, survivors and families of men lost pressed for the full details of what happened, and in 2017, for the first time, a largely unredacted version of the board of inquiry report was released and the true story emerged.

Still, there remained many unanswered questions, and apart from in *Sheffield*'s case, there were big redactions in the released versions of the official reports into the losses of ships during the conflict. In the case of HMS *Ardent*, even a heavily redacted version of the official report into her loss had not been released. Through freedom of information requests made by the author, most of the facts are now available, many of which are published for the first time in this book. As well as a wealth of previously unpublished detail about the events leading to the sinking of six British ships, there are startling disclosures about the reasons for the loss of *Ardent* and *Atlantic Conveyor*.

Disclosures requested by the author under the Freedom of Information Act were in some cases refused under the provisions of the act. Examples of such information included that which would endanger the physical or mental health of any individual, e.g. graphic details of the way in which a crewman died, which would be distressing to survivors who bore witness and relatives and friends of the victim; sensitive personal information about survivors; witness statements, which are withheld so that witnesses can speak freely knowing that their evidence will not be disclosed within their lifetimes; and information that would prejudice the capability, effectiveness or security of any relevant forces.

The accounts given in chapters 3–8 of this book (relating to the sinking of British ships) are based mainly on the board of inquiry reports and associated correspondence and the first-hand reports of those present (given for example in books that they published or in oral testimonies now archived in the Imperial War Museum). In the case of chapter 2 (the sinking of *General Belgrano*) official reports requested from the Argentine Navy were not made available, and the narrative is largely based on first-hand testimonies, Foreign and Commonwealth Office reports on the incident, the HMS *Conqueror* Report of Proceedings, and information revealed in books by Stuart Prebble and Mike Rossiter. The author has drawn conclusions about the reasons for the losses, which in some cases deviate from, or add to, those given in the board of inquiry reports. The first chapter provides an overview of key events in the conflict, whilst the final chapter draws broad conclusions from chapters 2–8 and identifies lessons learned.

Grateful thanks are due to the staff of The National Archives and the Ministry of Defence Freedom of Information Records and

Information Rights teams for their help in providing many of the documents on which this book is based, and to the senior officers present who published their accounts of the conflict. I would also like to thank my publisher at Osprey, Marcus Cowper, for his encouragement and helpful suggestions, my production editor, Gemma Gardner, for her attention to detail and bringing the book to production, and John Osmond (who served during the conflict), for discussions on fire control systems, weapons and sensors.

I

Going to War

The Falklands conflict came at a good time for the Royal Navy, some might say. Prolonged periods of peace are not always good news for the armed forces. Whilst few would want to be accused of war-mongering or welcome going to war, especially those who had experienced it, the attrition of resources in peacetime defence budgets meant reduced capability, fewer personnel and weaker promotion prospects. In the days of the sailing navy most of the fleet would be laid up, with many officers finding themselves 'on the beach' with only half-pay and no prospects. In the steel navy things were different, with more job security and a bigger active fleet during peacetime. In the post-war era, the Cold War, with its ever-present Soviet threat, provided a buffer, and the fleet was larger than it otherwise would have been, despite there being no direct combat. But as defence reviews came and went, the Navy got smaller and smaller.

The 1981 defence review was no exception, and was particularly brutal for the Navy, which would bear 75 per cent of the cuts. The United Kingdom faced a severe economic downturn, at a time when the USSR was continuing to build up its armed forces. The architect of the review was John Nott, the new Conservative defence secretary, who decided to place emphasis on ground and air forces and slashed the size of the future fleet, which would concentrate on its NATO anti-submarine role. The brand-new aircraft carrier *Invincible* would be sold to Australia. The assault ships *Intrepid* and *Fearless* would be withdrawn without replacement. Nine of the Navy's 59 escorts would be decommissioned, from the County, Leander and Rothesay classes, whilst others would be placed in reserve in the standby squadron, which was still declared as part of Britain's NATO commitment. Plans for a new class of air-defence destroyers were abandoned. With Trident set to replace the Polaris inter-continental ballistic missiles, greater reliance was once again to be placed on the strategic nuclear deterrent as the counter to the Soviet threat, together with an increased nuclear-powered attack submarine fleet, which would expand from ten to 17 boats, albeit at the expense of conventional submarine numbers.[1] The ice patrol ship *Endurance*, the Navy's only regular presence in the Falkland Islands and Antarctica, would be paid off, as would four Royal Fleet Auxiliaries. The cuts meant that parts of the Navy's infrastructure could be rationalized: Chatham and Gibraltar dockyards would be closed, whilst Portsmouth would be downgraded from a major dockyard to a much smaller fleet repair and maintenance organization. There would be a phased redundancy programme for Royal Navy personnel, with a total cut of between 8,000 and 10,000 personnel (about 13 per cent of the total) and large cuts in the dockyards' workforces.

On Friday 2 April 1982, Portsmouth dockyard workers arrived for work in the morning and many received their redundancy notices, part of cuts that would reduce the workforce there from 6,900 to 1,300. Ironically, on the same day, Argentina invaded the Falkland Islands, and unlimited overtime was immediately instituted in the dockyard to prepare ships for a task force which would be sent south to recapture the islands. The redundancy notices were withdrawn as the workforce set about preparing the aircraft carriers *Hermes*, which was undergoing a dockyard-assisted maintenance period, and *Invincible*, which was having operational defects put right whilst her crew were on Easter leave. Over that weekend aircraft were flown onto the two carriers as they were stored, loaded with armaments and fuelled, and the essential maintenance tasks were hastily completed. On Monday 5 April they sailed from the port on the 8,000-mile passage to the South Atlantic.[2] In Devonport,

Chatham and Gibraltar other ships were being hurriedly equipped for the task force, with the frigates *Alacrity* and *Antelope* sailing from Devonport, and *Yarmouth* and *Broadsword* from Gibraltar, on the same day that the carriers left Portsmouth, and many other ships were to follow.

The Falklands conflict took most people by surprise, although tensions between the United Kingdom and Argentina over sovereignty of the islands had recently escalated after two centuries of disputed ownership. The islands had first been sighted by a number of navigators in the 16th century, but the first British landing there was made in 1690 by Captain John Strong, of HMS *Welfare*, who named the strait between the two main islands Falkland Sound, in honour of Lord Falkland, Treasurer of the Navy. The islands offshore of South America had been confirmed as Spanish in the 1713 Treaty of Utrecht, but the French settled there in what they called les îles Malouines in 1764 and the colony was claimed for France, a step which brought strong protests from the Spanish. In the following year Captain John Byron of the Royal Navy claimed the islands for King George III, as the Falkland Islands, and in 1766 a British settlement was established on West Falkland. However, in 1767 the French accepted Spanish claims to the territory and their colony on East Falkland was handed over. In 1770 the small British marine garrison at Port Egmont was forced by the Spaniards to leave. Intensive negotiations between the two countries resulted in Britain returning to Port Egmont in 1771, but Spain subsequently reserved the right to sovereignty and the British settlement was abandoned in 1774, despite continued British claims to the islands.

The islands remained as the Spanish colony of Islas Malvinas until Argentina, which had achieved independence from Spain in 1816, laid claim to them. An Argentinian colony was established and a governor appointed, leading to protests by Britain in 1829, which reasserted its claims to sovereignty. In 1831 a dispute over the arrest of American sealers accused of poaching led USS *Lexington* to intervene and destroy fortifications at Puerto Soledad. The Americans declared the islands free of sovereignty before sailing away. In 1832 an Argentinian garrison landed in an attempt to re-establish Argentinian sovereignty in defiance of the British claims. HMS *Clio* and *Tyne* arrived under the command of Captain John James Onslow and evicted the Argentinian garrison with no loss of life, and reasserted British claims to the islands. The civilian population was invited to stay, and most did, to be joined by Scottish colonists who arrived to establish sheep farms after the islands were declared a crown colony in 1841.[3]

Argentina continued to lobby for the possession of the Falklands/Malvinas with varying degrees of intensity. In the 1960s the lobbying became particularly intense and there were also a number of unofficial and official incursions by small groups of civilian and military Argentines. In 1965 the United Nations passed a resolution specifying the islands as a colonial problem and called on Britain and Argentina to find a peaceful solution. Talks continued, on and off, for the next 17 years, with Britain showing some signs of flexibility in its stance but insisting that any solution had to meet with the approval of the Falkland Islanders. In October 1975, the British government tasked Lord Shackleton (son of the Antarctic explorer Sir Ernest Shackleton) with an economic survey of the Falkland Islands. The Argentinian government reacted furiously and refused permission for Lord Shackleton to travel via Argentina. Later the ship transporting Shackleton to the islands, the RRS *Shackleton*, was fired upon by the Argentinian destroyer ARA *Almirante Storni*. In 1976 Argentina set up a scientific base on Southern Thule in the South Sandwich Islands and stayed put despite diplomatic protests by the UK. This was a precursor to the South Georgia operation of March 1982. In late 1980 the Falkland Islanders rejected the one remaining solution of lease-back for a fixed period. They considered themselves British and saw no advantage from Argentinian control.

Amid economic turmoil and domestic unrest in Argentina new leaders came to the forefront of the military junta, which had gained power in 1976, and General Leopoldo Galtieri, commander-in-chief of the army, became president of the country in December 1981. Argentina was experiencing 13 per cent unemployment and 130 per cent annual inflation. The 'disappeared' of Argentina comprised many thousands of civilians abducted, tortured, imprisoned, or murdered. Popular sentiment that the 'Malvinas' were part of Argentina was whipped up. Diplomatic negotiations were ramped up, but the UK did not expect the Argentines to invade. Admiral Jorge Anaya, head of the navy, encouraged a military solution to the Falklands issue, and the subsequent invasion can be explained as a diversion to distract Argentines from poor economic conditions and harsh military rule. The Argentines did not expect the UK to retaliate and try to take back the islands. If there was to be a conflict, US and European military analysts at the time predicted that Argentina had a good chance of winning.

The first episode in the conflict started on 19 March 1982 when a party of about 41 scrap metal workers and some service personnel arrived at Leith, South Georgia, aboard the Argentine Navy transport *Bahía Buen Suceso* and raised the Argentinian flag. They came on the pretext that they would salvage scrap metal from the derelict whaling station at Grytviken, but their presence was provocative. In response, the ice patrol ship *Endurance* sailed from Port Stanley, the capital of the Falkland Islands, for South Georgia on 20 March, carrying two Wasp helicopters and her own Royal Marines detachment of 12 men, and arrived at Grytviken on 23 March to monitor the Argentinian activity. On the following day the Argentine Navy sent a corvette to take up station between South Georgia and the Falklands, in order to intercept *Endurance* if she succeeded in taking off the Argentines at Leith. The latter received more direct support the next day with the arrival of a party of Argentinian marines who landed at Leith from the naval transport *Bahía Paraíso*.

On 26 March a squadron of Argentinian warships, led by the aircraft carrier *Veinticinco de Mayo*, sailed for exercises with the Uruguayan Navy. Aboard the landing ship *Cabo San Antonio* was a marine infantry battalion, whilst the destroyer *Santísima Trinidad* had embarked a marine commando unit. It was on that day that the Argentinian junta made the decision to invade the Falklands in Operation *Azul*, targeting 1 April for the landings, a date that would be put back by 24 hours because of bad weather. In view of the escalating situation the nuclear-powered attack submarine *Spartan* was ordered on 29 March to embark stores and weapons at Gibraltar for deployment to the South Atlantic, and her sister ship *Splendid* was ordered to deploy from Faslane the following day. Rear Admiral John 'Sandy' Woodward, flag officer of the Royal Navy's First Flotilla, was at Gibraltar exercising with 16 destroyers and frigates, and was ordered to prepare plans for the deployment of a task group to the South Atlantic. On 31 March the UK government received intelligence of the planned invasion and the first sea lord, Admiral of the Fleet Sir Henry Leach, was instructed to prepare a task force to be sent south whilst diplomatic attempts to achieve a peaceful resolution continued. *Endurance* was ordered to return to Port Stanley after landing a party of 22 marines at Grytviken to protect the British Antarctic Survey personnel and maintain watch on Leith.[4]

The Argentinian assault on the Falkland Islands started at 03.00 on 2 April when the submarine *Santa Fe* landed 20 commandos to secure a beachhead at Stanley. Eighty commandos landed from the destroyer *Santísima Trinidad* and assaulted Government House and the empty Royal Marine barracks. After a brief resistance by the Royal Marines at Government House, the governor Sir Rex Hunt surrendered to the superior force. At 06.30 the main force of Argentinian marines disembarked from the landing ship *Cabo San Antonio* to help secure the airport and the harbour area. The aircraft carrier *Veinticinco de Mayo*, with 1,500 army troops on board, remained just outside Stanley harbour. Meanwhile Argentinian troops had landed by helicopter on South Georgia Island: the outnumbered Royal Marines shot down an Argentinian Puma helicopter and slightly damaged the corvette *Guerrico* before surrendering. On Sunday 4 April the nuclear-powered attack submarine *Conqueror* sailed from Faslane for the South Atlantic and on the following day the vanguard of the task force, including the aircraft carriers *Hermes* and *Invincible*, sailed from the UK, and was soon followed by more ships. On 9 April the requisitioned P&O liner *Canberra* sailed from Southampton carrying the 3rd Commando Brigade (3 Commando) under the command of Brigadier Julian Thompson.

Map 1: The deployment of the British task force to the Falklands, 1982

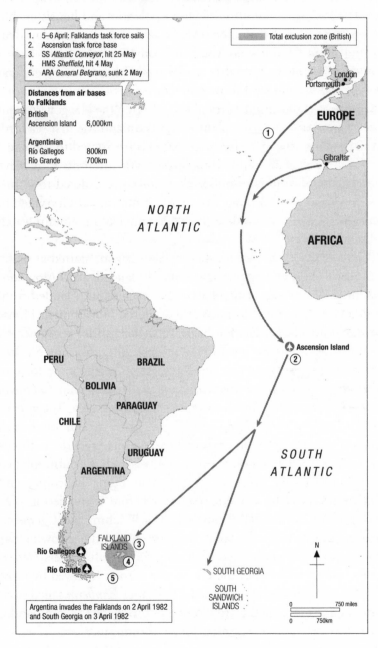

1. 5–6 April: Falklands task force sails
2. Ascension task force base
3. SS *Atlantic Conveyor*, hit 25 May
4. HMS *Sheffield*, hit 4 May
5. ARA *General Belgrano*, sunk 2 May

Total exclusion zone (British)

Distances from air bases to Falklands

British
Ascension Island 6,000km

Argentinian
Río Gallegos 800km
Río Grande 700km

London
Portsmouth

EUROPE

Gibraltar

NORTH ATLANTIC

AFRICA

PERU   **BRAZIL**

BOLIVIA

PARAGUAY

CHILE

URUGUAY

ARGENTINA

Ascension Island

SOUTH ATLANTIC

FALKLAND ISLANDS

Río Gallegos

Río Grande

SOUTH GEORGIA

SOUTH SANDWICH ISLANDS

N

Argentina invades the Falklands on 2 April 1982 and South Georgia on 3 April 1982

0   750 miles

0   750km

The Argentines used the period between invasion and the earliest likely date of British return to reinforce the islands both in supplies and in building up troop levels to approximately 11,000, as well as constructing defences. The airfield at Stanley was secured and warning radars set up. A significant garrison was established at Goose Green on the west side of East Falkland and an improvised air base was created on Pebble Island.

On the day of the invasion, many of the British destroyers and frigates involved in the large training exercise Exercise *Springtrain*, off Gibraltar under Rear Admiral Woodward, were ordered south. They were joined by *Hermes* and *Invincible*, carrying Sea Harrier fighters and helicopters, additional destroyers and frigates from the UK, as well as amphibious ships, Royal Fleet Auxiliary tankers and stores ships, and merchant ships that were taken up from trade for use as troopships, transports, salvage tugs and repair ships.

There were also the three nuclear-powered submarines to cover the surface ships and, when later stationed just off the Argentinian mainland coast, give early warning of air raids launched from mainland bases. In overall command of the South Atlantic Task Force, Commander-in-Chief Fleet Admiral Sir John Fieldhouse was

Command Structure for the South Atlantic Task Force

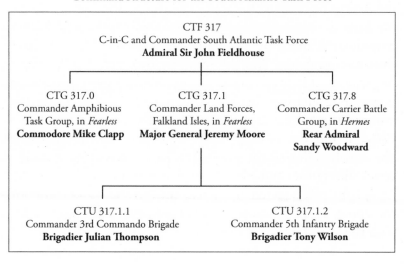

based at his headquarters at Northwood near London. Woodward commanded the carrier task group (also known as the carrier battle group) while Commodore Mike Clapp was in command of the ships of the amphibious task group. The Royal Marines of 3 Commando would be backed up by the 5th Infantry Brigade (5 Brigade) under Brigadier Tony Wilson, and Major General Jeremy Moore would take overall command of the land forces.

On 11 April a small group of British ships led by the destroyer *Antrim* left Ascension Island with Royal Marines and SAS troops on board to recapture South Georgia, which was achieved by 26 April. The Argentinian submarine *Santa Fe*, which had been re-supplying the Argentinian garrison on the island, was abandoned there by her crew and captured by the British forces following an attack by helicopters from *Antrim*, *Plymouth*, *Brilliant* and *Endurance*. The UK declared a 200-nautical-mile maritime exclusion zone around the Falkland Islands on 12 April and this was extended to a total exclusion zone on 30 April, which then covered aircraft and ships of all nations. It was on this latter day that the carrier task group entered the exclusion zone.

On 1 May Special Boat Squadron and Special Air Service troops were inserted on East and West Falkland. On the same day, Stanley was attacked by both Royal Navy and RAF aircraft, and the Argentines reacted with air raids on the warships of the task force. At the same time the Argentines were trying to conduct a co-ordinated attack by two groups of warships. One was led by their aircraft carrier and the other by their sole cruiser *General Belgrano*, an elderly ex-American ship. Meanwhile British nuclear-powered submarines had been trying to track both of these groups. The submarine *Conqueror* made contact with *General Belgrano* and her escorts, reporting this to fleet headquarters. She closely followed the group and later received permission to attack the cruiser outside the total exclusion zone. On 2 May *Conqueror* manoeuvred to attack, firing three straight-running torpedoes. Two hit, and the *General Belgrano* sank within an hour with the loss of over 320 lives.

On 4 May Sea Harriers attacked the Port Stanley and Goose Green air strips. The Argentines clearly wanted to avenge the loss of their cruiser and to do so they used the most capable weapon in their armoury, the air-launched Exocet missile carried by Super Étendard jets from a mainland base. The jets approached the task group at low level before going to higher altitude to gain radar contact on British ships. One ship was selected as a target and, despite detection of the jets by ships in the group, the Exocet missile found the destroyer *Sheffield*. The missile hit the ship centrally, causing widespread disruption and fires, and 20 deaths. *Sheffield* had to be abandoned and sank a few days later.

On 9 May two Sea Harriers attacked the Argentinian intelligence-gathering trawler *Narwal* operating within the exclusion zone. The crew abandoned ship and she later sank. Two days later the frigate *Alacrity* sank the Argentinian transport *Islas de los Estados* in Falkland Sound. On 12 May 12 Argentinian Skyhawks attacked the frigate *Brilliant* and destroyer *Glasgow*: two were shot down and a third crashed into the sea trying to avoid Sea Wolf missiles fired by *Brilliant*. *Glasgow* suffered damage from a bomb passing directly through her hull without exploding: this put her out of action for three days as temporary repairs were effected. On the same day the requisitioned liner *Queen Elizabeth 2* left Southampton with 5 Brigade, including mainly Gurkhas and Welsh Guards, aboard.

On 7 May the main amphibious task group set sail from Ascension Island for the Falklands. On 18 May the British Cabinet gave approval for amphibious landings, because the diplomatic negotiations brokered by the Americans and the United Nations had broken down. At an early point in the planning it became clear that a landing on East Falkland was desirable for several reasons, not least it being a little further from Argentinian air bases than West Falkland and also where the main occupying Argentinian forces were established. A number of options for the landing beach were considered, but San Carlos emerged as the best choice because its separation from Stanley gave the best chance of successful landing and build-up of troops. A further factor was the landlocked topography of the inlet, giving a degree of defence against Argentinian air attack. The amphibious force included two assault ships, five landing ships and a number of requisitioned merchant ships including the liner *Canberra*. These carried the landing force, which was formed of most of 3 Commando, largely consisting of Royal Marines and Parachute Regiment troops. The amphibious group also had a number of destroyers and frigates whose tasks included close escort of the amphibious force, naval gunfire support for the troops once landed and diversionary attacks to deceive the Argentines.

The force moved forward and entered Falkland Sound on the night of 20/21 May. Marines and paratroopers of 3 Commando made unopposed landings at four separate points around San Carlos: 4,000 troops were put ashore without any casualties. The Argentines reacted by launching air attacks. One frigate of the covering force, *Ardent*, was hit by bombs dropped by Skyhawks and subsequently sank, whilst the destroyer *Antrim* and frigate *Argonaut* were hit and seriously damaged. As the British troops consolidated their positions ashore, the ships defending the amphibious force came under further air attacks. On 23 May the frigate *Antelope* was hit, and two unexploded bombs became lodged within the ship. During attempts to defuse one of these bombs, it exploded and *Antelope* sank.

Ominously, 25 May was Argentina's national day, for which her aircraft carrier *Veintecinco de Mayo* had been named. The British expected that the enemy would make a special effort that day, and unfortunately this prediction proved to be correct. Fierce attacks by enemy aircraft led to the losses of the destroyer *Coventry*, which was bombed, and the aircraft transport *Atlantic Conveyor*, which was hit by two Exocet missiles whilst screening the two British aircraft carriers. A pair of Argentinian Super Étendard aircraft carrying Exocet missiles had attacked the carrier battle group and one missile was directed at one of the frigates, which deployed a cloud of distracting metal strips (chaff). The chaff did its job and the missile flew on, having lost its original target. The missile's radar then acquired *Atlantic Conveyor*, which was hit on the port quarter, starting huge fires. This led to the eventual abandonment

Map 2: The principal sinkings and troop movements during the Falklands conflict

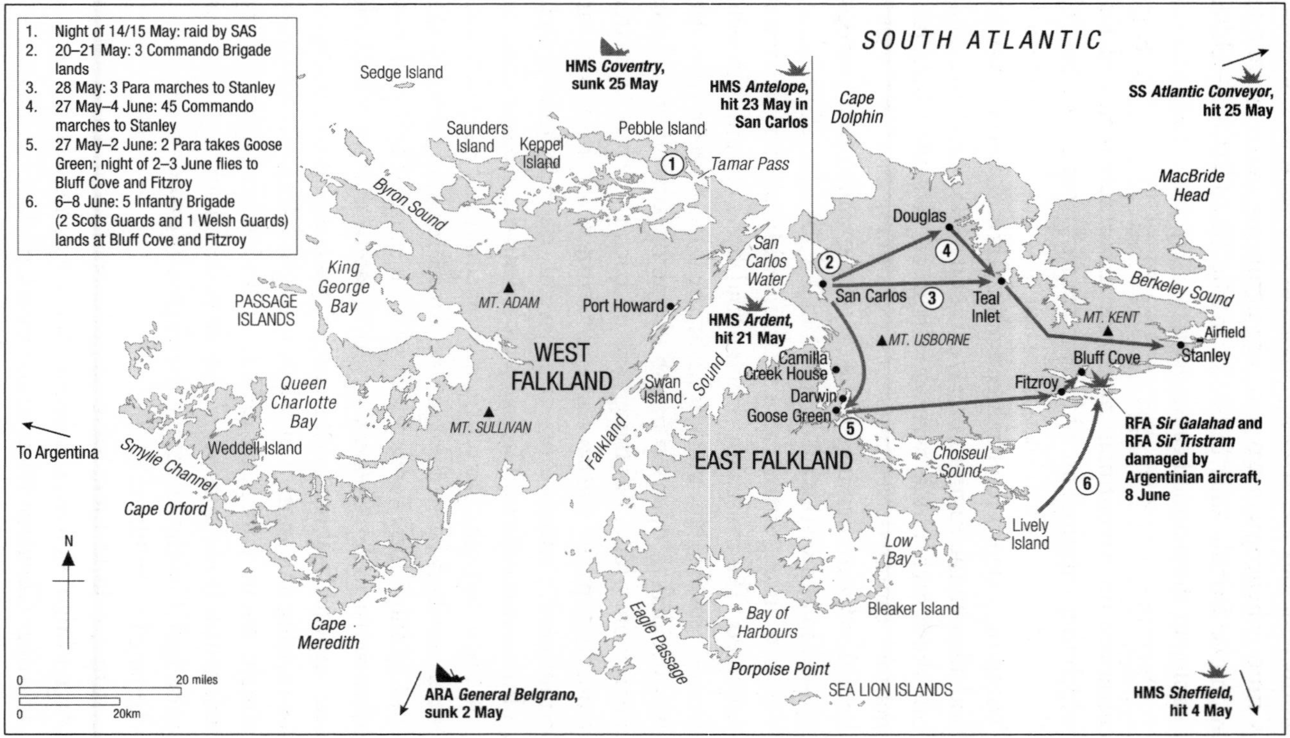
1. Night of 14/15 May: raid by SAS
2. 20–21 May: 3 Commando Brigade lands
3. 28 May: 3 Para marches to Stanley
4. 27 May–4 June: 45 Commando marches to Stanley
5. 27 May–2 June: 2 Para takes Goose Green; night of 2–3 June flies to Bluff Cove and Fitzroy
6. 6–8 June: 5 Infantry Brigade (2 Scots Guards and 1 Welsh Guards) lands at Bluff Cove and Fitzroy
SOUTH ATLANTIC
Sedge Island
HMS Coventry, sunk 25 May
HMS Antelope, hit 23 May in San Carlos
Cape Dolphin
SS Atlantic Conveyor, hit 25 May
Saunders Island
Keppel Island
Pebble Island
Tamar Pass
Byron Sound
MacBride Head
Douglas
San Carlos Water
King George Bay
PASSAGE ISLANDS
MT. ADAM
Port Howard
San Carlos
Teal Inlet
Berkeley Sound
MT. KENT
Airfield
Stanley
HMS Ardent, hit 21 May
MT. USBORNE
WEST FALKLAND
Camilla Creek House
Bluff Cove
Queen Charlotte Bay
Swan Island
Sound
Darwin
Fitzroy
Goose Green
MT. SULLIVAN
Falkland
RFA Sir Galahad and RFA Sir Tristram damaged by Argentinian aircraft, 8 June
To Argentina
Weddell Island
Smylie Channel
EAST FALKLAND
Choiseul Sound
Cape Orford
Lively Island
N
Low Bay
Cape Meredith
Bay of Harbours
Bleaker Island
Eagle Passage
Porpoise Point
0
20 miles
0
20km
ARA General Belgrano, sunk 2 May
SEA LION ISLANDS
HMS Sheffield, hit 4 May

of the ship and 12 men were lost. The loss of six Wessex and three Chinook helicopters was also very significant as they were intended to move British land forces from the San Carlos beachhead to Stanley in the planned campaign.

Over the next two days, troops of the Parachute Regiment advanced on Argentinian positions at Goose Green and Darwin, which they captured on 28 May in the fierce battle of Goose Green. Royal Marines began their advance on Stanley, mostly on foot – 'yomping' – deprived of helicopter lift. The hilly terrain was difficult and allowed the Argentines to maintain strong defensive positions, but these high points were to fall in succession. On 7 June the marines captured Mount Low, overlooking Stanley airfield. The liner *Canberra*, carrying 5 Brigade as the second-wave troops, had arrived in San Carlos on 2 June.

On 3 June Fitzroy, on the south side of East Falkland, was occupied. The campaign on land had been going fairly well with troops crossing the main part of the island from San Carlos. It was decided to open up a second line of advance in the south at Fitzroy on 3 June, but there was a setback there five days later. The landing ships *Sir Galahad* and *Sir Tristram* had been sent carrying equipment, ammunition and several military units, including soldiers of the Welsh Guards. On 8 June they were at anchor near Fitzroy in daylight. Before unloading could be completed, the ships were attacked by five Argentine Air Force A-4 Skyhawks. Bomb and cannon hits were taken on both ships causing fires, which were worst in *Sir Galahad*. Unfortunately, there was heavy loss of life, especially aboard *Sir Galahad*, with a total of 50 men killed or missing and more wounded. It might have been worse without timely rescue efforts by helicopter and boat, and rapid medical assistance. Both ships were abandoned and *Sir Galahad* became a total loss. On the same day the frigate *Plymouth* was bombed and damaged in Falkland Sound.

On 11 June there were major assaults on the outer ring of Argentinian defences around Stanley, and all succeeded. The destroyer *Glamorgan* was struck by a land-launched Exocet missile on 12 June, off Port Stanley, and was badly damaged. On the next two days heavy attacks by British troops led to the capture of most of the high ground around Stanley and a successful final assault on the capital was made, culminating in the surrender by General Mario Menéndez of the Argentinian forces there. A total of 9,800 Argentinian troops were made prisoners of war and were later repatriated to Argentina in the liner *Canberra* and ferry *Norland*.

The Royal Navy supplied most of the British airpower off the Falklands, in many different ways. Helicopters carried aboard most naval units were very versatile, providing anti-submarine defence, attack of surface targets, support for special forces and other land operations, medical and rescue support and the everyday but very necessary ability to move people and stores between the ships. Latterly, many helicopters were based ashore. Sea Harrier vertical-take-off-and-landing fighters provided the main longer-range air defence as well as attacking ground targets. They played a very large part in the reduction of Argentinian offensive airpower. The whole British airpower effort was characterized by an ability to improvise; for example, both aircraft carriers had far more than their normal peacetime complement of planes. The RAF provided airlift to Ascension Island and beyond, conducted maritime reconnaissance, provided airborne fuel and was able to bomb the runway at Stanley, though only very limited damage was inflicted. Further, Harrier GR3 aircraft, mainly for ground attack, were deployed both from sea and latterly on shore by the RAF. Royal Marines and Army Air Corps helicopters gave direct support to the land forces. The biggest threat to the British task force came from the air, and the British were never able to establish the air superiority that the amphibious landings needed. However, the 20 Sea Harriers from *Hermes* and *Invincible* inflicted serious losses on the Argentinian air forces, destroying 23 aircraft in air-to-air combat for the loss of none of their own number.[*] A further 17 enemy aircraft were destroyed by the task force's anti-air missile and gun defences. Destroyers

---

[*] Although no Sea Harriers were lost in aerial combat, two were lost to enemy ground fire and four were lost in accidents.

and frigates fired 7,500 rounds against Argentinian positions and provided valuable support for the troops ashore.[5]

The conflict lasted 72 days and claimed the lives of 236 British and 649 Argentinian servicemen, plus 19 British civilians from the Merchant Navy, RFA and Islanders. It was the largest naval and air combat operation between modern forces since the end of World War II. The Argentinian junta collapsed in the wake of the conflict, and the three commanders, including Galtieri and Anaya, were stripped of their ranks and imprisoned for human rights violations and mishandling of the 'Malvinas' war.

The next chapter will look at the events of 1–2 May, when the shooting war erupted around the Falklands and the first sinking occurred.

2

The Sinking of ARA *General Belgrano*

In the afternoon of 2 May the veteran Argentinian cruiser *General Belgrano* was steaming on a westerly course, skirting the total exclusion zone south of the Falklands, when a deadly, silent and unseen foe struck. Torpedoes raced towards the cruiser and two of them hit her on the port side. The old ship was mortally wounded and flooded rapidly, causing her to roll over and sink just 15 minutes after the last man had abandoned ship. Her assassin, the nuclear-powered submarine *Conqueror*, increased speed and went deep to avoid any attack from *Belgrano's* escorting destroyers, though they had in fact sped away from the scene.

Completed in 1939 at the New York Shipbuilding Corporation's yard in Camden, New Jersey as USS *Phoenix*, the Brooklyn-class cruiser survived the Japanese attack on Pearl Harbor in December 1941, putting to sea undamaged to search unsuccessfully for the enemy aircraft carriers. Her war service in the Pacific and Indian oceans saw her survive numerous *kamikaze* attacks and earn nine battle stars. When the war ended she was placed in reserve and, in 1951, sold to Argentina, being renamed *17 du Octubre* after the 'People's Loyalty Day' that was associated with the regime of President Juan Perón. In 1956, following the coup in which Perón was overthrown, she was renamed *General Belgrano* after General Manuel Belgrano, a founding father of the newly independent Argentina in 1819.[1]

Her main armament was 15 6-inch guns, arranged in five triple turrets, with a range of 12½ miles. Eight 5-inch guns were also mounted, mainly for anti-aircraft purposes, and in 1967–68 she had been modernized with two quadruple Seacat anti-air missile launchers and Dutch radars. She also had two twin 40mm Bofors guns, and in the hangar below deck aft could accommodate two helicopters – during the Falklands deployment she carried an Alouette. As was typical for a ship of her type and age she was heavily armoured, with up to 4-inch armour in the main belt, 3-inch in the turrets and 2-inch in her decks, whilst the conning tower armour was 8 inches thick. She displaced 12,200 tons at full load. *Belgrano's* eight boilers fed steam to her Westinghouse geared turbines, which had given her a speed of 32½ knots when new.[2] However, by 1982 her machinery and boilers were far from new and in less than perfect condition. As a result, they produced only 70 per cent of their original maximum output, unless in an emergency, and a maximum speed of 18½ knots had been imposed.[3]

General Belgrano was not part of the invasion force that captured the Falkland Islands on 1 April 1982 because at that time she was at Puerto Belgrano, the Argentine Navy's main base, 350 miles south of Buenos Aires, undergoing a period of general maintenance which included overhauling her turbines and boilers. She had recently returned from a summer training cruise which had taken her south to Tierra del Fuego and beyond. Following the invasion, and in the knowledge by 5 April that a British task force was being sent south, work on *General Belgrano* was speeded up so that the ship could take part in the war that might ensue. Also, extensive stores and ammunition were loaded to allow the ship to undertake an extended war cruise. The admiral's quarters at the stern of the ship became an intelligence centre where charts, details of enemy forces – their ships, aircraft and equipment – and intelligence gathered by Argentinian agencies were assembled.[4]

She was commanded by Captain Héctor Bonzo with Commander Pedro Luis Galazi as second-in-command. Captain Bonzo had joined the Argentine Navy in 1947 and worked his way up the ranks, travelling some 200,000 nautical miles. He trained and qualified in naval systems and taught in several Argentine Navy institutions. He had served on board the cruisers *La Argentina* and *9 de Julio*, the sail training ship *Libertad* and the ice breaker *General San Martín*.

To put the ship on a war footing the size of the ship's company was increased, with the addition of extra lieutenants and lieutenant commanders, and consisted of 56 officers, 629 permanent crew and 408 conscripts who were serving their mandatory 12 months of national service and most of whom had been on the summer cruise.[5]

Captain Bonzo attended planning meetings at the naval base in which war strategies and options for the deployment of the ship were discussed. It became known that the British were sending nuclear-powered submarines to the area and these presented a major threat to the Argentinian ships, which they would have difficulty dealing with. *Spartan* and *Splendid* were heading for the waters between the Falklands and the Argentinian mainland whilst *Conqueror* was going to South Georgia. The Argentinian government was warned by the British authorities that from midnight on 12/13 April a maritime exclusion zone would be established and their warships and merchant ships sailing within 200 nautical miles of the Falklands would do so at their own risk. The Argentines reacted by withdrawing their larger surface warships from the area, but continued to send in merchant ships of the state shipping line, supplying the garrison on the islands. These ships went unmolested by the submarines, since at this stage in the conflict it would have been unthinkable to sink a civilian ship without warning and a submarine's position would be compromised if it surfaced and ordered the merchant ship's crew to abandon ship before sinking it.[6]

The Argentinian plan was to defend the Malvinas by deploying a naval task force, which would comprise three task groups. The first, Task Group 79.1, would consist of the aircraft carrier *Veinticinco de Mayo* with its Skyhawk fighter bombers and Tracker anti-submarine aircraft, the destroyer *Santísima Trinidad* and the corvettes *Guerrico*, *Drummond* and *Granville*. The second group, 79.2, would contain five destroyers – *Hercules*, *Piedra Buena*, *Hipólito Bouchard*, *Segui* and *Comodoro Py*. In addition to their conventional armament of guns and anti-submarine weapons, all of the destroyers were fitted with Exocet ship-to-surface missile launchers, and both the Type 42s, *Hercules* and *Santísima Trinidad*, also had Sea Dart anti-air missiles. Both of these task groups were to be stationed to the north of the Falklands, where it was thought the British would concentrate their attack. The third group, 79.3, would be a single ship, *General Belgrano*. Bonzo's orders were to take up station off the Isla de los Estados (Staten Island), a small island to the east of Tierra del Fuego, and patrol the waters off Cape Horn to prevent British ships transiting from the Pacific to reinforce their task force off the Falklands, and – perhaps more importantly – to intercept Chilean warships if Chile decided to enter the conflict. He was to avoid any engagement with ships armed with ship-to-surface missiles, like Exocet, but otherwise his ship should be more than a match for other Royal Navy destroyers and frigates armed with 4.5-inch guns.[7]

On 23 April the British government sent the following message to the Argentinian government, making it clear that its terms would come into effect immediately:

> In announcing the establishment of the Maritime Exclusion Zone around the Falkland Islands, Her Majesty's Government made it clear that this measure was without prejudice to the right of the UK to take whatever additional measures may be needed in the exercise of its right of self-defence under Article 51 of the United Nations Charter. In this connection, HMG now wishes to make clear that any approach on the part of warships, including submarines, naval auxiliaries, or military aircraft which could amount to a threat to interfere with the mission of British Forces in the South Atlantic will encounter the appropriate response. All Argentine aircraft including civil aircraft engaging in surveillance of these British Forces will be regarded as hostile and are liable to be dealt with accordingly.

This was apparently intended to clarify or strengthen the earlier announcement of the maritime exclusion zone. After the conflict the government, when defending the decision to attack *General Belgrano*, was to say, 'It is clear from the above text that the warning applied outside the Exclusion Zone as well as within it.'[8]

On 16 April, a calm and sunny day, *General Belgrano* sailed from her home port and arrived at her patrol area on 19 April, where she cruised within the 12-mile limit close to the mainland Argentinian territory of eastern Tierra del Fuego, and conducted gunnery practice. On 22 April *General Belgrano* left her patrol area for Ushuaia, the port and Argentinian naval base in Tierra del Fuego, on the Beagle Channel. Here she loaded more ammunition, including live Seacat missiles, and refuelled, then sailed on 24 April and headed east. The uncertainty of British intentions now caused some redeployment of Argentinian ships. The destroyers *Piedra Buena* and *Hipólito Bouchard* together with the oiler *Puerto Rosales* were detached from group 79.2 in the north and sent to join *Belgrano* in group 79.3.

Britain announced on 28 April that the maritime exclusion zone around the Falklands would become a *total* exclusion zone, in which both warships *and aircraft* would be treated as hostile, effective from 30 April. Argentina retaliated by declaring a 200-mile exclusion zone around its territory, which the government said included the mainland, the Malvinas, South Georgia and the South Sandwich Islands.[9]

Meanwhile *Belgrano*, the two destroyers and the oiler had left their station off Isla de los Estados (Staten Island) and were steaming towards the southern edge of the total exclusion zone, south of the Falklands. By midnight on 1/2 May the group was in that area, poised to head north for South Georgia, not knowing that it was being closely followed by the nuclear-powered submarine *Conqueror*.[10]

Conqueror, commanded by 36-year-old Commander Chris Wreford-Brown, had sailed from Faslane naval base on the Gareloch in Scotland on Sunday 4 April, two days after the Argentinian invasion, with instructions to proceed south as fast as possible.[11] On 10 April she received a signal directing her to South Georgia, and crossed the equator on 12 April, when there was little time for the traditional ceremony. By 18 April she was nearing South

Georgia. She carried 14 marines of the Special Boat Squadron (SBS) and their equipment, who could land in South Georgia for reconnaissance work to identify possible landing sites for the operation to retake the islands. Arriving in the vicinity, *Conqueror* carried out inshore surveillance and reconnaissance work along the rocky coastline of the main island. On 24 April she was ordered to sink the Argentinian submarine *Santa Fe*, which had left her mainland base on 9 April and was believed to be carrying marines to reinforce the Argentinian troops on South Georgia. Although a likely contact was gained, it proved difficult to track and no engagement was made. That night *Santa Fe* docked at Grytviken and on the following day was captured by British forces. The islands were retaken without the involvement of *Conqueror*'s SBS men.[12]

Ordered on 28 April to proceed west to an area to the south-west of the Falklands, between the relative shallows of the Burdwood Bank to the south of the Falklands and Los Estados Island off the Argentinian mainland, where *General Belgrano* and her task group were thought to be operating, *Conqueror* entered the exclusion zone around the Falkland Islands at 16.45 the next day, tasked with finding and following *Belgrano*. Also on 28 April, the British government announced the establishment of the total exclusion zone of 200 nautical miles around the Falkland Islands. The announcement stressed that 'these measures are without prejudice to the right of the United Kingdom to take whatever measures may be needed in exercise of its right of self-defence under Article 51 of the UN Charter.' On 29 April a signal informed Commander Wreford-Brown that he would be working with Rear Admiral Woodward's task group, though Woodward still had no authority to determine the submarine's rules of engagement. On 30 April the rules of engagement then in force, which allowed Argentinian warships, naval auxiliaries and aircraft to be attacked inside the total exclusion zone, were amended to allow attacks to be made on the aircraft carrier *Veinticinco de Mayo* outside the exclusion zone in circumstances where it posed a threat to the British task force. This reflected the fact that an attack might be made by the ship's aircraft when the carrier itself was outside the exclusion zone.[13]

On 1 May the British task force came under attack for the first time from the Argentinian air forces, actually the fleet air arm operating from the mainland, during most of the daylight hours. During the night an RAF Vulcan had attempted to bomb the runway at Stanley, with very little success – only one of the 21 bombs dropped hit the runway, and it caused minimal damage. This was followed at 08.00 (Falklands Standard Time*) by Sea Harriers dropping bombs on the airfield. The ensuing Argentinian air raids on the task force were an Argentinian response to these events, but were repulsed by Sea Harriers from *Invincible* and *Hermes*, with one Mirage, one Dagger and one Canberra shot down by Sidewinder missiles, whilst a second Mirage was damaged and subsequently shot down over Stanley in error by the Argentines. The destroyer *Glamorgan* and frigates *Alacrity* and *Arrow* suffered minor damage, and the Seacat operator in *Arrow* was wounded. At Goose Green an Argentinian Pucará aircraft was destroyed and two others damaged beyond repair by Sea Harriers from *Hermes*.[14]

Shortly after entering her patrol area at 11.08 on 30 April *Conqueror* made sonar contact with a group of ships to the west, about 50 miles east of Staten Island, which correlated with intelligence reports indicating that the *Belgrano* group was in the area of this bearing, and would be heading east. *Conqueror* was about 75 miles east-south-east of the group, and maintained sonar contact, then at 07.40 on 1 May she went deep and increased speed to 15 knots for one hour to get to the area of the suspected task group. At 08.54 she made the first visual contact with the group, which consisted of the cruiser, two destroyers and the oiler. The submarine then shadowed the group, remaining between 9,000 and 14,000 yards from it at speeds up to 21 knots. She was instructed at 20.14 that day to intercept and attack

---

* Times in the Falklands region are given as Falklands Standard Time, which in 1982 was four hours behind Greenwich Mean Time. British ships' timekeeping adhered to GMT during the Falklands conflict, and this was known as Z or Zulu time. From 2012 the Falkland Islands government made Falklands Summer Time apply all year round. This is three hours behind GMT, in common with the Argentinian time zone.

General Belgrano if her task group penetrated the exclusion zone. At 10.00 on 1 May the submarine reported the sighting of the *Belgrano* group and gave their position as 54°07' south, 64°24' west, on a course of 125°, at a speed of 8 knots, with *Belgrano* in the process of refuelling from the oiler. When the refuelling was completed the tanker moved off to the west and the three warships increased speed to 13 knots and set off to the south-east. They steamed steadily south-eastwards and then east, avoiding the total exclusion zone by about 25 miles, but heading towards the shallow Burdwood Bank. A further signal was sent when the submarine next came up to periscope depth at midnight on 1/2 May, giving *Belgrano* group's position 55°20' south, 60°14' west, course 90°, speed 13 knots. During the night the task group burned no navigation lights, so visual contact was lost, and it was only regained at 08.50 the following morning. At 05.18 the commander-in-chief's staff at Northwood instructed *Conqueror* that *Belgrano*'s group was not to be attacked until allowed by the rules of engagement.[15]

'Early on the morning of 2 May,' Admiral Woodward later explained, 'all the indications were that the *Veinticinco de Mayo*, the Argentinian carrier, and a group of escorts had slipped past my forward SSN [nuclear-powered attack submarine] barrier to the north, whilst the cruiser *General Belgrano* and her escorts were attempting to complete the pincer movement from the south, still outside the total exclusion zone.' A Sea Harrier from *Invincible* had spotted a group of enemy ships, which possibly included the aircraft carrier, north of the Falklands, some 50 nautical miles outside the exclusion zone,* whilst the *Belgrano* group was known from *Conqueror*'s signals to be south of the islands, about 18 miles outside the exclusion zone. The main body of the British task force was some 120 nautical miles north-east of the Falklands, inside the exclusion zone.

The Argentinian operations commander in the South Atlantic at the time, Admiral Juan José Lombardo, later confirmed on a

---

* In fact, the position of the carrier group was already known to the British forces from the decoding of Argentinian signals and/or from intelligence from satellite surveillance being received from the United States.

Map 3: The sinking of ARA *General Belgrano*, 2 May

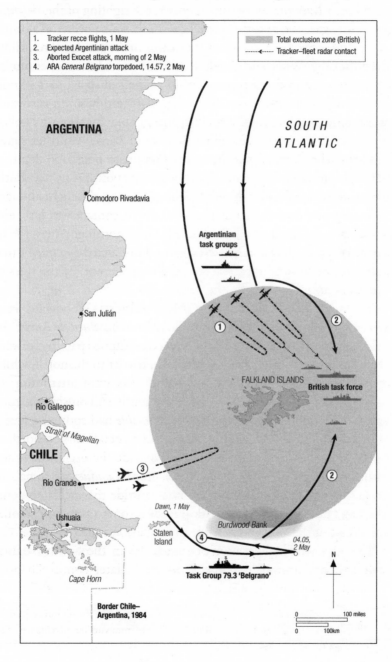

1. Tracker recce flights, 1 May
2. Expected Argentinian attack
3. Aborted Exocet attack, morning of 2 May
4. ARA *General Belgrano* torpedoed, 14.57, 2 May

Total exclusion zone (British)
Tracker–fleet radar contact

ARGENTINA

SOUTH ATLANTIC

Comodoro Rivadavia

Argentinian task groups

San Julián

FALKLAND ISLANDS

British task force

Río Gallegos

Strait of Magellan

CHILE

Río Grande

Ushuaia

Dawn, 1 May

Staten Island

Burdwood Bank

04.05, 2 May

Cape Horn

Task Group 79.3 'Belgrano'

Border Chile–Argentina, 1984

N

0   100 miles
0   100km

BBC Panorama television programme that the Argentine Navy was indeed attempting to engage in a pincer movement against the task force using his task groups in the north and south of the islands.[16] Commander Pedro Luis Galazi, executive officer in *Belgrano*, later stated that their plan was to move into the exclusion zone towards the British carrier battle group, in co-ordination with *Veinticinco de Mayo* and the other warships in the northern task groups, and attack surface ships with the destroyers' Exocet missiles. If any British ships were hit and damaged, only then would *General Belgrano* move in and attempt to sink them with gunfire.[17]

It was probably during the night of 1/2 May that the fleet commander's staff in Northwood realized that if the *Belgrano* group chose to make a dash across the shallows, *Conqueror* might not be able to keep track of all three ships, and they might get within Exocet range of *Hermes* and *Invincible* before anybody could take action to stop them.[18]

Spartan and *Splendid* in the north now had no contact with *Veinticinco de Mayo*, so Admiral Woodward wanted to take out *General Belgrano*. In response to the threat to the task force, he sought a change to the rules of engagement to allow *Conqueror* to attack *Belgrano* outside the exclusion zone, after having himself unilaterally decided to give *Conqueror* permission to attack, a signal that was countermanded by the flag officer, submarines, Vice Admiral Peter Herbert, who retained control of the submarines in the Falklands area. Actually, Herbert and Admiral Fieldhouse had already started the process of requesting a change to the rules of engagement.[19] The War Cabinet, meeting at Chequers, the prime minister's country residence, decided at 08.00 (13.00 London, British Summer Time) on Sunday 2 May that, on the basis that a real threat to the task force existed, the rules of engagement should be changed to permit attacks on all Argentinian naval vessels on the high seas, whether inside or outside the exclusion zone, as had previously been agreed for *Veinticinco de Mayo* alone.[20]

This change was signalled from Northwood to *Conqueror* at 08.38 (Falklands Standard Time), but it was not until 12.25 that the submarine was able to communicate its receipt and understanding of the signal, and to communicate her intention to attack. This delay was due to the limitations in communications between submarines in the far South Atlantic and Northwood and the fact that *Conqueror* had persistent problems with her radio mast. At 10.01 *Conqueror* reported that the *Belgrano* group had reversed course from due east to due west at 04.05 in position 55°20' south, 58°22' west, and increased speed; by the time the signal was made the group was at 55°16' south, 60°18' west, on a course of 270° at 14 knots, with *Conqueror* some 5,000 yards astern. The task group appeared to have started some gentle zigzagging. This was a major change, for it now meant that the *Belgrano* group was sailing *away* from the task force, outside the exclusion zone, rather than towards it, and was some 260 nautical miles from the nearest ship in the British task force. Wreford-Brown obseved, 'Although intelligence suggests that the group will enter the TEZ, they appear to have a different idea. Perhaps the bombing of Stanley airfield and the "splashing" of a Mirage may have made them wary of the TEZ?'[21]

Indeed, it appears that the military action on 1 May, in which seven Argentinian aircraft had been lost or damaged, may have concentrated minds in their high command. At 20.07 on that day the Argentinian warships were ordered to return to their bases, an order that was repeated in the early hours of the following morning at 01.19, though it was nearly another three hours before *Belgrano* reversed course.[22] After the conflict, stating that the intentions of the Argentinian task groups were to advance in a pincer movement and for their carrier's Skyhawks to bomb one of the British aircraft carriers and put it out of action, Captain Carlos Madero, weapons officer on *Belgrano*'s 5-inch gun batteries, said that there had been no wind on the night of 1/2 May and for the morning of 2 May, when the operation was to take place, the wind was forecast to be insufficient for the fully loaded aircraft to take off from the deck, so the operation was cancelled.[23] Other sources cite Rear Admiral Allara's evidence to the Rattenbach commission, an Argentinian inquiry into the performance of their forces in the conflict, which confirmed this decision and the reasons for it. The order for the ships to return to their bases was made by Vice Admiral Juan Lombardo, commander of the Argentinian fleet.[24]

For the British submarines, the changes to the rules of engagement made on 2 May widened the area in which an attack could be made:

All vessels positively identified as either [sic] an Argentine aircraft carrier, cruiser, destroyer, frigate, corvette or submarine may be attacked, except when the target is both north of 35° South and west of 48° West or within 12 nautical mile territorial waters.[25]

Prior to this, attacks by submarines could only be made on Argentinian warships, other than the aircraft carrier or submarines, if they were within the total exclusion zone or within 200 nautical miles of South Georgia or the South Sandwich Islands.

When the members of the War Cabinet took the decision to authorize the attack on it the cruiser group had already reversed course, although this information was not known to them. The report from *Conqueror* was sent two hours later; however, the Royal Navy was successfully intercepting and decoding all Argentinian signals, so it is probable that the order to reverse course was known to the Royal Navy high command. If he did know, chief of defence staff Admiral Lord Lewin did not tell the War Cabinet. *Conqueror's* report was not made known to ministers at the time because (it was later said), the *Belgrano* 'could have altered course again and closed on elements of the Task Force, acting in concert with the carrier to the north... [hence] the precise position and course of the *Belgrano* at that time were irrelevant.'[26]

Intermittently, the submarine slowed to 5 knots and rose to periscope depth to send or check for incoming signals, and then after diving deeper had to speed up to 18 knots to catch up with her prey. Wreford-Brown recorded, 'Aim is now to close TG 79.3 then work into a firing position. Preferred weapon Mk 8 Mod 4. If a good attacking position cannot be achieved because of the escorts, then I shall use a Mk 24.' *Belgrano's* anti-submarine tactics were described as 'pretty pathetic' by Wreford-Brown, and Captain Bonzo, who had no experience of what nuclear-powered submarines could and could not do, was thought by Woodward to be 'mentally not yet at war'. At 15.30 *Conqueror* reported that the *Belgrano* group had at 14.56 been at 55°27' south, 61°25' west, on a course of 280° with a speed of 11 knots, and that *Belgrano* had been successfully attacked with two hits from Mk 8 torpedoes.[27]

Conqueror had on board two types of torpedo – the very old Mk 8, which predated World War II, and the much newer Mk 24 Tigerfish. However, despite having a much longer range, the latter was unreliable, and the Mk 8 torpedoes had bigger warheads and therefore a better chance of penetrating *Belgrano*'s armour and anti-torpedo bulges, so the Mk 8 was chosen.[28] The submarine had closed to within 1,280 yards of *Belgrano*, on her port side because the two destroyers were on her starboard side. The destroyers did not have their sonars operating in active mode.[*][29] Three torpedoes were fired in a slight fan pattern on a track angle of 90°, but one did not hit the cruiser; instead, it is believed to have hit one of the destroyers, without exploding. The two that did hit *General Belgrano* did explode, one beneath the after superstructure and the other just aft of the bow. Chris Wreford-Brown was to recall, 'I looked through the periscope and saw two of the torpedoes hit. I distinctly recall seeing an orange fireball in line with the main mast – just aft of the centre of the target – and shortly after the second explosion I thought I saw a spout of water, smoke and debris from forward.' On board *Conqueror*, the ship's company let up a cheer when they heard each of the explosions.[30]

The two destroyers had orders to flee if there was an attack, but apparently returned to the area later and were sighted by *Conqueror* when she slowed and came up to periscope depth three hours after the attack. The submarine had rapidly gone deep and increased speed after firing the torpedoes, and a number of large bangs were heard which the crew imagined were depth charges. It later emerged that the destroyers deployed no mortar bombs or depth charges, so the explosions heard probably came from the sinking cruiser.[31]

---

[*] Argentinian warships had been ordered not to use active sonar as it would reveal their position to British nuclear submarines, but they could use passive sonar.

On board *Conqueror*, feelings about what they had done were mixed. Later in the same day as the attack, supply officer Lieutenant Narendra Sethia wrote in his diary:

> I am still overwhelmed by it all. I can hardly believe the enormity of what we have done. We can't go back and apologize now – it's too late. I wonder how many died. I wonder, even more, what the reaction will be? The lads have taken it very well – a couple were frightened outwardly, and the rest of us made do with being frightened inwardly.[32]

Commander Wreford-Brown led a service with his crew to pray for the enemy dead only hours after the sinking. When they heard that the enemy destroyers had left the scene without picking up survivors, the initial euphoria of *Conqueror*'s crew turned to horror.[33]

A few months after the sinking, Wreford-Brown was to comment, 'The Royal Navy spent thirteen years preparing me for such an occasion. It would have been regarded as extremely dreary if I had fouled it up.'[34]

Wreford-Brown also reflected:

> Afterwards I had a certain amount of regret about the loss of life. I did not know the numbers involved, but one presumed it was considerable. But I feel we did just what we were invited to do and I would have no hesitation in doing it again. It is a fact of life that if you want to go to war, you must expect losses.[35]

* * *

When the first explosion came, Captain Héctor Bonzo knew it was a torpedo. The ship came to a dead halt and all electrical power was lost, plunging everywhere into darkness. 'There was a terrifying silence,' he said. He opened a door and looked towards the bow, but there was now no bow. The second torpedo had hit the ship 50ft from the bow, just forward of the first main gun turret. The bow section was destroyed and fell into the sea, but the main bulkhead didn't fracture. The first torpedo had hit underneath the middle engine room, just abaft the second funnel. The explosion ripped open the hull of the cruiser and created an orange fireball that burst upwards through four decks, killing everyone it encountered in the senior ratings' mess, the petty officers' mess, the dining room and the area known as the Soda Fountain, a relaxation lounge where the refreshment bar was manned by the only two civilians in the ship, who were brothers. Before leaving port the brothers were told they could disembark, but chose not to, saying they were part of the ship's crew, in bad times as well as good. One of them made it to the upper deck, but went back down to find his brother and they were never seen again. It is believed that 272 men died in the explosion and many others received severe burns. A quick assessment of the damage control prospects was made by Lieutenant Commander Norberto Bernasconi, one of the senior engineering officers, who concluded that there was no hope, and communicated this to Captain Bonzo and Commander Galazi in the bridge. The ship was listing at a rate increasing by one degree a minute, and by 15.21 had reached 30°. Captain Bonzo gave the order to abandon ship.[36]

Twenty-four-year-old marine Captain Carlos Madero was on the 5-inch guns. He was astonished at the large explosion, but there was no panic and everyone followed the procedures in which they had been trained. Madero went down to the lowest decks to rescue people. In the ship's last few minutes men were still going below, risking their lives and sometimes dying, to find friends. Some were in flooded cabins and had to swim under water to escape. Others were trapped dead in doors and had to be prised out of the way to allow survivors to escape.[37]

Quickly, life rafts were released into the sea, where they automatically inflated. The wind was strong and the seas were picking up. Men lining the sides of the ship jumped, many landing in a life raft but others landing in the freezing water and struggling to reach the comparative safety of a life raft. By 15.40 almost everybody had left the ship, and Captain Bonzo walked down the main deck in a shocked and dazed state, close to mental collapse.

A young petty officer, walking along the sloping deck, spotted him and called out, '*Vamos, comandante!*' He then dragged his captain to the guardrail, where they walked down the side of the ship into the sea and swam for about 100 yards to a life raft. Bonzo was too cold and weakened to hold a rope, but was bundled over the side into the packed raft.[38]

For those in the rafts the situation was still perilous: some rafts were carried by waves into the fractured bow of the ship, where they were punctured and had to be abandoned by their occupants. Marine Captain Madero was in one of those – all 20 occupants had to swim through the very cold water to another raft, in the course of which the most senior person, a lieutenant commander, lost consciousness and was hauled into the raft in very bad shape. Some of the rafts were overcrowded, which at least meant the men could huddle together for warmth, but others contained as few as two men, who were thrown around violently in the tossing raft and suffered badly from the cold. There were many injured men in the rafts, and some men were finding it difficult to cope with the stress and shock of their experiences. There were no rescue ships or aircraft in sight, and although they did not know it at first, many of the survivors would spend up to 48 hours in their raft before rescue came. The two destroyers had sped north for 30 miles, as they had been ordered to do if attacked by a submarine. They signalled the commander of the task force, Rear Admiral Gualter Allara, saying that they had lost contact with *Belgrano* and feared she had been disabled. For the men in the water who could not make it to a raft the shock of immersion in the cold water and subsequent hypothermia meant they could not stay alive for long, and they drowned or died within minutes: 28 men were lost in this way.[39]

The two destroyers later returned to the scene but could find no trace of *Belgrano* or survivors, and soon their search became hampered by darkness. The night was stormy with mountainous seas. Neptune aircraft joined the search and at 09.10 the following morning one of them spotted a large oil slick. As the search narrowed a Neptune spotted the first life rafts at 13.15, but the nearest ships were 30 miles away. At 17.30 the ocean-going tug *Gurruchaga*, equipped with powerful searchlights, made contact with the first life rafts and hauled the desperate survivors onto the low stern deck of the vessel. Marine Captain Madero had to jump from his raft onto the rescue ship, but the water was up to his knees in the life raft and he found his legs wouldn't work. He fell in the water in a frozen state and struggled to grasp a life ring that was thrown to him; with great difficulty, thinking he was going to die, he finally managed to get hold of it and was pulled up to safety. The two destroyers and the icebreaker *Bahía Paraiso* arrived to assist, but many of the survivors had to live through a second night, when some men lapsed into unconsciousness and the condition of others was deteriorating seriously. The raft containing the 25-year-old ship's doctor, Lieutenant Commander Alberto Levene, a 19-year-old petty officer and ten young conscripts was one of the last to be rescued, in the late afternoon of 4 May, after 48 hours adrift, including two nights of 15 hours' darkness. By the next morning the search was completed: 770 crew members had been rescued alive, but 23 men had perished in the life rafts, and 28 in the water. The total loss of life was 323 from a ship's company of 1,093, the biggest loss of life in any incident in the Falklands conflict. Memorials to the dead have been erected in Buenos Aires, Ushuaia and Puerto Belgrano.[40]

* * *

After the conflict there was considerable political fallout from the *Belgrano* sinking. John Nott, the hapless British defence secretary, had announced the action 36 hours after it took place:

> The next day, 2 May, at 20.00 London time, one of our submarines detected the Argentine cruiser *General Belgrano*, escorted by two destroyers. This heavily armed surface attack group was close to the total exclusion zone and was closing on elements of our task force which was only hours away... The threat to the task force was such that the task force commander could ignore it only at his peril.

As Stuart Prebble noted in his book *Secrets of the Conqueror*, there was hardly anything in this statement that was true. *Belgrano* had not been detected at 20.00 London time on 2 May: she had been detected 34 hours earlier and closely followed for the entire time (29 hours) until she was attacked; so any suggestion that the decision was made in the heat of battle could be discounted. She was not close to the exclusion zone – when sunk she was well over 30 miles outside the zone and had been carefully avoiding it. Furthermore, *Belgrano* was not closing on elements of the task force – for 11 hours she had been sailing in the opposite direction. Even if she had reversed course and advanced on the task force at full speed she would have taken at least 15 hours to get within range of it. Anyway, she was under orders to return to her base and at any time could have been sunk by *Conqueror* if she became a more immediate threat.[41]

Inconsistencies soon emerged between the government's account of events and statements made by Royal Navy officers, including Wreford-Brown and more senior officers. Smelling a rat, the Labour MP Tam Dalyell, supported by the shadow defence secretary Denzil Davies, relentlessly probed the issue in letters to the prime minister and parliamentary questions. A number of journalists and the broadcasting media joined the fray, and soon the government was very much on the back foot.

Answers to various questions were sought. When and why were the rules of engagement changed, and by whom? Who gave the order to attack the *Belgrano*? Why was the order given when in fact the *Belgrano* was outside the exclusion zone and steaming away from the Falklands? What course was the *Belgrano* steering when she was torpedoed? Did ministers know the course had reversed? At the time when the decision was made, what was the state of progress on the Peruvian peace plan and when was it communicated to the government? Wasn't the sinking of *Belgrano* deliberately intended to scupper the peace plan?

Where answers were given, they were often inaccurate or incomplete. For example, *Belgrano* was said to have made many changes of course on 2 May, whereas she only made two (the reversal of course and a change from 270° to 280°), and it was said that the cruiser was zigzagging, but it had now been confirmed that she was not.

The prime minister, Margaret Thatcher, was grilled by a member of the public, Diana Gould, in a question and answer session on a BBC television programme during the general election campaign of May 1983, and had a very uncomfortable time. Mrs Gould highlighted the facts about the cruiser's course and position, and when asked by the presenter Sue Lawley what she thought was the motivation for the sinking she replied that it 'was in effect sabotaging any possibility of any peace plan succeeding, and that Mrs Thatcher had fourteen hours in which to consider the Peruvian peace plan that was being put forward to her.' Mrs Thatcher replied that the peace proposals, which were only in outline, did not reach London until after the attack.[42] This was later clarified, saying that the proposals reached London from Washington at 23.15 London time (BST), over three hours after the attack on *Belgrano*.[43] The British view of the proposals was that they 'seemed only vague and indeterminate and provided no basis on which to do business.'[44]

A book by Arthur Gavshon and Desmond Rice, *The Sinking of the Belgrano*, gave an incisive account of events and the government's untruths. Further disclosures came from the diary of Lieutenant Narendra Sethia, supply officer in *Conqueror*. Tam Dalyell was suspended from parliament for calling the prime minister a liar, referring to her version of the timing of the Peruvian peace plan. However, despite the damaging allegations that had swirled around regarding the *Belgrano* affair, in the general election of June 1983 Mrs Thatcher won a landslide victory, reflecting public approval of her conduct of the Falklands conflict.

The Foreign Affairs Select Committee now weighed in with its own questions, seeking detailed information on events. Clive Ponting, a senior civil servant, who had been responsible for compiling a dossier on the affair, which became known as the 'Crown Jewels', became incensed when he realized the committee was not being given the information it wanted. He decided to leak some of the information to Tam Dalyell. His motive for revealing the documents was that he felt parliament was being denied information, to the extent that it was being misled. He was suspended from his job, arrested and was prosecuted by the government for leaking confidential documents, allegedly in breach of the Official Secrets Act. Ponting's defence was that the matter and his disclosure of the information to an MP were in the public interest. Despite the judge's summing up, which made it clear that he thought that Ponting should be found guilty, the jury unanimously reached a verdict of not guilty.

* * *

Interviews conducted by Martin Middlebrook for his book *The Fight for the Malvinas* indicated that Argentinian naval officers understood that the intent of the announcement by the UK on 23 April of a maritime exclusion zone was to indicate that any ships operating near the exclusion zone could be attacked. Argentinian Rear Admiral Allara, who had commanded the task force of which *Belgrano* was part from aboard *Veinticinco de Mayo*, said, 'After that message of 23 April, the entire South Atlantic was an operational theatre for both sides. We, as professionals, said it was just too bad that we lost the *Belgrano*.'

The modified British rules of engagement permitted the engagement of *Belgrano* outside the exclusion zone before the sinking. In his book, *One Hundred Days*, Admiral Woodward makes it clear that he regarded the *Belgrano* as part of the southern part of a pincer movement aimed at the task force, and it had to be sunk quickly: 'The speed and direction of an enemy ship can be irrelevant, because both can change quickly. What counts is his position, his capability and what I believe to be his intention.'[45]

Admiral Enrique Molina Pico, head of the Argentine Navy in the 1990s, wrote in a letter to *La Nación*, published in the 2 May 2005 edition, that the *Belgrano* was part of an operation that posed a real threat to the British task force, that it was holding off for tactical reasons, and that being outside of the exclusion zone was unimportant as it was a warship on a tactical mission. This, he said, is the official position of the Argentine Navy.[46]

In the controversy that followed the sinking, Captain Bonzo, in spite of Argentinian claims of a deliberate 'criminal action', always maintained it was 'an act of war'. 'The sinking of the cruiser was an act of war. It was not a crime. It was a legal, most unfortunate and lamentable action... We were in the front and we suffered the consequences', he said at the time. 'As of April 30 I was given orders to open fire and if the submarine should have been before me having emerged for repairs, I would have opened fire with the fifteen guns until it sunk.' He also described the 323 Argentinian sailors that went down with the old cruiser as 'heroes'.

In an interview in 2003, Bonzo said, 'Our mission in the south wasn't just to cruise around on patrol but to attack. When they gave us the authorisation to use our weapons, if necessary, we knew we had to be prepared to attack, as well as be attacked. Our people were completely trained. I would even say we were anxious to pull the trigger.' According to Bonzo, the *Belgrano*'s move before dawn on 2 May was only a temporary manoeuvre. Admiral Woodward later commented: 'I think a lot of people outside didn't understand how important a threat *Belgrano* and her destroyers were.'

Commander Christopher Wreford-Brown, who had taken command of *Conqueror* three weeks before she sailed from Faslane for the Falklands, was awarded the Distinguished Service Order for his role in the successful attack, and Acting Petty Officer Graham Libby, the chief diver aboard the submarine, received the Distinguished Service Medal for his bravery in a later incident during the Falklands campaign when an aerial wire became wrapped around *Conqueror*'s propeller, and he risked his life for the benefit of his ship far beyond any call of duty (see Appendix).[47]

* * *

General Belgrano had fallen victim to the deadly efficiency of the nuclear-powered attack submarine for which she and her escorts were no match. She was old, ill equipped for modern combat and reportedly in poor material condition. Her escorting destroyers, which were almost as elderly, having been built for the US Navy in 1944 and sold to Argentina in the early seventies, failed to detect the shadowing *Conqueror*, even though the submarine had shadowed the group for 29 hours. This was despite the destroyers reportedly having been modernized for anti-submarine work, with variable depth sonar and helicopter facilities (though no helicopter was carried), although retaining their obsolete Mk 32 homing torpedoes and Hedgehog anti-submarine mortars.[48] They might at least reasonably have been expected to detect *Conqueror*'s presence, which would have allowed some form of evasive action to have been taken. Instead, both destroyers were positioned on the starboard side of *Belgrano*, allowing *Conqueror* to approach on the port side to within 1,280 yards of the cruiser and fire her torpedoes. Had one of the destroyers been positioned on the port side, its sonar (had it been in active or passive mode, which reportedly it was not) should easily have been able to detect the submarine. *Belgrano*'s anti-submarine tactics were woeful and her captain had no knowledge or experience of nuclear submarines. As Woodward would later comment, the cruiser should have been zigzagging in a *determined* way and varying its speed with periods of high speed and occasional slow speed rather than 'dawdling along' at a constant 13 knots. It should also have edged up towards the shallower water of the Burdwood Bank, making it less likely that a submarine would approach from that direction, thus simplifying the task of the escorts.[49] Damage control procedures aboard *Belgrano* were inadequate and the rapid flooding of the ship following her torpedoing could not be countered. All of this indicated that Captain Bonzo and his group were not on a warlike footing, and were apparently oblivious to the warnings given by the British and the known presence of nuclear-powered submarines in the area. After her sinking, the Argentinian surface navy effectively retired from action, but the country sought revenge, which would have disastrous consequences for HMS *Sheffield*, as described in the next chapter.

3

The Loss of HMS *Sheffield*

Two days after the sinking of *General Belgrano*, on 4 May 1982, a British warship positioned off the south-east of the Falkland Islands suffered a sudden, unexpected and devastating hit as a French-made missile launched by an Argentinian aircraft sliced through her hull and clouds of black smoke and fire erupted from the gaping hole in her side. The loss of the ship sent shockwaves through the fleet, whilst back at home in the United Kingdom people incredulously watched the pictures on their television screens, showing the stricken HMS *Sheffield* in her death throes. The timing of the attack was not a coincidence, for it was seen as a reaction by the Argentines to avenge the loss of their cruiser. *Sheffield* was the first British warship to be lost in combat since World War II, and the first to be lost to guided missile attack. How could a ship that had been designed to protect the fleet by detecting and intercepting aircraft and missiles have fallen victim to them herself?

HMS *Sheffield* was the first of class of the Sheffield (or Town) class of Type 42 destroyers. Ordered in November 1968, her keel was laid at Vickers (Shipbuilding) Ltd at Barrow-in-Furness on 15 January 1970. She was launched by the Queen on 10 June 1971, commissioned on 28 February 1975, and undertook a number of first of class trials until 1976.[1] Alone in the class, *Sheffield* was completed with an unusual funnel designed to reduce the infrared signature.[2]

Intended to provide area defence for a task force, the design of the Type 42 was heavily influenced by cost constraints. The ship was limited in length to 392ft, with too short a run in from the bow to the point where the full width of the hull was needed to accommodate the missile magazine. As a consequence, the ships were very wet forward, which affected the maintainability of the Sea Dart missile launcher and 4.5-inch gun, something that was to cause problems for *Sheffield*'s sister ship *Coventry* later in the campaign. To overcome this, the last four Type 42s, built after the Falklands conflict, were given a longer hull and forecastle and were wider in the beam. Some of the economies in the original design that affected equipment fit were later to be reversed, so, for example, the ships entered the Falklands with both the SCOT satellite communications system and sensors to detect radar emissions. However, these two pieces of equipment were too close together, and to prevent interference when transmitting on SCOT the radar emissions sensor had to be turned off. Hull strength was inadequate because too many longitudinals were omitted as a weight-saving measure, so deck reinforcements became necessary. The all-gas turbine propulsion was innovative, following successful trials in the frigate *Exmouth*, and gave many advantages over a steam turbine installation including weight and space saving, reduced engine room complement, reduced fuel consumption, and faster acceleration to maximum speed. Another bonus was that working conditions in the engine room were greatly improved.[3]

In her trials and work up *Sheffield* experienced many problems with equipment and systems, which required fixing, and so she did not become operational until early 1978.[4] In 1978/79 she worked with other NATO warships as the Royal Navy's contribution to the Standing Naval Force North Atlantic, prior to her first refit in Portsmouth Dockyard from June 1979 to November 1980. This long first refit lasted 74 weeks, and included alterations and additions to equip *Sheffield* for the Lynx helicopter, to provide deck edge stiffening, to fit UAA1 (the sensor for detecting radar emissions from enemy aircraft, missiles or ships), and to incorporate a considerable number of improvements to her other sensors.[5]

She emerged from this refit with a standard Type 42 weapon and equipment fit, apart from the absence of STWS, a shipborne torpedo weapon system firing the Sting Ray anti-submarine torpedo, which was fitted to all the other ships of the class. Thus, she had one 4.5-inch Mk 8 gun, a twin Sea Dart medium-range anti-air missile launcher (22 missiles were carried), two single 20mm Oerlikon guns, and a Lynx Mk 2 helicopter equipped with Sea Skua short-range anti-ship missiles and Mk 46 anti-submarine torpedoes. She bristled with radar scanners: one Type 965R for long-range air search, one Type 992Q for medium-range surveillance and target indication, two Type 909s for Sea Dart target tracking and fire control, and one Type 1006 for navigation and helicopter control. However, she lacked a close-range point defence system: the need for this had been identified in the mid-1970s, and a proposal to fit a Sea Wolf missile system, at the expense of the 4.5-inch gun and the after Type 909 radar, was considered but discarded as too demanding on dockyard resources and operational time for the ships.[6] She also mounted a Type 184M sonar for detection of submarines. *Sheffield* was powered by four Rolls-Royce gas turbines (two Olympus for high speed, in the forward engine room, and two Tyne for cruising, in the after engine room), which gave her a top speed of 29 knots on her Olympus engines and a range of 4,000 miles at 18 knots on her Tyne engines. The operations room was buried in the hull for protection, rather than being set adjacent to the bridge. Her normal ship's company consisted of 21 officers and 249 ratings.[7]

The ship's material state, on completion of the refit, was assessed in November 1980 as generally satisfactory, although significant difficulties with the Type 909 radar, which controlled her Sea Dart missile firing control and targeting, were noted. Following post-refit trials *Sheffield* and her crew started working up to full operational efficiency at Portland in April 1981. Here the poor state of internal communications was the only initial and immediate area of concern, and her programme of sea training was judged to be most successful. Rejoining the fleet, in June 1981 she participated in Exercise *Roebuck*, which was followed by a period of shore leave for her crew, then high-seas firing of five Sea Dart missiles, Exercise

Ocean Safari, pre-deployment leave and an assisted maintenance period alongside at Portsmouth. She sailed in November 1981 for the Indian Ocean, and carried out Gulf Patrol (Operation *Armilla*) in the Arabian Gulf from approximately 14 to 24 December, and from 27 December to 4 January. During a self-maintenance programme at Mombasa, Kenya on 26 January 1982 Captain J. T. F. G. Salt RN relieved Captain P. J. Erskine RN in command. Captain Salt (a submariner), and his second-in-command (an anti-submarine helicopter observer), who was appointed concurrently, had little or no relevant surface ship experience, and both were very inexperienced in air defence, the main role of *Sheffield*.

Captain 'Sam' Salt, as he was always known, was born on 19 April 1940 in Yeovil. He was the son of Lilian and Lieutenant Commander George S. Salt, a Royal Navy officer who was lost in action six months after his son's birth while in command of the submarine HMS *Triad* on a Mediterranean patrol during World War II. The young Salt received his early education at Wellington College, Berkshire. On enlisting in the Royal Navy he received a commission as an officer after passing through Dartmouth in 1958–59. Salt married Penelope Walker in 1975 and had four sons. After an early career in surface vessels in the 1960s, he volunteered for the submarine service in which his father had lost his life. He commanded the conventional submarine *Finwhale* (1969–71), was executive officer of the Polaris submarine *Resolution* (1973–74), and commanded the attack submarine *Dreadnought* (1978–79).[8]

Homeward bound, on 12/13 March 1982 *Sheffield* had passed through the Suez Canal and visited Piraeus and Gibraltar before participating in Exercise *Spring Train* in the Atlantic.[9] The exercise was shortened and, on 2 April, the ship was ordered to prepare for deployment to the South Atlantic as part of the Falklands task force. She was short of many supplies and was paired with the home-going frigate *Active* for stores transfer, receiving a large quantity of supplies and ammunition to help equip her for a war situation, including 4.5-inch ammunition, chaff rockets, medical items, food and canteen stores. The ammunition then carried exceeded her normal outfit, possibly by as much as 100 per cent in some categories. However, it was all stowed in magazines, although not always in approved locations. For example, 4.5-inch ammunition was stowed on the deck in the 4.5-inch magazine and also in the air weapons magazine adjacent to the hangar. In accordance with war orders, pictures were removed, carpets below 1 deck were taken up and loose fittings were stowed away. Due to the danger of misidentification of the ship as an Argentinian Type 42 destroyer, thick vertical black marks were painted on the funnel, screen and ship's side, both port and starboard. Ship's company were issued with medication for use in the event of chemical attack, as part of steps to increase their awareness of the reality of the threat. Lectures, training programmes and briefings were carried out. The removal of beards was considered but was not enforced. However, a strong enough line on personal kit and soft furnishings was not taken: privately owned boats were left stowed on the upper deck, and carpets were not removed from cabins and messes on 1 deck and above, and all of these caught fire in the attack.[10]

Following passage south in company with *Antrim, Glamorgan, Coventry, Glasgow, Brilliant, Arrow, Plymouth* and Royal Fleet Auxiliaries (RFA), *Sheffield* arrived at Ascension Island on 10 April. A large quantity of stores was ashore awaiting transfer using a Wessex helicopter. The stores' organization ashore was described by the ship's officers as chaotic, no doubt caused by the huge amounts of stores received for a large number of ships in a short space of time. The stores flown to Ascension included many items which were only required for the planned assisted maintenance period and were of no importance to a ship proceeding to a war zone.[11]

After a short period in the local exercise areas, during which *Sheffield* 'was particularly sharp, hitting her missile target with a perfectly executed Sea Dart shot first time',[12] she sailed from Ascension on 14 April and proceeded south at about 25 knots to a position near 35° south 38° west, in company with *Brilliant, Glasgow, Coventry* and *Arrow*, later joined by RFA *Appleleaf*. While some other ships had considerable propulsion problems during this fast passage, *Sheffield*'s main machinery remained generally serviceable. This group joined the *Hermes* and *Invincible* battle group and entered the total exclusion zone (200 nautical miles around the Falkland Islands) on 1 May.[13]

On Saturday 1 May the task group commenced operations in the total exclusion zone. On that first day *Sheffield* went to action stations on numerous occasions at Air Warning Yellow (when an air threat was thought possible). However, because radar detection ranges on Argentinian aircraft of some 160 miles were being achieved, and because attacks by them were made only on the naval gunfire support ships inshore, this routine was subsequently modified and action stations were delayed until Air Warning Red (when an air raid was definitely developing or likely). *Sheffield* and other ships were dogged by what they considered to be false alarms, believing that the radar of Argentinian Mirage III jets was being wrongly identified by the UAA1 sensor as the Agave radar (nicknamed Condor) of the Argentine Navy's Super Étendard (Super E) jets, because of the almost complete similarity between the radar parameters of the two aircraft. *Sheffield* did successfully acquire some of the aircraft on its Type 909 radar when they closed within 100 nautical miles and did fire one reduced pattern of chaff, a missile decoy fired to produce a cloud of small aluminium pieces. After an uneventful night the ship went to action stations on Sunday 2 May anticipating retaliatory air raids on the task group in light of the heavy Argentinian losses of five aircraft the day before over the Falklands, but nothing happened. Thereafter 2 and 3 May were quiet and the ship settled into a defence watch routine and the Air Warning remained Yellow throughout.[14]

The ships of the task group were provided with a large amount of intelligence data, the first of which had been received on board *Sheffield* on or about 21 or 22 April and was described as 'a sizeable and daunting bundle' that required sorting out to understand the threat. Prior to this the ship's officers had researched available intelligence documents held on board, particularly copies of the standard reference books *Jane's Fighting Ships* and *Jane's All the World's Aircraft*, highlighting for example the French-designed and operated Mirage III and Super E jets. On the critical question of whether Argentinian Super Es had air-to-air refuelling and Exocet capabilities, and hence whether British ships were vulnerable to Exocet attack, *Sheffield* had intelligence information, received from the task group commander on 26 April, showing that such an attack was quite possible, because the five Super Es that were capable of firing Exocet had a refuelling pod, and if refuelled in mid-flight had a radius of action which extended as far out as South Georgia. This covered the whole of the total exclusion zone and would permit reasonably protracted low-level operations east of the Falklands. Without refuelling, their radius of action bisected the Falkland Islands. The Argentines were thought to have some ten Exocet missiles.[15]

On 4 May *Sheffield* and other ships received from the task group commander information that five Super Es were operating from the Argentinian mainland base at Río Grande. It was thought that probably only one Super E was fully equipped to launch Exocet, although all could carry them. This modified the ship's appreciation of the risk, and the implications were said to have been well understood. The task force commander later told the board of inquiry that Super E/Exocet attack had been well recognized by all for some days as the most potent threat, with Super Es operating from southern Argentinian air bases.

However, *Sheffield* rated the Exocet danger lower, and the submarine threat higher, than did the carrier group. *Sheffield*'s captain regarded the area as a 'submariner's paradise' and, with an Argentinian Type 209 submarine thought to be operating in the area, in the prevailing calm weather, Sam Salt rated the submarine threat to be *as great* as the air threat.[16] The Type 209 was a fairly small German-designed conventional submarine equipped with eight torpedoes. Two such boats had been assembled in Argentina from sections shipped out from Germany and completed in 1974[17] and were regarded by Captain Salt as sophisticated vessels. Although *Sheffield* had not dismissed the possibility of an airborne Exocet attack, the experiences of 1 May, when they believed the alleged Super Es were actually Mirage IIIs, probably lulled the ship into a belief that future raids might well develop along similar lines to those seen then, attacking the inshore naval gunfire support ships rather than the offshore ships.[18]

When the attack came, on the afternoon of 4 May, *Sheffield* was the southerly of three British Type 42 destroyers that formed an air defence arc about 18 miles to the west, up threat from the carrier battle group, the other two destroyers being *Glasgow* and *Coventry* (see Map 4). The anti-air warfare commander (AAWC) was in *Invincible* and the flag officer, Rear Admiral Woodward, in *Hermes*. The weather was fair with a calm sea and 2-metre swell, and visibility of 7 nautical miles. *Sheffield* was making 12 knots on her two Tyne gas turbines, with both Olympus gas turbines on standby at two minutes' notice, and was transmitting on radar, sonar, and HF, UHF and SHF radio. On board the atmosphere was understandably tense, but no one was uptight; morale was high and everyone's mood good – they were said to be keen and ready to fight. However, some were beginning to get bored and a little frustrated from lengthy periods of inactivity.

The starboard defence watch came on duty at 12.00 and shortly afterwards the AAWC in *Invincible* broadcast a situation report confirming Air Warning Yellow, with no known hostile air activity within 200 nautical miles of the task group. The captain visited the operations room at about 12.45 to update himself and then returned to his cabin where he remained until the missile impact. The anti-air warfare officer (AAWO), Lieutenant Commander Nick Batho, left the ops room at about 13.40 to go to the bridge to check the cloud-base, and then went to the wardroom and had a cup of coffee. His assistant, Able Seaman Burns, also left to 'visit the heads' (relieve himself), as had one of the target indication operators, whilst the air picture reporter was still in the ops room but not at his desk. Thus, the AAWO and three of his air team of eight were out of the ops room or out of position, severely depleting the manning.

At about 09.00 (Falklands Standard Time) two Super Étendards of the Argentinian 2nd Naval Fighter and Attack Squadron, each with one Exocet missile under the starboard wing, took off from the Río Grande air base on the island of Tierra del Fuego. Piloted by Lieutenant Commander Augusto Bedacarratz and Lieutenant Armando Mayora respectively, they flew due east at a speed of about

Map 4: The Exocet missile strike on HMS *Sheffield*, 4 May

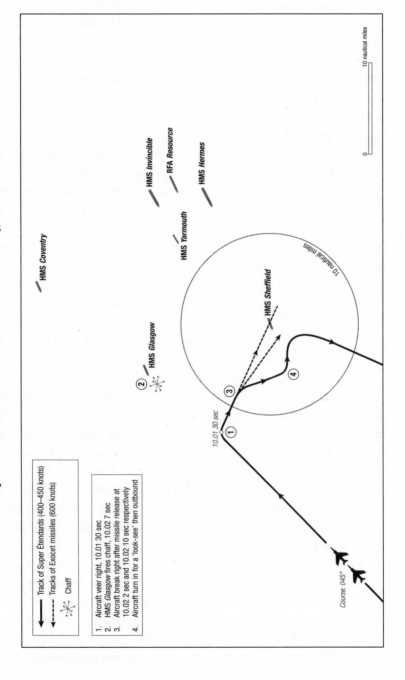

Track of Super Étendards (400–450 knots)

Track of Exocet missiles (600 knots)

Chaff

1. Aircraft veer right, 10.01 30 sec
2. HMS *Glasgow* fires chaff, 10.02 7 sec
3. Aircraft break right after missile release at
   10.02 2 sec and 10.02 10 sec respectively
4. Aircraft turn in for a 'look-see' then outbound

HMS *Coventry*

HMS *Invincible*

RFA *Resource*

HMS *Hermes*

HMS *Yarmouth*

HMS *Glasgow*

HMS *Sheffield*

10 nautical miles

10.01 30 sec

Course: 045°

0   10 nautical miles

400–450 knots, with extra fuel tanks under their port wings. They climbed to 15,000ft to rendezvous with a Hercules tanker aircraft for air-to-air refuelling some 150 miles out from their base. When about 280 miles from the British battle group, they began their gradual descent for the final approach and attack, when they would fly at about 50ft above the sea, so that the curvature of the earth masked them from the long-range radar of the British destroyers. They 'popped up' briefly to about 200ft for a quick look with their radar to see if any targets presented themselves. If the men in the operations room of the destroyers were alert, they might detect the radar emissions from the planes and spot them on their destroyers' radar screens.[19]

Sure enough, the raid was first detected on UAA1 by *Glasgow* at 09.56 30 sec and was correctly assessed as Super E Agave radar by the ship's commanding officer and the anti-air warfare officer. Like everyone when the ship was at action stations they were wearing their yellowish cotton anti-flash hoods and gloves to prevent serious flash burns to the face, head and hands if a missile or shell got through.[20] At 09.58 *Glasgow* reported the Agave/Condor contact on AAWC UHF and HF radio, and this was heard in *Sheffield* on UHF. At 09.58 06 sec *Glasgow* intercepted two further Agave sweeps and nine seconds later gained two distinct Type 965 radar contacts with the aircraft at about 40 miles. These were followed by two contacts on her Type 992 radar 30 seconds later. *Glasgow's* captain, Paul Hoddinott, was in his operations room monitoring all developments and directing responses, as was Captain David Hart Dyke in *Coventry*, but in *Sheffield* neither Captain Sam Salt nor his second-in-command was in their ship's operations room. Hoddinott had banned the daytime use of his satellite communications system (SCOT), which could block out detection of the Étendard's Agave radar.[21]

Glasgow reported the raid from the south-west on AAWC radio at 10.00 00 sec (which was received in *Sheffield*), went to action stations 23 seconds later, and fired chaff at 10.02 7 sec. However, she did not fire Sea Dart missiles at the intruder. Radar 'paints' were seen in *Invincible* at 50 and 30 miles, which correlated with

Glasgow's report. Two Sea Harriers on combat air patrol were told to investigate and set off west, but then, from just over 100 nautical miles behind them, *Hermes* called the pair back to their combat air patrol position. This was because the AAWC in *Invincible* did not accept *Glasgow's* classification of the raid and declared the contacts to be spurious, with Air Warning remaining at Yellow: this was despite the fact that *Glasgow's* AAWO on watch, Lieutenant Commander Nick Hawkyard, persisted in trying to convince AAWC that it was a genuine raid, to no avail. Shortly afterwards, two other Sea Harriers on combat air patrol to the south of the first pair were ordered by a controller in *Hermes* to proceed 120 miles to the south-west to carry out a visual surface search for enemy surface units, even though they could have just flown about 20 miles in that direction and then used their radar to sweep the target area. The removal of this combat air patrol left a large hole in the outer defence ring of the group.[22]

In *Sheffield* at 10.01 45 sec the order to 'stand to' was given to the crews of the Sea Dart, 4.5-inch and light guns. Ten seconds later the approach of the aircraft was indicated to *Sheffield's* forward Type 909 radar but not to the aft 909, which had clear arcs to the aircraft initially and to the missile throughout. A further seven seconds later the first Exocet missile was fired, prompting *Glasgow* to fire chaff five seconds later. The second missile was fired at 10.02 10 sec, just eight seconds after the first.[23] *Glasgow* found herself unable to fire Sea Dart missiles at the intruders because of a failure to acquire the small, fleeting targets on the Sea Dart's 909 fire control radar in time.[24] Such frustrations were not uncommon with Sea Dart, which relied on rather clunky electronics systems, causing delays or failure to react, and the fire control radar was designed to pick up long-range high-flying targets, not the low-level close-range targets that often presented themselves in the Falklands conflict. Eight days later, when *Glasgow* was under attack from Skyhawks the Sea Dart loading system failed safe,* the launcher computer refusing to

---

* The system responded to a malfunction in a way that prevented damage to the equipment or personnel: this is known as a fail-safe design feature.

accept the two missiles, and *Glasgow* was hit by a 1,000lb bomb.[25] *Coventry* also experienced at least one Sea Dart system failure, when attempting to engage an Argentinian Boeing surveillance aircraft.[26]

At 10.01 30 sec the two attacking Super Es had swung to starboard, away from *Glasgow* and towards *Sheffield*, which was about 15 nautical miles away; this turn was observed in the ops rooms of both ships. In *Sheffield* the UAA1 sensor, which covered the Étendard's Agave radar and the Exocet missile head radar, was blanked out by the ship's own transmission on SCOT (the satellite communication system). Neither the principal warfare officer nor the AAWO were aware of this transmission and had not given permission for it. The AAWO was still out of the ops room as were two important members of the air team, and AAWC radio was not being manned. At 10.02 15 sec missile smoke (from the Exocet boosts) was sighted visually from the bridge and reported to the ops room. However, officers on the bridge were mesmerized by the sight and did not broadcast a warning to the ship's company. Chaff was not fired and attempts to acquire the targets on the forward 909 radar (controlling the Sea Dart anti-air missiles) were unsuccessful. The captain was not called, the ship was not called to action stations, and did not turn towards the incoming missiles in order to minimize the ship's profile. At 10.01 45 sec *Sheffield*'s missile/gun director, Chief Gunnery Instructor Adamson, ordered 'stand to' and the Sea Dart, 4.5-inch gun and 909 radar crews quickly moved to their stations. The target was indicated to the forward 909 but was not acquired by it, in part because an unnecessarily long procedure was used.

At 10.01 40 sec the AAWO (who was chatting to stewards in the wardroom) had been called over the ship's voice system by the principal warfare officer, and returned to the ops room at 10.02 10 sec, very shortly before the Exocet missile struck, though many witnesses put the time he returned as much later, at within 5 or 10 seconds of missile impact. He misidentified the raid as Mirage III because he did not believe *Sheffield* was within range of Argentinian Super Étendard aircraft. He was too late to fire chaff or otherwise influence events, and at 10.03 00 sec the missile struck the ship at 2 deck on the starboard side between the galley and the forward auxiliary machinery room and forward engine room.[27]

* * *

On the bridge the officer of the watch, Lieutenant Peter Walpole, had seen something coming towards the ship, trailing smoke, but had great difficulty recognizing what it was:

> We had only a matter of seconds before impact... I knew it wasn't coming straight for me but to the centre of the ship, so I had the possibility of surviving... I shouted twice down a handset to the ops room, 'Take cover!', and wanted to go to the bosun's mate position to activate the main broadcast alarms, but I never got there, and at the moment of impact was lying on the deck. It really was the most frightful crash, a very strange sensation, like a bad car accident but ten times worse – the pressure wave and the sound of such a terrific explosion.[28]

In a second the perfect working ship was irrevocably changed. Only the urgent tone of the request to the AAWO to return to his station had given any warning to the majority of the crew of the imminent attack. A probable second missile missed and ditched in the sea close by. The Argentinian aircraft that had launched the missile flew over the ship, perhaps to observe the results of the attack. The AAWC in *Invincible* remained unaware that *Sheffield* had been hit and continued denying the existence of the raid for some 12 minutes. Many in *Sheffield*, including the principal warfare officer, still did not realize this had been an Exocet attack.[29]

Sam Salt had been writing his diary in his cabin when he heard a bang, 'not spectacular at all', and dashed straight up to the bridge. 'By the time I reached it we had lost 50 per cent of electrical power, nearly all communications, and the ship in darkness. Smoke was starting to come straight up to the bridge. All in a matter of seconds… and we could not tell the ship's company what was happening.'[30]

As the Exocet had approached, Chris Purcell, a 22-year-old able seaman, had just stepped back on deck after asking the chefs in the galley below to make some tea. He was talking with the pilot on the bridge wing, when they saw a huge fireball approaching. The pilot yelled 'Exocet!' and a broadcast shouted 'Take cover!' Purcell dived behind an ammunition box and heard a thud into the ship's side. Within seconds the upper deck was covered in thick smoke, and all the chefs he had been talking to were dead by then.

Captain David Hart Dyke, in the ops room of *Coventry*, recalled that the three Type 42s were talking to one another by radio and his ship became aware of the threat from *Glasgow*. Suddenly there was silence from *Sheffield*, and then, as 18-year-old missileman Able Seaman Martin 'Izzy' Isaacs, who was on watch on *Coventry*'s bridge, recalled, 'a radio operator from *Sheffield* came over the air in plain language and screaming, "We've been hit", and we could see the thick black smoke on the horizon.' Hart Dyke recalled that aboard *Coventry* the ship's company was shocked by the sudden reality of war and struggled to overcome their feelings and fears. Nevertheless, their confidence quickly returned and they were able to face the battles ahead with a steely resolve to hit back at the enemy as soon as they possibly could.[32]

* * *

Shortly after the missile impact, personnel manning *Sheffield*'s starboard side light guns heard the sound of an approaching aircraft, but their view was obstructed by smoke. Assuming it to be hostile, the starboard 20mm and light machine guns blindly engaged the aircraft until it was realized by the flight commander on the forecastle that the noise was that of a friendly helicopter. The engagement was then terminated on the orders of the flight commander and the Sea King was seen to take drastic evasive action by diving and turning away: fortunately, it was not hit. In a short time smoke made the bridge untenable and it had to be evacuated. The captain shouted up from the forecastle deck to ask Peter Walpole if he was in communication with the tiller flat, so the rudders could be controlled locally instead of from the bridge. Salt said that if the ship could be steered and was still running on some engines they could head to South Georgia, which Walpole interpreted as being somewhere where it could be repaired, but he never did get control of the rudders.[33]

The missile's impact left a 15ft by 4ft hole in the ship's side and caused widespread minor shock damage, especially in the forward engine room, forward auxiliary engine room and galley, typically the buckling of doors and hatches and the collapse of ladders. Initial evidence indicated that the warhead did not detonate, with few reports of shrapnel, but this was questioned by later analysis in an MOD paper that concluded that it had exploded.[34] This remains in doubt. Large fires broke out immediately in the forward engine room and auxiliary engine room area, and there was a very rapid spread of acrid black smoke through the centre section of the ship, and upwards to the bridge. This very quickly forced evacuation of the machinery control room, main communications office and the bridge, followed after a few minutes by the ops room and later the complete forward section of the ship and the forward superstructure. Missile propellant and burning diesel fuel from the ruptured forward auxiliary service and ready use tanks were the main sources of this smoke, which was responsible for the early and almost complete loss of the ship's fighting capability. Smoke clearance* was unsuccessful forward and only partially successful aft.[35]

Without orders, as a natural reaction, most of the ship's company immediately tried to get to their action stations. They were hampered by smoke and jammed doors, and many never reached their positions. Several casualties were seen within seconds of impact and this added to the total surprise, shock and general bewilderment. Several key officers and ratings were suffering from

---

* Smoke clearance is intended to redirect smoke to the outside of the ship in order to minimize smoke in escape routes and allow easier access by firefighting parties.

shock, which was not immediately apparent. It was 10 to 15 minutes before effective control was established. The physical shock of the missile impact tripped the computer, forward 909 radar and the main machinery room, rendering the ship defenceless for the few minutes required to bring all this equipment back on line. This showed that a single hit could prevent defence against a continuing attack, a worrying implication.[36]

The weapon engineer officer, Lieutenant Commander John Woodhead, his computer section officer and three senior ratings stayed at their posts in the computer room after the remainder of the forward end of the ship was evacuated. At the time of the missile impact, Woodhead had directed damage control action near the operations room. He then went below to the computer room and with the crew there began to assess the damage to his weapon systems. Smoke caused the operations room above, and then the forward sections of the ship, to be evacuated, but Woodhead continued at his post and carefully and with extreme determination co-ordinated attempts to restore power to essential weapon equipment and succeeded in restoring the computer facility. Tragically, all five men in the computer room perished.[37] Those who died were Lieutenant Commander John Woodhead, Sub-Lieutenant Richard Emly, Weapons Engineering Artificer Anthony Eggington, Chief Weapons Engineering Mechanician Michael Till and Weapons Engineering Mechanician Barry Wallis, all having been overcome by the dense smoke.[38]

Peter Walpole and others reassembled on the upper deck and looked after some of the upper deck crew who had been closer to the impact and had flash burns that made them unrecognizable; the doctor set up a first-aid post on the forecastle. Flames were leaping nearly 100ft into the air from the ruptured fuel tanks: this died down quickly into a smoking sort of fire, which was raging inside. Walpole climbed onto the bridge top to try to establish some sort of command position and see if any further attack was coming. He felt like someone's prey, trapped and unable to move, fearing a fresh attack. A Harrier flew over, which was a great relief.[39]

The fire main was ruptured on impact, removing any real chance of tackling the fires, which gained quickly, spreading to the rest of the ship. Firefighting in the forward section was largely restricted to external boundary cooling, using portable pumps and buckets, with little or no effect on the fires raging within the ship. Re-entry attempts were made in several places: these were well-briefed, determined attacks by men wearing fearnought fireproof suits and breathing apparatus, but all were beaten back by heat and smoke. One casualty had his leg trapped in a buckled quick-release door which had thick black smoke billowing past it, near the forward auxiliary machinery room. Three attempts were made by ratings wearing breathing apparatus to free the casualty but they were driven back by heat and dense smoke. In brave efforts to salvage damage control and firefighting equipment from the forward section, several men were overcome by smoke and Petty Officer David Briggs died of asphyxiation. He was wearing an anti-gas respirator, which allowed him to keep his eyes open in the smoke but did not supply oxygen (as breathing apparatus would do).

Firefighting efforts in the aft section were a little more successful, with reasonably effective smoke clearance established. Pressure to the hoses was provided by a Rover gas turbine pump, supplied by the frigate *Arrow** alongside to port, right up until the order to abandon ship was given. On the upper deck buckets were being used and, later, hoses from submersible pumps hung over the ship's side. The ship's Gemini craft was launched and used hoses from one of the submersible pumps on the forecastle to direct water into the hole in the ship's side where a mass of flames could be seen. This was later augmented by hoses supplied from *Arrow*'s fire main, and *Arrow* did an excellent job of boundary cooling. Conditions for *Yarmouth*, to starboard, were less easy. Both ships' efforts were bedevilled by frequent spurious submarine and torpedo alarms; on nine occasions *Yarmouth*'s crew thought they detected a torpedo in the water, causing them to move away from *Sheffield*, and on two

---

* The frigates *Arrow* and *Yarmouth* were in the vicinity and were summoned to assist *Sheffield*.

occasions they fired their ship's anti-submarine mortars. Suspecting that the threat was imagined, Admiral Woodward sent a very ratty signal to Commander Tony Morton, captain of *Yarmouth*. It was later deduced that the propeller noises they kept hearing on their sonar came from the outboard motor of *Sheffield*'s Gemini inflatable dinghy.[40]

Yarmouth's position was made difficult by being on the windward side and was also affected by the swell. She encountered considerably more difficulty than *Arrow* in achieving a satisfactory alongside position, and in fact never really did so. The support provided by helicopters, particularly in supplying firefighting equipment and evacuating casualties, was invaluable despite flying conditions being made extremely difficult at times by smoke, and their operations centred on *Sheffield*'s flight deck and forecastle. But Rover gas turbine pumps collected from several ships performed outstandingly badly: of the five pumps eventually tried on board *Sheffield*, only one operated successfully.

Eight duty watch chefs were in the galley at the time of impact and were probably killed outright. If not, they died of asphyxia from the very dense acrid smoke. The man trapped in a door died, probably from asphyxia; he had been comforted by a first-aider, who unfortunately carried no morphine. One man last seen in a stores area failed to escape with the two survivors from that space. Another died at the foot of a ladder, unable to climb it, and may have been injured: a survivor tried to pull him out but was unsuccessful because of smoke. Petty Officer Briggs, who died of asphyxiation trying to retrieve damage control equipment in the forward section, was working with Marine Engineer Mechanics Chiplen and Tancock, all three wearing anti-gas respirators. Tancock took some of the equipment forward but collapsed at the bottom of the escape ladder. Michael Chiplen remained in the damage control store with Briggs and collected up a further load which he took forward, leaving Briggs in the store. When he returned he found Briggs unconscious, but was himself having difficulty breathing and could not pull him out. He therefore retired to seek help. Three other men who were not sighted immediately before or after impact could not be accounted for, and were presumed dead. Four men sustained serious injuries.[41]

In the forward machinery room one man was thrown down on the deck plates and probably knocked unconscious. Recovering, he was unable to reach the normal access ladder due to a major fire. His overalls were on fire; he beat these out, turned forward and, with the compartment full of smoke, found a wall of flame. He covered his face with his hands and traversed the fire, then made it up another escape ladder. He proceeded forward and received first aid and medical treatment, having sustained serious 44 per cent burns. Another man made a difficult escape from the forward engine room, suffering flash burns and burns to his hands from a ladder that was too hot to hold. In the main communications office, one man was blasted by a blinding flash that blew his trousers off completely and left him with flash burns to his hands, face and both legs. He was blown 6 feet and covered in debris. Another man in the same space was blown 4–5 feet and sustained flash burns to his face, legs and ankle. Amongst the more minor casualties, two were unconscious and were resuscitated by the medical officer and his petty officer assistant. Others recovered in the fresh air.[42]

Petty Officer Medical Assistant Gerald Meager gave immediate first aid treatment to the more serious casualties and his first aid teams established a very effective casualty centre in the hangar. He provided excellent direction and encouragement where it was needed, comforted those who were suffering from shock and later organized the evacuation of casualties by helicopter. At one point, receiving a report that a man below decks had been overcome by smoke, Meager donned breathing apparatus and rescued the unconscious Weapons Engineering Mechanic Glaseby in very difficult circumstances. He found the body of Petty Officer David Briggs, but the smoke was very thick and, not knowing how much air he had left in his breathing apparatus, he went to get help. Surgeon Lieutenant David Ward despatched Leading Seaman Davies and Able Seaman Shaw in breathing apparatus to recover the body to an area where Ward and Meager attempted resuscitation, though unfortunately this was unsuccessful.[43]

Mark Snow, a 19-year-old chef at the time, says had he not overslept that afternoon, he probably would have died in the blaze:

> I should have been up making coffee and tea for the watch changeover before my watch started at 12.00. The first thing really was the smoke, and then someone shouting 'fire, fire, fire!', and then smoke started drifting down, and I heard screams, and shouts of 'casualty, casualty!'. I don't think the enormity of it occurred to me whatsoever – you just knew that something was wrong, and you were doing a job. It wasn't until about halfway through the afternoon that I saw one of the ship's company die... things were happening that you never thought you would experience.[44]

After fighting the fire for nearly four hours, and with the situation deteriorating, the captain became convinced that the ship's fighting capability was irredeemably destroyed, and at 13.50 40 sec he ordered 'abandon ship'. Most men climbed over to *Arrow*, whilst a few went to *Yarmouth* by Gemini. Peter Walpole recalled having to get aft, crossing the central area of the ship that was blazing with fire. He clambered down onto the port waist and made a dash through the hot centre section to the flight deck, where people were jumping across the perilous gap to *Arrow*, being encouraged by others to jump as the gap opened and closed whilst the two ships rolled into each other. Some, including Sam Salt and the warfare officers who had been on watch, were flown by *Sheffield*'s Lynx helicopter to *Hermes*, where the admiral's staff were keen to learn what had actually happened. ITN reporter Michael Nicholson saw this group when they arrived on board *Hermes*, looking shocked; Sam Salt was in tears, devastated by the loss.[45]

Salt received a rather frosty reception from Admiral Woodward, who said, 'Sounds as though you've been pretty careless, Sam', and felt that the loss should not have happened. It did not help Salt's rock-bottom morale. Salt found the next two nights really fearful. 'I started to have the most ghastly guilt complexes. What could I personally have done? Why wasn't I down in the ops room? Would I have been able to do anything different?'[46]

Two officers and 18 ratings had died in the attack and its immediate aftermath: some, such as those in the galley area, were killed on impact. Others were asphyxiated, attempting to escape, re-entering the ship or staying at their quarters to try to restore the ship's fighting capability, as in the computer room. Twenty-six men were injured, mostly suffering burns, shock, wounds from flying debris or smoke inhalation, all of whom were later thought to have made a satisfactory recovery. The casualties were taken to *Hermes* where they received treatment from that ship's surgical support team before being transferred on 12 May to the hospital ship *Uganda*, which had much better facilities. The *Sheffield* casualties were the first to be treated in *Uganda*, a P&O liner which had been taken off a Mediterranean cruise and hurriedly converted in Gibraltar Dockyard for her new role.[47] After ten days they were all transferred to the tanker *British Esk* and taken to Ascension Island.[48]

Sheffield's starboard Tyne gas turbine was shut down after the missile impact, but the port Tyne was still running when the ship was abandoned because access to the machinery control room had been impossible. On the three consecutive days after the incident, with fires still burning in parts of the ship, small parties of men were winched down from helicopters onto *Sheffield*'s flight deck or forecastle to recover firefighting equipment that had been transferred from other ships and the arming pins for the helicopter's Sea Skua missiles, without which the missiles were useless. The body of Petty Officer Briggs was also recovered. *Sheffield* was taken in tow by *Yarmouth* on the morning of 9 May and reached the edge of the total exclusion zone. However, the sea had been entering the ship through the hole in its side and a list developed. At around 03.00 on 10 May the ship rolled over on its side and sank in about 1,000 fathoms, six days after the attack.[49] The wreck is a war grave and is designated as a protected place under the Protection of Military Remains Act 1986. The 242 survivors were taken by sea to Ascension and then flown home. Now, located on a southern cliff on Sea Lion Island in the south-east of the Falklands archipelago, a large cross commemorates the sinking of *Sheffield*.

* * *

Decorations for bravery were awarded to Lieutenant Commander John Woodhead, Distinguished Service Cross (posthumous) for exceptional leadership, dedication to duty and courage; Petty Officer David Briggs, Distinguished Service Medal (posthumous) for leadership, bravery and devotion to duty; and Petty Officer Medical Assistant Gerald Meager, Queen's Gallantry Medal for selfless dedication to duty and professionalism which undoubtedly saved life and minimized many injuries (see Appendix).[50] Petty Officer Briggs' body was transferred to *Hermes* on 6 May and was committed to the deep in a moving ceremony later the same day.[51]

When the awards were first announced, the press rang Salt up at midnight saying, 'Captain Salt, what is your comment on the fact that you are not included in the list of awards?' Salt replied that he was not the slightest bit proud of himself: he would not want a decoration for losing a ship.[52]

* * *

A board of inquiry into the loss of *Sheffield* was convened at HMS *Nelson*, Portsmouth, and comprised Captain J. J. R. Oswald (president), Commander J. Astbury, Commander R. J. Rolls, Commander C. W. Pile and Surgeon Commander J. R. Harrison. Their report was presented to the commander-in-chief, fleet, on 22 July 1982.[53]

The board concluded that, when the attack came, *Sheffield* was not fully prepared for it. Some vital members of the defence watch operations room team, including the AAWO, were absent from that room. The 909 radar did not acquire the missile target (a fast, low flyer) and an unnecessarily lengthy process was used. Neither Sea Dart nor 4.5-inch gun engaged the missile or the firing aircraft. The crew of the 20mm and light machine guns were not alert:

despite the 'stand to' order their weapons were neither manned nor loaded and were not able to engage the missile. The raid was not well handled by the AAWC in *Invincible*. If all the right reactions had been taken, very quickly indeed, and in particular if chaff had been fired by *Sheffield* on receipt of the warning from *Glasgow*, the board concluded that it might just have been possible to frustrate this 'determined and very professional' Super E Exocet attack.[54]

One of the shortcomings of the Type 42 design was the lack of a close-range (point) defence system such as Sea Wolf, which was fitted in Type 22 frigates, or the Phalanx 20mm motorized cannon that had been in service in the US Navy for two years. Other shortcomings were the lack of a jammer to block the missile's radar, the very high reliance demanded of a number of operators if a Sea Dart or 4.5-inch gun versus sea-skimming missile engagement was to have any chance of success, and inadequate training simulator provision, particularly for realistic 909 radar low target acquisition practice. In the 'hot washup' of the attack by *Sheffield*'s officers, the Super E attack profile was described as 'quite unlike that expected', because they all thought it would be launched at long range and high-ish level.

Three minutes had elapsed after the first indication of the strike by *Glasgow* before the missile hit *Sheffield*. *Glasgow* had reacted quickly and correctly to the threat, but *Invincible* failed to broadcast an air attack warning and the responses in *Sheffield* were critically deficient. The principal warfare officer in *Sheffield* did not react to the signal from *Glasgow*, failing to call the captain, pipe the ship to action stations and raise the damage control state: according to the report this was 'partly through inexperience, but more importantly from inadequacy'. Amongst the many lessons learnt, the inquiry reported, were the supreme importance of timely firing of chaff; the need for constant vigilance of all on watch; instant, full reaction, in accordance with standard tactical doctrine and teaching, on first indication of a possible attack; speedy 909 radar acquisition, even for a fast, low flyer; the realization that improvements made in recent years to ships' habitability (e.g. carpeting and furnishings) had been made at the expense of firefighting considerations; and the urgent need for an improvement to the Type 42's point-defence capability against sea-skimming missiles. Also, the need for airborne aerial warning became very obvious to the board.

Two days after the incident, the commander of the task group, Rear Admiral Sandy Woodward, signalled ships with a list of 15 lessons learned. Amongst these was: 'Beware of ignoring the advice of the ship in contact', with which the board agreed and commented, 'As the AAWC one cannot afford to stand on dignity. Montgomery said, "It is upon the initiative of subordinates that the battle is finally won."' Woodward also advised, 'If in doubt always assume the worst situation and react accordingly', 'In war no-one is ever to leave his post', and that the chaff firing panel should never be left unattended. He considered that, 'Ample warning was in fact available for ASXD [anti-ship missile defence]', to which the inquiry report added, 'Had *Sheffield* been properly organised she might have successfully fended off this very professional attack.'[55]

It seems clear from the inquiry report that the ship had not been put on a vigilant, alert and responsive war footing, and that this failing extended to the senior officers (such as the AAWO), who – from captain down – were of course also responsible for instilling the necessary war discipline amongst the ship's company.

The board found two officers, the principal warfare officer (Lieutenant Tolley) and the anti-air warfare officer (Lieutenant Commander Nick Batho), were guilty of negligence, but they escaped courts martial and did not face disciplinary action, a decision made by Commander-in-Chief Fleet Admiral Fieldhouse, apparently to avoid undermining the euphoria that gripped much of the UK at the end of the war.[56]

Nine critical deficiencies in damage control and fire-fighting arrangements and equipment in Type 42s came to light, including a shortage of breathing apparatus and forward escape manholes that were too small for passage by men wearing breathing apparatus. The use of gas masks (rather than breathing apparatus) when re-entering areas was contrary to regulations: they filtered out fumes but the filters probably became blocked in heavy smoke and were also ineffective against carbon monoxide, causing one death, two cases of unconsciousness and two who were close to unconsciousness. The firefighting and other activity lacked cohesion: no emergency headquarters was established, it was not clear where command of the ship was located, the control of personnel was unco-ordinated and, in particular, inadequate checks were made on which quarters had been abandoned and which were still closed up. By the time it was realized that the computer room crew and the supply officer were missing, it was too late.[57]

There were many fine examples of individual bravery in the efforts to save *Sheffield*. The five men in the computer room and Petty Officer David Briggs, all of whom died, were singled out as particularly praiseworthy.[58]

* * *

Captain Salt's background as a submariner and his lack of air defence and recent surface ship warfare experience, along with his appointment to *Sheffield* after the ship had worked up and participated in major fleet exercises, meant he was not well prepared and lacked experience for command of an air defence unit facing a potent threat in a war situation. Similarly, the first lieutenant, Lieutenant Commander Norman, a helicopter observer, lacked relevant in-depth experience of surface ships. After impact, he was somewhat at a loss, albeit in extremely difficult and demanding circumstances, and he was not able to control manpower effectively or direct effort decisively. That these two appointments had been made concurrently was unfortunate, the board said.[59]

Admiral Fieldhouse's view on the performance of Captain Salt and his second-in-command was that 'none of the failings revealed amount to negligence, since without the relevant experience I would not have expected more from these capable and conscientious officers, especially Captain Salt, who had been in command for only a limited period and at a time of restricted employment for the ship.' But Fieldhouse noted that a recent report (April 1982) from Flag Officer Sea Training stated that 'With the ever-increasing complexity of warfare, it is essential for commanding officers to be appointed in relation to both their specialisation and to their past experience and, whenever possible, at a time when they are "in date" operationally'. A similar sentiment had been expressed by the Naval Secretary in February 1982. Fieldhouse concluded by saying, 'The loss of *Sheffield* accentuates the need to pursue this policy to the utmost.'[60] It is therefore rather surprising that Captain Salt's next seagoing appointment was to another Type 42 destroyer, *Southampton*: his experience in *Sheffield*, whilst no doubt instructive, could hardly be described as extensive.

* * *

Sheffield was a modern ship expressly designed for air defence: despite some potential shortcomings in her missile fire control system, she should not have fallen victim to Exocet if all the right actions had been taken promptly. Her crew displayed an almost complete lack of war discipline, with a watch that was far from vigilant and an anti-air warfare officer and other key personnel missing from their posts when the attack came. It did not help that the sensor that could detect the radars of the incoming Super Étendard and the Exocet missile head was blanked out by the ship's own transmission on the satellite communication system, something which could have easily been avoided. The captain was not in the operations room or bridge and the ship was not called to action stations by the principal warfare officer after the warning from *Glasgow* was heard. No meaningful response to the missile threat was initiated: chaff was not fired and the point defence weapons were not manned; the missile target was not acquired by the Sea Dart fire control system because of the over-lengthy procedure that was erroneously used. If *Sheffield* had fired chaff when the warning was given by *Glasgow*, the ship might well have escaped being hit. In *Glasgow* the imperfections of the fire control system meant that no Sea Dart missiles were fired at the Exocet. The warning from *Glasgow* was not broadcast by the anti-air warfare co-ordination team in *Invincible*, who believed it to be spurious. This led to two Sea Harriers, which had been told to investigate and set off west, being called back to their combat air patrol position by *Hermes*, and a second combat air patrol being diverted elsewhere: another opportunity to avert the disaster had been missed.

The experience of *Sheffield*'s loss was a sobering influence on other ships' officers and men: the reality of war and the need to be constantly awake to the threats, and assiduous in their responses, were brought home even more strongly than before. It was to be another 17 days before the next ship, HMS *Ardent*, was lost. She was the first of four British ships lost in the space of five days in the dangerous period covering the amphibious landings of troops and their immediate deployment.

4

The Loss of HMS *Ardent*

On the evening of 20 May, HMS *Ardent*, which had been escorting the amphibious force south, sped through the narrows at the northern entrance to Falkland Sound, some two hours ahead of the force. She proceeded to her assigned station in Grantham Sound: here she would bombard the enemy airstrip at Goose Green, where Pucará aircraft posed a threat to the landings, and would act as a diversion from those landings in San Carlos Water. The expected Argentinian air raids began as soon as dawn broke. In her exposed position in the broad waters of Grantham Sound, with no other British ships nearby, *Ardent* was very vulnerable. After fending off the first attacks she fell victim to two raids by Skyhawks which swept in from the west, and within hours lay crippled and abandoned. The true story behind the abandoning is revealed for the first time in this chapter.

Ardent was the seventh Type 21 frigate of the Royal Navy and entered service on 13 October 1977. She was built by Yarrow (Shipbuilders) Ltd, Glasgow, where she was launched by the Duchess of Gloucester on 9 May 1975. Her armament consisted of one 4.5-inch Mk 8 gun, two 20mm Oerlikon guns, one quadruple Exocet missile launcher, one quadruple Seacat missile launcher and two triple Mk 46 torpedo tubes. The 4.5-inch gun could fire 25 rounds per minute and had a maximum range of 24,000 yards, whilst the Exocet had a horizon range.[1]

Ardent carried a Lynx helicopter armed with anti-submarine torpedoes. In addition, she was equipped with two chaff decoy launchers and a Type 184 hull-mounted sonar. Powered by two Rolls-Royce Olympus and two Rolls-Royce Tyne gas turbines, *Ardent*'s top speed was 32 knots, with a burst speed of 37 knots. She displaced 3,250 tons at full load, or 2,750 tons at standard load, and had a complement of 15 officers and 181 ratings. Her homeport was Devonport.[2] For the Falklands operation she sailed with her commanding officer, 15 other officers, 181 ratings and two supernumeraries (one Chinese laundryman and one Royal Artillery naval gunfire support officer), a total of 199.[3] The ship's motto was 'Through Fire and Water'.

Type 992 surveillance radar sat atop the foremast and was used for surface and air warning as well as target indication. It had a range of 70 miles for air contacts, but surface contacts could only be obtained out to horizon range, which is about 20 miles. Type 978 radar was fitted lower down the foremast, for navigation and helicopter control purposes. Two Type 912 radars situated just forward of the foremast and just aft of the funnel provided target tracking for air and surface targets and were linked to the ship's WSA4 fire control system.[4] They controlled the 4.5-inch gun (GSA4) and Seacat (GWS24) and allowed two targets to be engaged simultaneously from a fire control console in the ops room.

The targets were selected and tracked at a CAISS (computer assisted action information system) display in the ops room, which provided a labelled overlay on the surface and air radar pictures. Six of these consoles were installed in the ops room, each being used for a particular role such as weapon direction or anti-submarine helicopter direction. Information from the ship's sensors was corrected (e.g. for ship's movement) by the computer and stored. A track was built up from a succession of inputs, and the course and speed of a potential target was computed and stored (so that updating could continue by dead reckoning if the target was lost for any reason). Tracking could also be monitored and controlled manually from the Seacat and gun controllers' consoles in the ops room using a joystick. The 912 radar aerials incorporated a camera supplying CCTV pictures, allowing the missile or gun to be fired, acquired and, in the case of the missile, guided from the ops room. With the camera centred on the target, the Seacat missile's flight was automatically gathered onto the camera's sightline and the angular displacement of the missile from the target sightline was automatically calculated. Bearing and elevation commands were then transmitted by radio to the Seacat to guide the missile all the way to the target, in automatic mode. In a variant of this mode, once the missile had been automatically 'gathered' onto the camera sightline the Seacat controller in the ops room could take command and steer it via a joystick on his console. Alternatively, an aft-mounted unstabilized pedestal sight fitted with a missile control joystick allowed visual target indication and complete 'manual' operation of Seacat if the primary computer broke down or was damaged, or if the target had not been acquired by the radar – for example as an emergency mode when an aircraft had unexpectedly appeared.[5]

Exocet was fired in fully automatic mode and incorporated radar in its warhead so that it could guide itself to the target. The ship pointed in the rough direction of the target, the approximate range and bearing of the target was fed into the setting panel, allowing the post-launch flight to be programmed, and the distance from the target that the missile was to switch on its own radar was set. The missile could then be launched at the turn of a key. It then guided itself, switched on its radar to lock onto the target and steered a course to the target. A radio altimeter controlled altitude, which could be pre-set to give a sea-skimming height.[6]

The Type 21 frigates were unusual in having been designed by commercial shipbuilders – Vosper Thornycroft and Yarrow – rather than by the Navy's own naval constructors, and in having aluminium superstructures, rather than steel. They were intended to be cheaper than the Leander-class frigates that they superseded, and to require a smaller ship's company. Based on a Vosper Thornycroft frigate design for Iran, they were the first all gas turbine frigates built for the Royal Navy. This form of propulsion offered large savings in engine-room personnel. As an interim design they would fill the gap before the Type 22 and 42 designs were ready. The Type 21s proved to be popular ships in the Navy; well liked for their speed and sleek appearance, they also had unusually large wardrooms and the accommodation space per man was 15 per cent more than in the Leanders. A big disadvantage was that their size offered only a limited margin for additional equipment and so they were never modernized.[7]

Shortly after being promoted, Commander Alan West took command of *Ardent* in 1980; aged only 32, he was at the time the youngest commanding officer of a Royal Navy frigate. Born on 21 April 1948 in Lambeth, London, he was educated at Windsor Grammar School and Clydebank High School. In 1965 he entered Dartmouth as an officer cadet. He served in the commando carrier *Albion* and circumnavigated the globe in the frigate *Whitby*, taking part in the Beira Patrol off Mozambique. In 1973 he married Rosemary Anne Linington Childs, an artist, and they had two sons and one daughter (all aged under seven at the time of the Falklands conflict). After his command of the patrol vessel *Yarnton* in Hong Kong in 1973, he qualified as a principal warfare officer in 1975 and served as operations officer in the frigates *Juno* in 1976 and *Ambuscade* in 1977. Promoted to lieutenant commander on 1 April 1978, he qualified as an advanced warfare officer before being appointed to the destroyer *Norfolk* in 1979.[8]

On 8 December 1980 *Ardent* sailed from Devonport for the Gulf of Oman, where she arrived on 30 December and carried out two Armilla patrols interspersed with an assisted maintenance period in Mombasa. On 28 March 1981 she left the Gulf for passage to the UK, which included a visit to Haifa. Arriving at Devonport on 23 April, the ship entered a period of assisted maintenance and shore leave. In June she carried out gun and missile firings and remained in home waters for the rest of the year, visiting Amsterdam in December with her sister ships *Alacrity*, *Arrow* and *Amazon*.[9]

On 11 January 1982 she arrived at Portland for Continuation Operational Sea Training (COST). By the end of this, on 4 February, all areas were assessed as satisfactory apart from communications and diving, which were below standard. It was

THE LOSS OF HMS *ARDENT*

reported that the ship's company had made good use of their time at Portland, were enthusiastic throughout and responded very well to training. The anti-air warfare team demonstrated an above average capability in basic and tactical practices but now needed to progress to more advanced practices. This team was generally sound at director and controller level, but junior operators were very inexperienced. Production of a valid air picture proved to be a weak area; as the air picture team improved, more effective weapon control was achieved, but more training in air picture compilation and reporting was needed. A defect in the 4.5-inch gun system hampered progress in firing practices, particularly in the second sea week. However, the ship achieved some firings in all modes by the end of the period. The fire control system (GSA4) was proved in all modes of fire, but firings across all range brackets were not achieved due to a defective forward 912 radar. The Seacat missile fire control system (GWS24) was proved in auto mode, with two missiles fired effectively. Sonar operating improved, but anti-submarine warfare procedures and weapon co-ordination in multi-threat situations needed more practice. Other areas requiring more training included communications procedures (especially voice), night diving, and helicopter weapon loading drills. The marine engineering department was well administered and organized, and did particularly well in machinery breakdown drills. Weapons engineering was a soundly run department and worked very hard to overcome shortcomings and defects. Routine maintenance of breathing apparatus was inadequate and on at least three occasions the first breathing apparatus sets chosen for use were unusable.[10] The weakness in the communications sub-department was to be at least partially remedied by the replacement of the radio supervisor when the ship called at Ascension Island on the way south to the Falklands.[11]

On completion of COST, the ship proceeded to Portsmouth for Staff College harbour days. After that, two weeks in late February were spent on an intensive Joint Maritime Course off the Scottish coast, involving practice in anti-submarine and anti-aircraft warfare, and naval gunfire support. Afterwards, *Ardent* proceeded to

Stavanger, Norway, for work on the NATO calibration range there. Following a visit to Narvik on 5 to 7 March the ship embarked on Exercise *Alloy Express*, a NATO amphibious exercise in northern Norway with HMS *Invincible*, HMS *Fearless*, USS *Guadalcanal* and others including Norwegian, Danish and Dutch warships. This was a rehearsal for the ships' roles in the event of a Russian advance through Norway. On conclusion of the exercise, on 17 March, *Ardent* laid a wreath on the sea at the position where her namesake and predecessor, the destroyer *Ardent*, was sunk on 8 June 1940 by the German battlecruisers *Scharnhorst* and *Gneisenau*. The ship then engaged in surveillance of a Soviet intelligence-gathering ship, which had been monitoring the amphibious exercise, off northern Scotland. On 21 March *Ardent* was off Aberporth, Wales for Exocet firing on the missile range there. She then sailed to Devonport for an assisted maintenance period and shore leave.[12]

These first three months of 1982 had given the ship good training in many of the activities which were to be required in the Falklands campaign. However, in neither the Joint Maritime Course nor *Alloy Express* were aircraft engaged by Seacat or the 4.5-inch gun in the emergency (visual or manual) mode; instead, the more normal auto mode had been employed. However, *Ardent* had done particularly well in missile and gunnery exercises: in fleet competitions she was winner of the Seacat Trophy for the period 1 March 1981 to 28 February 1982 and Surface Gunnery over the last two six-month periods; she was runner-up in Naval Gunfire Support for 1 September 1981 to 28 February 1982 and Anti-Aircraft Gunnery in one of the last two six-month periods. The ship was held in high regard by both squadron and flotilla staffs. By the time *Ardent* sailed for Operation *Corporate* in the Falklands the ship's company and officers were pleased with their general state of training. The passage south was regarded as a period for intensive further training, during which emphasis would be placed on those skills most likely to be needed in the forthcoming operation. The state of marine and weapons engineering equipment was good.[13]

Whilst at Devonport, news of the Falklands invasion on 2 April convinced the ship that they would be deployed to the South Atlantic in the near future. They were repeatedly told that they would not be going, but continued to prepare for war. At one stage they did stop preparations temporarily, so strong were the views expressed by the staff of the commander-in-chief, fleet, at Northwood. However, on 15 April word came that *Ardent* was to sail south on Monday 19 April. By that date the ship was fully stored with 14 weeks' dried, 12 weeks' frozen and four weeks' fresh provisions, and in a high state of operational readiness. Approximately half of these provisions had to be stored outside the provision rooms, in various spaces. After one topping-up replenishment at sea, the ship was to enter the area of operations with about ten weeks of food. Before sailing the captain decided that they were likely to be employed in the naval gunfire support role and so carried as much 4.5-inch ammunition as possible, amounting to 650 rounds. By the time she entered the operations zone she also had on board 28 Seacat and four Exocet missiles, nine Mk 44 and 13 Mk 46 torpedoes, 93 3-inch chaff rockets, and 3,750 20mm Oerlikon rounds.

The Lynx helicopter underwent rapid modification to carry Stingray torpedoes and Sea Skua missiles. Three Stingray torpedoes were embarked in Devonport, adding to the other torpedoes, and two Sea Skua missiles were later embarked by helicopter from *Antelope*. The helicopter could not carry AS12 missiles and none were embarked. *Ardent* requested the supply of four general purpose machine guns (GPMG) but was only allowed one before sailing. By the time the ship entered the operations zone she was carrying 8,000 GPMG rounds, 13,000 ball and 1,200 tracer light machine gun (Bren) rounds, and 4,800 Sterling machine gun rounds.[14]

The prime threat likely to be encountered in the Falklands area was considered by Commander Alan West to be Argentinian fighter/ ground-attack aircraft, low-level bombing from Mirage and Skyhawk aircraft and medium- to high-level bombing from Canberra aircraft. It was known that there would be threats from surface warships and submarines, but he believed that these would be of a much lower order in the immediate vicinity of the islands. He was mildly concerned at the threat of both mines and shore bombardment on passing through Falkland Sound but did not think these would be serious problems thereafter. *Ardent* had experienced air attack close inshore during Exercise *Alloy Express*, and West was well aware of the ship's operational limitations in such restricted environments. He thought that the ship was likely to be employed close inshore in the naval gunfire support role, where the 4.5-inch gun and Seacat were unlikely to work in their primary (auto or radar controlled) mode because of the proximity of land; instead the emergency, visual, mode would have to be used for both systems.

The anti-air training requirement on the passage south was therefore to exercise the 4.5-inch and Seacat visual direction teams in emergency modes with the operations room, and to exercise the 20mm Oerlikon, general purpose machine gun and light machine gun crews. Nevertheless, training in all other aspects of operations would also need to be undertaken. There were no Sea Harriers available to *Ardent* as targets during the passage south and the ship had to use the Lynx helicopter to simulate fixed-wing aircraft. Commander West's appreciation of the risks was apparently much better than that of Admiral Woodward or Commodore Clapp, neither of whom emphasized the threat of low-level air attacks in the confined waters of Falkland Sound in their threat assessments.[15]

On 19 April *Ardent* sailed from Devonport at 10.00, and in the afternoon carried out firing against an anti-aircraft target before rendezvousing with the frigate *Argonaut*, RFA *Plumleaf* and RFA *Regent* at 19.00, and arrived at Ascension Island on 30 April. On that passage the ship carried out equipment checks and electronic warfare exercises in co-ordination with *Argonaut*, and a variety of other training drills and exercises. On 26 April a refuelling at sea was undertaken from RFA *Plumleaf*. Off Ascension Island *Ardent* shadowed a Soviet spy ship for three days, conducted anti-submarine warfare operations, and carried out gunnery drills.

At Ascension the ship only needed to top up with armament stores and duly sailed on 6 May, escorting the requisitioned merchant ships *Canberra* and *Elk* towards Rio de Janeiro before crossing back to join up with the rest of the amphibious group led by *Fearless*, on 10 May. During this phase, to escape detection, they avoided contact with all other shipping, using the Lynx helicopter to search ahead of the ships. A number of gun and Seacat missile firings were made for exercise purposes, and other exercises included one that simulated an Exocet hit at night. On 11 May *Ardent* replenished at sea from RFA *Stromness* and practised anti-Exocet drills. The need for such drills had been emphasized by the strike on *Sheffield* on 4 May. On passage towards the total exclusion zone (TEZ) there were many more drills and exercises, replenishment from the Royal Fleet Auxiliaries *Pearleaf*, *Tidepool* and *Stromness* (again), and rendezvous with the aircraft carriers *Hermes* and *Invincible* for cross-decking.

On 19 May the ships reached the edge of the TEZ, and in the afternoon of the following day, 20 May, the amphibious group began its run-in to the northern end of Falkland Sound with close escort provided by *Ardent* and six other destroyers and frigates. At 16.10 (Falklands Standard Time) *Ardent* and the destroyer *Antrim* detached from the convoy when about 100 miles north-east of the entrance to the Sound and proceeded independently, ahead of the amphibious force, to reach their ordered positions in Falkland Sound. It was a clear, dark night with a force 3 wind from the north-west and a calm sea. All members of *Ardent*'s ship's company had been issued with a life jacket and a once-only survival suit and were briefed on taking cover. At 19.30 *Ardent* went to action stations and entered Falkland Sound at midnight, at 30 knots, and fortunately remained undetected by the enemy and untroubled by mines.[16]

Shortly after this the after first aid point was moved by Petty Officer Writer Trevor Quinton from the senior rates' dining hall to the junior rates' dining hall, as he believed this would be a safer site. This separated the first aid point from most of their equipment in the sick bay and from their telephone link. Neither the sick bay nor the forward first aid party were made aware of this move. At 01.00 a second change was made when Leading Medical Assistant Bob Young was ordered by the medical officer to move to the after first aid point, thus reducing the risk to them both being injured simultaneously. The forward first aid party were not notified of this change. Quinton remained in charge despite being less knowledgeable than Young, who appears to have kept himself separate from the first aid party until the subsequent attacks.[17]

Ardent proceeded to Grantham Sound, her fire support area, which lay on the east side of Falkland Sound between San Carlos and Darwin/Goose Green, and was ready for calls for fire support by 21.00. Having established her patrol uneventfully, she then went to 'action stations relaxed' to give her crew opportunity for rest while it was still dark, and went onto Tyne engines to reduce funnel smoke and fuel consumption.

Her prime gunfire targets were the airstrip at Goose Green (which was 22,000 yards from the ship), Camilla Creek House and the routes out of the Darwin/Goose Green area towards the San Carlos amphibious operating area. *Ardent* had been chosen by Commodore Mike Clapp for this duty as she was his only ship with a gun capable of hitting at such a range. He later commented, 'She was a sitting duck to air attack, I knew it and so did her commanding officer.' The army spotter ashore eventually contacted the ship at 02.00 on 21 May, but surprisingly no calls for fire were received until 07.26, after it had become light. From then until 13.00 *Ardent* expended 150 shells on Goose Green and other targets with excellent results: three Pucará aircraft were immobilized on the ground and the Argentinian troops in the area remained firmly in their trenches. However, at least four pairs of Pucarás managed to get airborne. Various air actions took place during this gunfire support period and the ability of the fire control system to switch from shelling the land positions to anti-air warfare and back was proved to be outstandingly good.[18]

With landings now under way, the enemy's air forces unleashed their fury on targets in the San Carlos area under a clear blue sky with excellent visibility and light wind, ideal conditions for air attacks. Soon after dawn the first Pucará aircraft was seen to fly out into San Carlos Water from the land and retreat rapidly amid a hail of fire. At about 08.30 two Pucarás from Goose Green closed *Ardent* from the south-east, over land. On crossing the coastline they were engaged by the ship's Seacat and 4.5-inch gun, both in emergency mode. The Pucarás turned tail on sighting the Seacat missile, flew back over the coast and disappeared behind a ridge just ahead of the Seacat, which hit the top of the ridge.[19] At 08.45 *Ardent* recovered her Lynx helicopter, which had fired one Sea Skua missile at an Argentinian merchant ship in Fox Bay during a 1½-hour search to the south of Falkland Sound, setting it on fire: no other shipping was reported.[20]

Warning of air raids from the mainland was being obtained by radar at about 80 miles, but soon after that the aircraft were lost in the land mass of West Falkland. Immediate warning of their approach was therefore limited to some 5 or 6 miles when they reappeared, and the landlocked environment then, as expected, largely inhibited radar tracking and target acquisition. The first of the major air attacks on the landing force was detected at about 09.00. A lone Mirage from the north-west flew towards *Ardent* but on being engaged with Seacat (again in emergency mode) turned and paralleled the shore. The high crossing rate of the aircraft defeated the Seacat. Other Mirages flew north and low up Falkland Sound towards San Carlos, passed west of *Ardent* and were engaged by the 4.5-inch gun. At around 09.45 two Pucarás came over land from the south-east and, like the earlier pair, turned back as soon as Seacat was fired, with the missile chasing them over the ridge.[21]

Two Pucarás, probably the same ones, appeared from the same direction at 10.10. They turned south on crossing the coastline but then almost immediately headed back towards *Ardent*. Seacat fire was deliberately held until the range had markedly closed, but at 2,000 yards the aircraft suddenly turned away to the east. Three Sea Harriers rapidly appeared across *Ardent*'s bow, the first to be seen by the ship in the Sound, and they engaged the Pucarás. One Pucará of Argentine Navy Grupo 3 was shot down by Commander 'Sharkey' Ward in one of the three Sea Harriers of 801 Naval Air Squadron, using 30mm cannon. The pilot Major J. Tomba ejected and made it back to his Goose Green base on foot.[22]

A lull followed, and at around 12.00 the task group went to Air Raid Warning Yellow. Almost immediately a single A4 Skyhawk was sighted a mile south of *Ardent*, heading low out from the shoreline against which it was effectively camouflaged. It flew straight over *Ardent*, dropping two bombs, one about 10 yards off the bow on the port side and the other some 30 yards off the starboard quarter. It was engaged with 20mm and machine gun fire from the ship, though no hits were seen. The 4.5-inch gun, trained on the port beam, could not be slewed round fast enough and the Seacat was not engaged, although Commander West had put the helm hard over to allow it to bear. Neither bomb seems to have exploded, and the only damage done was to *Ardent*'s 992 radar aerial, which was forced over at a 30° angle by either the jet blast or an underwing tank as the aircraft flew low over it. However, this radar continued to operate without significant loss of efficiency.[23]

At about 13.00 *Ardent* was informed that there were no further naval gunfire support targets for her in the Goose Green area. She then called the frigate *Broadsword*, as the surface and sub-surface co-ordinator, and asked for any other targets. She was ordered with the frigate *Yarmouth* to 'split attacks from the south' (though it was later unclear who gave this order). The meaning of this order was not clear to Commander West, but it resulted in *Ardent* taking a patrol line to the east, and *Yarmouth* to the west, of an area near North West Islands at the northern entrance to Grantham Sound. *Ardent* proceeded north-west to the new area at 12 knots and was on her new patrol line there by 13.35, fully aware that there were still some three hours of daylight and thus potential for air attack left. Although there was now some cloud around, the day remained fine with good visibility and moderate wind. Other than *Yarmouth*, the nearest ship was *Broadsword*, some 4 miles to the north where she was stationed with *Antrim* on the southern side of the entrance to San Carlos Water.[24] At about 13.15 there were further air raids over the amphibious operating area, and the frigate *Brilliant* called for more combat air patrols over that area.[25]

Ardent had fought off attacks against her whilst on her gunfire support station and had achieved considerable success in that operation shelling the Goose Green area, despite the frequent interruptions during air attacks from which she had escaped unscathed, and much credit was due to the operations teams and the captain for this, and indeed to the flexible design of her fire control systems. But her station in Grantham Sound was clearly isolated and she lacked mutual support from other ships. Her primary task was now the protection of the amphibious landing area from attacks from the south and it seemed that this isolation had to be accepted. The air attacks had been satisfactorily handled by the ship so far, although they were lucky with the single Skyhawk attack, whose two near misses re-emphasized the dangers to ships operating close inshore. Unfortunately, *Ardent's* luck was not to hold.[26]

At about 13.40, with *Ardent* on a westerly course in her new patrol line, four Argentine Navy Skyhawks of the 3rd Fighter-Attack Squadron from Río Grande airbase, Tierra del Fuego, were sighted bearing about 240° coming low off West Falkland and over Falkland Sound on an easterly heading. Led by Lieutenant Commander Alberto Philippi, each plane carried four 500lb bombs. *Ardent* increased speed to 17 knots, the maximum achievable on her Tyne engines, and came hard to port into wind on a course of 200°.[27] On confirming the aircraft's heading, going left across the bow at low level, the captain ordered hard to starboard to maintain both 4.5-inch and Seacat arcs and then back hard to port again as the aircraft circled the ship anti-clockwise at about 3 miles. Three aircraft then turned in on *Ardent's* port quarter and ran in to attack. The 4.5-inch gun was trained to follow the aircraft as they flew from right to left but ran into blind arcs as the aircraft closed, despite the ship turning to port with full rudder. The Seacat, in emergency mode, was engaged but there was no sound of the expected 'whoosh' because it also had failed to fire (probably because the sight was depressed below the launcher's minimum safety angle), and despite close-range fire from the ship's 20mm and three light machine guns to port, the aircraft's attack was pressed home with cannon fire and bombs.[28]

Thus, at 13.44 six or more 500lb bombs were dropped, all aimed aft of the funnel, and two or three hit the ship; the others missed. One of the bombs penetrated through the diving store and into the after auxiliary machinery room, unexploded, whilst one (or possibly two) that did explode demolished the hangar, blew the Seacat launcher from atop the hangar onto the flight deck, and seriously damaged the Lynx helicopter, killing the aircrew (flight commander Lieutenant Commander John Sephton and observer Lieutenant Brian Murphy) by shrapnel and debris in the hangar area. They were acting as lookouts on the flight deck, with Murphy also manning a light machine gun there, since it had been decided that the helicopter had no useful contribution to make to the air defence battle.

Cannon fire impacted the port side of the flight deck from aft to the vicinity of the port shipborne torpedo weapon system. The after switchboard was hit with resultant loss of power including normal supplies to the 4.5-inch gun, and the diving store was demolished. Fifty per cent of the lighting in the ship, and power supplies to equipment aft, were lost. There were several other casualties aft, notably of flight deck personnel, fires started in the hangar area, and some flooding occurred below decks due to cracked fire mains. A submersible pump was rigged to pump out the ship control centre, later augmented by a second similar pump, whilst another pump was started up in the beer store. Water in the junior rates' dining hall, which was immediately below the flight deck, had reached a depth of about 14 inches in one corner and a bucket chain of men was established to bale it out.[29]

In the flight deck and hangar area, initial efforts went into extricating those pinned by debris (Aircraft Mechanics Andy Schofield and Bill Bailey) and to assist the injured (Schofield and Aircraft Mechanician 'Scouse' Lacey). The help was given by flight personnel taking cover in the ship's office flat, Leading Aircraft Mechanic Mark 'Speedy' Ball and Aircraft Mechanic John 'Wally' Wallington. After some discussion with Leading Medical Assistant Bob Young, Petty Officer Writer Trevor Quinton ordered his after first aid party to move from its base in the junior rates' dining hall to the hangar, and they were followed by Quinton. The senior rating in charge of the after damage control party was informed of the move, but the sick bay and the forward first aid party were not. Contrary to the leading medical assistant's belief, no member of the first aid party remained to act as a communications point or to tend any who might be injured in the damage control party.

The two first aiders found Aircraft Mechanic Allan McCauley lying dead under debris on the starboard side of the hangar, and the supply officer, Lieutenant Commander Rick Banfield, who was also the flight deck officer, lying semi-conscious and severely wounded with blood running from the leg of his flight deck suit, on the starboard side of the flight deck where he had been hit by the dislodged Seacat launcher. Quinton left 'on the pretext of' obtaining stretchers and ensuring that access to the sick bay was clear. Hearing from Quinton of the casualties aft, the medical officer Surgeon Lieutenant Simon Ridout left the sick bay and headed aft but encountered the injured Andy Schofield (supported by Bill Bailey and another rating) as they left the hangar and, with Bailey, escorted him to the sick bay where his perforated ear drum and damaged ribs could be attended to. They had probably just arrived when Captain Bob Harmes (Royal Artillery), the naval gunfire support liaison officer, came in and told them that they should move out because of the approaching smoke, although at this time there was very little smoke in the undamaged sick bay. Everyone in the sick bay left, taking with them only two first aid bags, extra field dressings and a first aid box, and moved forward to just outside the forecastle door.

Simon Ridout decided that it was too cold there and instructed the party to move into the wardroom. No one appears to have been informed of their location and the wardroom contained no medical equipment or supplies other than those brought from the sick bay. However, later casualties did find their way to the wardroom. Ridout returned to the flight deck after being summoned there by Leading Weapons Electrical Mechanic Pat Norris, and *en route* examined McCauley in the hangar and found him to be dead. He examined Lieutenant Commander Banfield and found him to be *in extremis*. Together with Bob Young and Writer Mark Bogard, who were already on the scene, he attempted to remove Banfield's life jacket using Petty Officer Pete Brouard's knife as none of the first aiders had any cutting instrument. Very shortly afterwards the final bombing attack was launched.[30]

Three hoses had been rigged to fight fires on the port side of the hangar, mostly by men from the ship's mobile repair party. The fires were shortly brought under control and two of the hoses had been switched off and were being reeled up when the next attack occurred. From the lessons learned from *Sheffield*, the action state of the fire main had been altered to isolate it into two independent sections to make the whole system less vulnerable to a single incident, and this had proved to be a wise change. Marine Engineering Mechanics Stephen 'Florrie' Ford and Alistair 'Buzz' Leighton – two firesuitmen with breathing apparatus – and their controller briefly appeared from the forward damage control base, and being told that they were not required they went to the after damage control base.[31]

The first lieutenant, Lieutenant Commander Andrew Gordon-Lennox, was visiting the ship control centre at the time of the second Skyhawk attack and took cover there. He went and checked the after switchboard and noticed holes in the deckhead and deck, then proceeded through the dining hall (the aft damage control base) and through the hatch onto the flight deck. There he confirmed damage to the hangar, attended to the flight deck officer, Lieutenant Commander Banfield, and identified the bodies of the two aircrew. He saw a torpedo hanging out of the starboard shipborne torpedo weapon system and attempted to release it, visiting the bridge for the key to the release button padlocks. Whilst on the bridge he gave a report on what he had seen to the captain. By the time the second attack struck, the captain had a fairly clear and accurate picture of the extent of the damage, obtained in the main from messengers, the first lieutenant and other visitors to the bridge. The captain gave the instruction to Marine Engineering Mechanic Keith 'Jessie' Owens (who was one of the messengers) that the Olympus engines were to be started.[32]

Ardent had survived the ordeal, but was now rather a lame duck. The ship still had main engines and steering, and was under control but largely defenceless, with her Seacat system destroyed and power lost to the 4.5-inch gun. A slight list to starboard (about 2°) developed, but the fire and flooding was virtually under control. The captain informed Commodore Clapp of his situation and was ordered to make for San Carlos Water at best speed. The ship turned north at 17 knots and Owens went below to order the starting of Olympus engines, all communications with the ship control centre having apparently failed. Power for the gun was quickly restored by switching to an alternative supply, but the gun could not be controlled in either primary or emergency mode. Whilst this problem was being investigated, the ship was to be hit for a second time. The 992 radar system was also down and could not be restarted.[33]

At about 14.00, as *Ardent* adjusted course to 020° to pass a mile off North West Islands, a further five or six Skyhawks, which also turned out to be of the Argentine Navy, were seen closing from the north-west from the direction of Mount Rosalie (see Map 5). Again, they ran down *Ardent*'s port side at some 2–3 miles' distance to stay out of Seacat's range. One group of three turned in very fine on the port quarter, while another two went broad round to starboard, coming in just abaft the starboard beam (see Map 5). With no Seacat, power lost from the 4.5-inch gun, and no light machine guns aft, the ship was almost helpless, and had only the starboard general purpose machine gun, port forward light machine gun and both 20mm Oerlikons to fend off this attack. One of the Skyhawks was hit on one wing by a burst of machine gun fire delivered by Petty Officer John Leake, a former regular soldier who had been enrolled as a petty officer NAAFI manager six days earlier. He had run through the carnage on the hangar deck to take over the gun as there was now no one to fire it.

The aircraft engaged with cannon, retarded bombs and some larger bombs. In all, about 16 bombs may well have been dropped. Between two and four bombs hit the ship and exploded aft of the hangar, some unexploded bombs probably hit the ship from the hangar aft, and many missed, some exploding close by in the water. Some of the bombs fell in the water forward: one bomb almost certainly struck the starboard side of the forward auxiliary machinery room a glancing blow about 3 feet underwater and failed to explode. Multiple shocks shook the ship, which whipped

Map 5: The third Skyhawk attack on HMS *Ardent*, 21 May

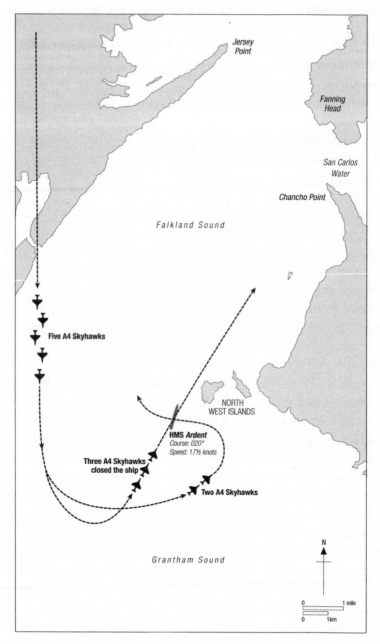

heavily. It was possible that further bombs that did not explode penetrated the ship near the canteen and after switchboard. The ship was also raked by cannon fire in the area of the flight deck and further forward. Steering was lost, but the main engines continued to run. From the hangar area aft to the stern, with the dining halls and associated compartments, was wrecked and the ship took on a list of over 5° to starboard. Two Sea Harriers intercepted the fleeing Skyhawks: one of them was shot down with the loss of its pilot, Lieutenant Marquez, and another, the one damaged by *Ardent's* fire, was destroyed after being subjected to further damage: the pilot, Lieutenant Arca, had to eject and was rescued. Throughout the raids, the captain gave a running commentary from the bridge on general broadcast and saying 'take cover' as bombs were released.[34]

During this attack, the helicopter, Seacat launcher and debris from the second Skyhawk attack were blown off the flight deck. The port after end of the flight deck was torn from the bulkheads and ship's side, and was bent upwards by about 8ft, whilst the starboard after end was buckled and depressed below the ship's side. A residual fire in the hangar, from the previous attack, re-ignited. There was very extensive damage in the junior rates' dining hall from bomb explosions and a large hole had been made in the ship's side above the waterline near the after end of the senior rates' dining hall. The hole extended below to the sonar instrument room, medical store and Avcat pump space, and there was a large fire in the area, probably centred on the Avcat pump space. The galley was heavily damaged and galley equipment, probably ovens, was blown into the passageway outside the servery. The deckhead of a store in this area was at least partially blown off. Further damage was caused to the canteen and after switchboard room by either cannon fire or an unexploded bomb.[35]

The ship's starboard side was damaged about 3ft below the waterline and a small split was causing seepage of water into the forward auxiliary machinery room. The marine engineering officer, Lieutenant Commander Terry Pendrous, left the ship control centre and checked its flat, with men still taking cover there. He saw water in the after switchboard room and pouring into the after auxiliary machinery room, and possibly through a split in 2 deck into the fridge flat. He saw very heavy damage in the dining hall area and the fire burning in the port after side of the junior rates' dining hall.[36]

Thick black smoke from the fire in the port aft area of the junior rates' dining hall spread quickly through the ship, filling 2 deck forward to the Olympus flat and 1 deck forward to the sickbay flat. There was a total loss of lighting from the Olympus flat aft on 2 deck and in the machinery space below. Smoke from this fire was rapidly thickening in the ship control centre flat, making breathing difficult.

Pendrous returned to the ship control centre and ordered its evacuation, but no instructions were given as to where to evacuate to; he also ordered the evacuation of the electrical generation control party. The Tyne engines were still running when Petty Officer Marine Engineering Mechanic Mick Langley passed through the ship control centre after the last men there had left. He heard an order for the telegraph to ring zero so he tripped both engines. He also heard a call from the forward auxiliary machine room asking what was happening, and in reply said he thought they were 'getting off'. This was also heard by the forward and aft engine rooms, and all of these groups decided to leave, and on reaching 2 deck were informed of evacuation back aft.[37]

On the flight deck, Leading Medical Assistant Bob Young was wounded and thrown into the flight deck netting, whilst Surgeon Lieutenant Simon Ridout was blasted overboard (to be rescued some 20 minutes later by *Broadsword*). Writer Mark Bogard, who was with them attending to Lieutenant Commander Banfield, managed to take cover and was uninjured: he made his way forward to the boat deck, where he treated the injuries of Leading Cook Dave Trotter. Steward Frank Walmsley, the other member of the after first aid party, was also uninjured and made his way to the wardroom, where the sick bay had been re-located. Bob Young, having recovered consciousness in the flight deck netting, assisted with firefighting in the hangar and tended two injured men who emerged from below out of the devastated dining hall before he moved, with those remaining in the area, to abandon ship.[38] Petty

Officer Pete Brouard, the captain of the flight deck, and Steward Shaun Hanson (whose action station was in the weapon repair party as runner and keyboard operator) were killed by cannon fire on the flight deck, where Lieutenant Commander Banfield also passed away.[39]

In the forward first aid party, Petty Officer Steward Dave Burr was in charge and sent Stores Accountant Tony Allison aft, having heard that first aid assistance was needed there. Allison was waylaid to assist Weapon Engineering Mechanic Kevin MacDonald, whom he took to the wardroom sick bay, and stayed there until told to abandon ship. Burr sent another first aider, Leading Steward Bob Brooks, to assist aft, and he arrived on the flight deck just in time to take cover in the starboard waist from the final attack, in which he was wounded. He was able to make his own way to the wardroom and thence to the bridge. Dave Burr continued to treat minor casualties until he was told to leave and prepare to abandon ship. The forward damage repair party assisted in the evacuation of the wounded men.[40]

Those in the after damage control party who had survived the attack and struggled free made their way out of the dining hall forward or through damage holes on to the upper deck or overboard. In the flight deck and hangar area, a small motley team was attempting to hose water onto the major fire coming from between decks through the damage on the port after corner of the flight deck. Despite the fact that they must have been badly shaken by the nearby explosions, they showed determination in sticking to the task, urged on by the leadership of Marine Engineering Artificer Jeff Curran and the cool example of Marine Engineering Mechanic Dave 'Brum' Serrell. They were later joined by two survivors from near the centre of the explosions between decks, Lieutenant David Searle and Leading Stores Accountant Kevin Johnson, as they attempted to deal with the damage, but were thwarted by the short length of hose available. They fully expected to be reinforced very quickly from forward, but when no help came and their efforts were having little effect Curran ordered the team to withdraw forward.[41]

When they left the flight deck, fire-main pressure was still available. They arrived on the boat deck to find it crowded with men in once-only survival suits, preparing to leave the ship. The forward damage control party initiated a blanket search, but this was not completed in detail below 3 deck: no damage was discovered in the compartments checked. The sound of water running into the hull outfit compartment was heard, but this could not be investigated before the order to abandon ship was given over the intercom. This water may have been from a split in the hull or from a fractured pipe or hose.[42]

Fifteen ratings died in the devastated dining hall: Derek Armstrong, Andrew Barr, Richard Dunkerley, Michael Foote, Stephen Ford, Sean Hayward, Stephen Heyes, Simon Lawson, Alistair Leighton, Michael Mullen, Andrew Palmer, John Roberts, Garry Whitford, Stephen White and Gilbert Williams; Gary Nelson died in the tiller flat.[43] All four fearnought* men, in firesuits and breathing apparatus, were in the junior rates' dining hall with their controllers, as part of the after damage control party, and were amongst those who perished. Ford and Leighton, and their controller Mullen, had relocated there from the forward damage control party, joining Williams and Armstrong, who with their controller Whitford were part of the after damage control party.[44]

Lieutenant Commander Pendrous went from the ship control centre to the bridge, where he met the first lieutenant, Lieutenant Commander Gordon-Lennox, and discussed the damage situation before reporting to the captain on the bridge. He then went down to the ship's office flat but was driven back by smoke from going further aft or below, and returned to the flag deck. Gordon-Lennox had taken cover under the Cheverton boat during the attack. He viewed the flight deck aft from the after 912 tracker platform, noting that the helicopter and Seacat launcher had disappeared, and that the flight deck was badly damaged, and concluded that the stern

---

* The fearnought suit is an overall firesuit made from white, flame-retardant woollen cloth (200 layers of compressed wool) and is used by Royal Navy personnel for firefighting on board ships. The men also wore anti-flash hoods and firefighting gloves.

was missing. He went below decks to the ship control centre flat, which he found empty and full of smoke. He later described the area aft of the ship control centre as devastated. On the way to the bridge he met Lieutenant Commander Pendrous, who was already concerned about the amount of water he thought was entering the ship aft, and his concern was amplified by news of the state of the stern, which was reported by Gordon-Lennox as missing. Before reaching the bridge he met Chief Stoker Andy Andrew, who told him 'the forward auxiliary machinery room is wrecked.'[45]

Immediately after the attack, the captain attempted unsuccessfully to establish communications with the ship control centre. The ship was heading for North West Islands with no steering, so the way needed to be taken off the ship. The engine telegraphs were not working, but results were finally achieved by running the lever setting switch on the bridge down to zero. The reply gong rang in answer, and once the engines had been tripped the ship stopped very quickly and Commander West ordered the anchor to be let go.

No damage picture was immediately available on the bridge, but it was clear that there must have been considerable damage because of the number of bombs which had hit and the whip experienced. The captain's first information about the damage came shortly after the ship had stopped, when he was informed from the ops room that they were 'abandoning ship aft'. He reacted strongly to this, saying the order to abandon ship had not been given and calling for a full damage report. Lieutenant Commander Terry Pendrous arrived on the bridge a couple of minutes later and informed the captain that there was tremendous damage down aft and that the ship was in serious danger of plunging by the stern very quickly, that she was free flooding from the after auxiliary machinery room aft, and that the stern had been lost.

West queried with Pendrous whether it would be possible to ballast flood forward to reduce the risk of plunging and was told there was no way of doing this because there was no fire-main pressure. Pendrous said he didn't think the ship could be saved. Lieutenant Commander Andrew Gordon-Lennox, who had arrived on the bridge with, or shortly after Pendrous, added that the forward auxiliary machinery room was wrecked, all power was lost and fires around the AS12 missile magazine and torpedo body room were causing him great concern. 'I don't believe we can save her, sir,' he said. At this stage the list to starboard had increased and there was the odd lurch, making the ship feel tender. Faced with all this evidence, the captain, without questioning its validity other than once again to ask, 'Are you sure?', ordered the ship to be abandoned and called *Yarmouth* alongside at 14.15 to take off survivors. *Yarmouth* came alongside at 14.30 and five minutes later *Ardent* let go her port anchor.[46]

By the time of the captain's order to abandon ship, a large number of men were already congregating on the boat deck and putting on survival suits. These included the people who had vacated the after section of the ship, but they had also swept up many other people *en route*. Others joined them as they prepared to leave the ship. Master-at-Arms Lenny Yeatman and Chief Marine Engineering Artificer Mick Cox started to search the ship on their own initiative, but, having covered only 01 deck (the midships deck one level higher than the forecastle deck – 1 deck) and the forward section of 1 deck, made no further attempt to go below to 2, 3 and 4 decks, and returned to the bridge and boat deck. Meanwhile, the first lieutenant, hearing of their search, went to follow them. He went down to the ship's office and Tyne flats, found heavy smoke that stopped him, and then returned. On Yeatman's return to the bridge, the captain was informed that a search of the ship had been completed, but was not given the extent of that search. With the considerable damage down aft, all concerned clearly felt that there was little likelihood of there being any survivors from that area. The first lieutenant saw two people jump from the port quarter, but at the time these were the only people that he knew had survived from down aft.[47]

According to the board of inquiry report, no serious consideration was given to enter the damaged compartments to look for survivors, nor was the hangar area, where a small party was still fighting fires, considered for search.[48] In a book published in 2000 (18 years after the event) it was reported that Yeatman and Cox tried to enter the dining halls to go aft to the tiller flat where Leading Physical Trainer Gary 'Ginger' Nelson would have been, but were unable to because of smoke. They turned back and entered the ship beneath the Cheverton boat and down a ladder into the ship's office flat on 2 deck, from where they were prevented by smoke and flames from descending another ladder into the workshop flat on 3 deck. They then tried to get below through the hangar, but the doors were blocked.[49] This apparent contradiction of the board of inquiry report can probably be explained by the lack of a 'serious' attempt to search the damaged compartments by men wearing fire-suits with breathing apparatus, which Yeatman and Cox were not wearing.[50] The 2000 account also reports that Petty Officers Robert 'Paddy' McGinnis and Chris Waspe made a search of a number of forward compartments.[51]

No formal check of persons present on the upper decks was carried out, the emphasis being on getting off the ship before it plunged. Personnel started to board *Yarmouth* straight away, from the forecastle and down ropes from the port side of 01 deck. Hoses from *Yarmouth* were boundary cooling from outboard over her quarterdeck in the vicinity of *Ardent*'s torpedo body room and AS12 magazine (which was being used to store 4.5-inch shells). Although there was a need for speed, the abandon ship process was carried out calmly and without major difficulty. Commander West was the last survivor to leave *Ardent*, at about 14.55.

Broadsword had arrived to assist, and recovered Surgeon Lieutenant Ridout from the water using a swimmer. A Wessex helicopter from *Canberra* picked up Marine Engineering Artificer Ken Enticknapp and Able Seaman John Dillon from the icy cold water and took them back to *Canberra*, where the other survivors had also been sent. Enticknapp had been knocked unconscious by falling debris while taking cover in the dining hall, had lost a finger, had a gash a foot long in his back, and blood was pouring from his head. Trapped beneath a section of ventilation trunking, he thought he was going to die. But his first baby was about to be born... he could not die, he willed himself not to die. Around the dining hall there were a lot of moans. Pain. 'Help.' 'Mummy.' 'Help me, help me.' Enticknapp was rescued by 17-year-old John

Dillon, who lifted the heavy debris clear despite having an injured arm himself. Fighting for their breath, and unable to get forward, the pair moved aft and crawled through a small gap underneath the winch for the Type 182 torpedo decoy. With no time to don their survival suits, they jumped into the water, but Dillon's life jacket did not inflate because it was punctured, and he struggled to survive in the cold water.[52]

Surgeon Commander Rick Jolly[*] recalled the incident in an interview with *The Plymouth Herald* in 2007:

As Senior Medical Officer with 3 Commando Brigade, I had been scrambled to a Wessex helicopter to help search for casualties from the ship. As the helicopter approached the listing HMS *Ardent*, we found it hard to spot survivors in the water as plumes of thick, black smoke towered into the sky from the fires on board. But as we hovered closer to the ravaged Type 21 frigate, the co-pilot saw a man struggling to stay afloat. The seawater was breaking over his face and it was clearly evident that he wasn't going to survive for too much longer. I knew then what I had to do. I tapped my crewman on the arm, leant across and shouted 'Me – down'. I sat in the doorway and contemplated what I had to do. I looked at what I was wearing and suddenly remembered I didn't have my immersion suit on. As well as my uniform, the only extra bits of kit were a pair of gloves and a thin lifejacket; I hadn't intended to go for a swim. Suddenly everything went quiet, as your body does when it prepares itself for serious demand. I stepped out and began to be winched down 30 feet or so. I just remember thinking, 'If I don't act now this man will die.' I dropped into the ocean and it was freezing: barely 2°C. My heart slowed down and my vision changed like I was in a tunnel. I was then dragged through the water and soon reached

---

[*] Jolly was Senior Medical Officer of 3 Commando Brigade, Royal Marines, and commanded the field hospital at Ajax Bay. There he and his team worked in the basic and hazardous conditions of a ramshackle former refrigeration plant: Rick Jolly, Wikipedia, https://en.wikipedia.org/wiki/Rick Jolly (retrieved 27 Sept 2019).

the sailor. I bear-hugged him and before I knew it we were back in the helicopter cabin. I literally jumped on the sailor and he vomited up all the seawater. He was alive. I was exhausted. I felt a sense of pride and relief having saved John Dillon's life.

But no sooner had I caught my breath than the Royal Marine corporal in the cabin beckoned for me to come closer. He pointed down and gave me a sort of smile; I knew exactly what he meant. Taking a deep breath, I prepared myself for the second plunge. I began to be lowered down and the wire became twisted. It was a very strange sight, spinning round seeing *Ardent* on fire, HMS *Yarmouth*'s crew on deck close by in their immersion suits and everything else going on. I dropped into the water and I was too weak to lift him. He was in a terrible state, with a huge gash in his head and blood all over his face. I submerged myself under water and placed a hook through his life jacket. He was in such a bad state, I'm not even sure he was aware he'd been saved. He was Ken Enticknapp, then a Chief Petty Officer, now a Commander. I will never forget the welcome the survivors received from marines as they stumbled on board *Canberra* for treatment. Members of 42 Commando were waiting to climb aboard their landing craft and go ashore. I couldn't help but shed a tear as each marine patted the *Ardent* survivors on the back as they walked past. I'll always remember one marine saying to one of the survivors, 'You gave them hell; we're going to do the same.' It really was a special moment.[53]

As *Yarmouth* turned into San Carlos Water, Commander West looked back at his ship and saw that it was still afloat, which surprised him as the evidence given to him by his marine engineering officer indicated that the ship would sink very quickly. All the survivors were transferred to *Canberra*, and the final number of dead and missing was determined as 22.[54] In the second Skyhawk attack three officers and one senior rate died. In the final attack two senior rates and 16 junior rates died, making a total of 22 men lost. Three officers, 15 senior rates and 19 junior rates were wounded.[55]

Alan West considered that he might not have been informed correctly about the ship's state and later spoke to Gordon-Lennox about getting a team together to go back on board. However, *Canberra* sailed to get clear of the area and any chance of returning to *Ardent* slipped away. The survivors were on their way home. The fires aft steadily enveloped the ship and a major explosion seen at 19.15 was probably the Seacat and torpedo magazines igniting, which in turn initiated slow flooding through splintering of the ship's bottom. By 02.00 on 22 May the bridge structure was ablaze and there was fire in the region of the loaded Exocet launcher. *Ardent* is believed to have sunk some time between 02.00 and 07.00 on 22 May, i.e. between 11 and 16 hours after she was abandoned. Reports by divers from the minehunter *Ledbury* on the wreck indicated that the ship was flooded aft by internal pipe fractures and perhaps some small holes or cracks in the ship's side by the time of abandonment, but was in no danger of sinking by flooding at that time.[56]

Commander Nigel 'Sharkey' Ward, commander of 801 Squadron in *Invincible*, was to be critical of the Sea Harriers' involvement in the final attack. *Hermes'* combat air patrol aircraft, of 800 Squadron Red Section, were to the south at high altitude and Ward asked the control ship, the frigate *Minerva*, to tell them to come down fast and get involved, as he was too far behind the Skyhawks to get them himself. Although two of the Argentinian aircraft were destroyed, Ward said that if the Sea Harriers had been at low level, 'where they should have been', and where Ward's Sea Harriers always were, the Skyhawks would not have gone for *Ardent* and would have gone home. Admiral Woodward's staff's orders to *Hermes'* 800 Squadron to come down on the enemy *after* they'd done their business were, in Ward's view, incompetent.[57]

* * *

The *Ardent* survivors were transferred from *Canberra* to *Queen Elizabeth 2* at South Georgia and received a spectacular welcome on 11 June when the Cunarder sailed into the Solent. They and the *Antelope* and *Coventry* survivors, who were also on board, were greeted by a gun salute fired by the frigate *Lowestoft* in the presence of the Queen Mother in the royal yacht *Britannia*.[58]

A board of inquiry was convened in the language school at HMS *Drake*, Plymouth, on 28 June 1982, and comprised Captain Brian Turner (president), Surgeon Commander G. H. G. McMillan, Commander R. H. Coward, Commander W. K. Hutchinson and Commander R. F. James. Their report was presented to the commander-in-chief, fleet, on 6 August 1982.[59]

On medical matters, the board noted that a commendably high proportion (43 per cent) of the ship's company had been trained in first aid, every man carried a field dressing, and morphine had been issued to members of the first aid parties, six officers and seven senior ratings. The sick bay was rigged as an operating and resuscitation area. However, it was critical of the medical organization. The wardroom should have been equipped to become a casualty collection and recovery area linked to the sick bay. In the event of one or both first aid points being damaged, it could then have been used as an alternative first aid point. There were relatively few non-fatal casualties, yet within a very short time there was a virtually complete breakdown of the organization, with effectively the loss of its only two fully trained members, the medical officer and the leading medical assistant. Whilst there was no evidence that this led to any lack of treatment of the existing casualties, there would have been no skilled care available to any later casualties. The organization had shown a lack of appreciation of the importance of communications, which were entirely by exchange telephone and thus required one from each first aid party to remain at base. The move of the after first aid party to the junior rates' dining hall weakened these links, and the senior rating in charge of the aft damage control party did not tell the damage control party communications rating or the ship control centre of this move. As a result of these failings, two first aiders were deployed unnecessarily from the forward first aid party. One diverted, quite properly, to treat a casualty, but failed to report this. The other was injured, and so the forward first aid point was under-manned.[60]

The medical officer had moved to the flight deck without due cause, the board said. He had responded to the call for assistance himself rather than ensuring that he was really needed and otherwise sending a first aider or ensuring one was already in attendance (as was the case). He tended one walking wounded then evacuated the sick bay without due cause before returning to the flight deck where he allowed himself, the leading medical officer and another first aider to remain in an exposed position treating a man he knew was dying before his eyes. He should have used the stretcher that was immediately to hand to move the dying man to a place of relative safety for all concerned. In consequence, he and his assistant were incapacitated during the final attack and the organization was left without any leadership. The medical officer, who had joined the ship just before she sailed from Plymouth, responded to a call for assistance as he had been trained for several years to do and the board conceded that it might be unreasonable to expect medical officers to subjugate this training immediately and adopt a more hardened approach, especially when the severely injured and clearly 'unsalvageable' casualties were concerned, but nevertheless this is what he should have done.[61]

The board recommended that combat casualty care training of medical officers should be intensified and extended, that the wardroom of all ships should contain stores to allow it to be adapted to a sick bay role, and medical and first aid organization in all ships should incorporate portable communications so that personnel could be more effectively controlled. Also, first aid training should include searching for casualties in a damaged area, as there had been confusion as to whether first aid parties should do this or merely wait for casualties to be identified to them.[62]

The board noted that before abandoning the ship there had been ineffective searches. Although the master-at-arms and chief marine engineer artificer had set off on a search, they covered little of the ship where people may have remained. The captain was clearly convinced by their reports that a search had been conducted. However, it was unlikely that anyone later found to be missing was in the undamaged part of the ship. The lack of any organized attempt to enter and search the dining hall area for survivors was less understandable. It stemmed from the general opinion that the area was devastated and ablaze, but although it was not fully appreciated by the captain and first lieutenant at the time, some eight persons had actually walked or climbed out of the area by various routes. Indeed, the first lieutenant saw two people (presumably Enticknapp and Dillon) jump from the port quarter into the sea. There was a possibility that others were remaining trapped but alive. None of this was appreciated at the time, when it was thought that no one could have survived. It was again clear that few people in authority on board were able to think clearly or act responsibly. The lack of a full search was later to be very much on the consciences of those who survived. Fifteen ratings died in the junior rates' dining hall and one died in the tiller flat.[63]

The board noted that after the ship went to action stations to enter Falkland Sound, fatigue coupled with periods of relative inactivity could have significantly affected the performance of some of those in the ops room and on the bridge if this danger had not been appreciated and steps taken to counter it, which, however, they were. Fatigue may have affected the performance of the lookout aimer sight operator, Leading Seaman Tony Langridge, who by the time of abandoning had had no sleep in comfort for 24 hours and should have been relieved. Whenever possible, men were allowed to sleep at their action station or adjacent to it. Most managed to doze and found this refreshing, but those forward and those who had to sleep in passageways found it most difficult to sleep because of cold.[64]

Commander West had fully appreciated the limitations of the ship's systems in the inshore environment and in particular of the 4.5-inch gun in emergency mode. While Commodore Clapp's staff were probably aware of the limitations of the radar when acquiring targets in inshore situations and the necessary use of emergency modes, it is unlikely that they understood the full limitations of the 4.5-inch gun in this mode. However, even full knowledge of this would probably not have altered the commodore's decision on the tasking of *Ardent*.

There were only three aircraft acquisitions by the ship's 912 trackers during the day, and on each occasion the aircraft turned away or flew low over land and the radar lock was lost. Although no hits were achieved with Seacat, the GWS24 fire control system was operating well at first, in the emergency mode, and the 4.5-inch gun was firing in the emergency mode with its very minimal anti-air capability (considered to be a last resort in such circumstances). In this mode the lookout aimer sight (LAS) operator had to visually aim ahead of the target since there was no computation of a predicted target position, and the term 'rifle mode' was also used in these circumstances. While tracking fast-moving crossing aircraft targets such as the Mirage, the LAS operator had problems with the relatively slow training rate of the sight, which often meant he could not keep up with or aim ahead of his target. Also, the limited field of view within the LAS binoculars did not allow adequate aim off ahead of the target to resolve the prediction problem. This resulted in the operator 'shooting from the hip' visually, unaided by the LAS binoculars. No Seacat hits were obtained because during each firing the Pucará target turned away. The pedestal sight operator was a petty officer with long experience of visual Seacat firings. When he attempted to engage the lead aircraft during the second Skyhawk attack, the missile failed to fire and the Seacat system was destroyed by bombs. This failure to fire was probably due either to the missile boost failing to initiate or the elevation being above 80° in a blind arc. The general purpose machine gun was loaded with tracer, as was one of the ship's light machine guns, but the other three were not despite it being policy to do so. The two loaded machine guns were fired and the one manned by Leake damaged one of the Skyhawks. The 20mm Oerlikons worked satisfactorily but caused no known damage.[65]

Ardent's change of station after the gunfire support operation is something of an enigma in that no one subsequently admitted to originating this move. There seems to have been some confusion over command and control within the amphibious task group during this period due to ship damage and the pace of events. The order apparently came from either Commodore Clapp's staff or from *Antrim*, to whom the anti-air warfare co-ordinator task was delegated by *Broadsword*, the senior escort ship; the intention was to provide anti-air defence against raids approaching the landing area from the south. The result of the change of station was that *Ardent* was pushed out into the mainstream of Argentinian air raids, where other ships had been for much of the day, and this exposed her to greater threat. However, the prime task was then to help defend the landing area against air attack and perhaps she could have been better positioned. *Ardent* received sufficient warning of the final attacks to respond in emergency mode to the threat. Both attacks were conducted very professionally from the quarters by the Argentinian pilots and pressed home with conviction. The failure of Seacat to fire on the first approach was a disaster, but whether taking out the first aircraft of such an attack would have deterred the rest is open to doubt. Had several bombs not failed to explode in each raid, the damage could have been even more severe. In essence, the ship's armament was inadequate to meet such a threat from determined adversaries. The ship handling during the attacks was sound, but was not able to keep up with the fast circling aircraft. The decision to remain on Tyne engines was deliberate, to avoid the effects of Olympus funnel haze over the Seacat deck.[66]

The third Skyhawk attack caught the ship just as order was returning after the previous attack. The explosions were more serious and more prolonged, and they left virtually everyone in a dazed or shocked state, for the whip was felt throughout the ship. The board felt that Lieutenant Commander Pendrous's order to 'Get out' from aft was given before many men had had a chance to re-orientate themselves and was obeyed before there was any chance to take stock rationally of the situation. The order to get out spread very quickly along both 2 and 1 decks, and because no directive had been given as to where to reassemble there was a general exodus to the upper deck. Only those personnel relatively remote from the centre of this exodus had time to even begin to take stock. The net result was that very little damage control was exercised and there was virtually no attempt to communicate internally. Because of this, the picture of the damage that emerged in the inquiry analysis was much less clear and concise than after the second attack. In particular, the full extent of the fire in the after section could not be ascertained accurately. In addition to the major fire in the port after corner of the dining hall, there were unconfirmed reports of fire in the canteen and in the area of the 992 metadyne compartment, though it was likely that this was mistaken for the fire in the hangar. What was clear, however, was that at the time the decision to abandon ship was taken, if these other fires existed, they were of considerably lesser magnitude than the fire in the dining hall area.[67]

The board concluded that everyone suffered some degree of shock and disorientation from the effects of the attack, and this explained the lack of any attempt at damage control by many. They were obviously frightened by the situation, and the general clamour to get out spreading from aft gave them the opportunity to back off from further attempts between decks. All those in the ship control centre had their judgement impaired by the effects of the explosions, but were physically uninjured and were ready and capable of obeying any rational instructions. What was missing here was a clear-headed objective assessment of what to do next. This would have had to come from someone who had not been exposed to the explosions. An alternative damage control headquarters should have been established and manned when the ship went to action stations, the board suggested. Against this background, Marine Engineering Artificer Geoff Hart and Weapon Engineering Artificer Cliff Le Good showed creditable firmness in insisting that their crews remained closed up until a firm instruction to leave the ship had been given.[68]

Both forward generators had remained on load supplying the forward switchboard. Both No 1 and No 2 fire pumps would still have been supplied with power after the third attack, and it was clear that fire-main pressure was still available at least to the hangar while the ship was being abandoned. However, Marine Engineering Mechanic Les Pearce in the forward auxiliary machinery room claimed that No 1 pump had stopped after that attack. The board found no confirmation of this and thought that the evidence of the continued ballasting forward and fire-main pressure remaining on the flight deck (being fed from the forward section) contradicted this. What was clear, the inquiry found, was that no attempt was made to restart the pump.[69]

Lieutenant Commander 'Paddy' McClintock, the weapon engineering officer, who was stationed in the operations room, found himself caught between the demands of his primary task, to liaise with the captain and principal warfare officer on weapon system availability, and his secondary task, to keep them informed of damage control incidents and actions as relayed to him on the ops room communication line. Immediately after the second Skyhawk attack, McClintock became absorbed in the actions to restore control to the 4.5-inch gun and hence failed to get and communicate a full picture of the action damage. His problem was exacerbated by the original ops room communications operator, Leading Seaman John Goddard, who, the board said, became very confused after the second Skyhawk attack. Because he had not got a full picture of damage control, Lieutenant Commander McClintock was unable to contribute positively to the discussion leading to the abandon ship decision. The inquiry found that this was more the fault of his tasking than of his own capability and performance: he was clear in his own mind that weapon repair was his priority. The damage control parties had tended to neglect all areas above 2 deck in their work, due to a misconception that it was the work of the weapon repair team, whom they often referred to as the 'upper damage control party', despite weapon repair being that team's priority.[70]

Before the decision was made to abandon ship there had not been a proper attempt to take stock, the inquiry found. The statement by Chief Stoker Andy Andrews that the forward auxiliary machinery room was wrecked was wrong, as proved by a subsequent diver's report on the ship's wreck. The forward generators were still working and the fire main was still available. It would still have been quite feasible to check the compartment as part of damage control assessment. Also, a check of the flight deck would have shown that the nearest fire to the AS12 missile magazine and the torpedo body room was that around the Avcat station, and that had already been contained. Such checks would also have shown that the trim of the ship was such that it was in no danger of plunging. It may also have been possible to see that the stern was intact, as later photographs proved. These photographs, taken with *Yarmouth* alongside, indicated that the stern was down by just under one foot compared to the average action state, and the heel was about 10°. Such a state would mean that the level of flooding aft was nothing like as serious as assumed by the marine engineering officer, though the loll (heel, due to the large area of free surface water inside the hull) was a worrying aspect which could not be neglected. It had not, however, reached dangerous or uncontrollable proportions and with sensible precautions it need not have done so. The diver's reports indicated that the only holes aft were caused by the bomb damage above the water line.[71]

Could the ship have been saved? The board said it was impossible to be categorical about this, but the important point was that no attempt was made to save her. At the time of the decision to abandon ship, the greatest danger came from the fire aft on the port side, but the basic resources to fight the fire, two generators and two fire pumps, with power and fire-main pressure, were available. There must have been a fair chance that *Ardent* could have been saved by determined action. The board's firm belief was that had the fire been contained *Ardent* would not have sunk, for it was not until the torpedo/Seacat magazines exploded later that night that splinter holes in the machinery spaces finally, yet slowly, caused a loss of buoyancy.[72]

The board concluded that the assessment of damage passed to the captain immediately prior to the abandon ship decision was exaggerated in vital areas, being based on unverified assumptions and conclusions. Faced with the assessments presented to him, the captain believed that there was little chance of saving the ship. His first priority was saving life, and a further air attack was more than possible. It was not surprising that he ordered 'Abandon ship', and the inquiry found that his decision, based on the evidence presented to him, was justified; it added that his state of mind was affected by the bombing and lack of sleep, but to a degree that could not be assessed.[73]

However, there were adequate resources to tackle the fire that was the greatest danger to the ship. The main problem was the loss of some breathing apparatus aft and the loss of charging facilities for breathing apparatus (the damage from the second Skyhawk attack had rendered all breathing apparatus charging points inoperative), but this could have been overcome with assistance from other ships. The recognition of the limitations in the use of breathing apparatus should have raised awareness of the need for discipline in its use and control, but the actual control was poor. Breathing apparatus not being worn was found abandoned on more than one occasion, and the senior rates in charge of parties were not aware of the use or whereabouts of the apparatus normally stored in their section.[74]

There was a total breakdown of damage control command and control when the order was given by the marine engineering officer to 'get out' of the ship control centre: the crew there were very badly dazed and disorientated after the third attack and a true assessment of the situation could only have been made by personnel further removed from the damaged area. Knowledge of ship stability criteria and behaviour was lacking amongst the command and heads of department. The marine engineering officer's understanding was overshadowed by a pre-occupation with the risks of plunging. The rapid spread of smoke along 1 and 2 decks exacerbated the confusion and lack of damage control effort after the final attack. Blanket searches following action damage, although practised, were not well organized or complete. Damage control communications proved very vulnerable to failure of power supplies from key transformer rectifier units.[75]

The board's excoriating summary of the ship's company's performance pulled no punches:

> The shock of the bombing clearly seriously affected many people and their effectiveness was reduced, in some cases to zero. The majority of officers and senior rates in the fringes of the damaged area became shadows of their normal selves and failed in their observation, thought processes and leadership. Many wandered rather aimlessly around the ship. Others were deliberately evasive.

The instruction by the MEO [marine engineering officer] to 'get out' was all that many senior and junior rates needed to move as quickly as possible to the upper deck. Others followed like sheep. Yet it is equally clear that most would probably have responded to good leadership and got on with the necessary damage control action had it been asked of them straight away. Remarkably those knocked unconscious in the damaged area seem to have responded more actively than most on recovering their senses… The poor performance of so many personnel must raise questions about the Royal Navy's preparation of personnel for the mental and physical stresses of battle.[76]

The inquiry considered that, with the benefit of hindsight, the Lynx should have been airborne during the air attacks. It hypothesized that the problem for the aircraft attacking *Ardent* would have been much more difficult if the Lynx had been airborne somewhere about 4 miles from the ship, armed with two Sidewinder missiles (though of course these were not available in the ship). Consideration should be given to making this standard practice during Air Raid Warning Red.[77]

The board's recommendations included the setting up of an alternative damage control headquarters when the ship was at action stations; that smoke curtains be provided for between deck bulkhead doors and doors to key compartments; and that a back-up network of sound-powered telephones should be installed linking key damage control positions. Further instructions on stability performance should be given to heads of department prior to joining the ship, and the stability characteristics of each ship should be provided in a form more readily appreciated from the practical aspects and observable viewpoint than hitherto. The Type 21 frigate should be fitted with additional short-range weapon systems. Further studies should be undertaken to provide a basis for improving methods of preparing men for the stresses of action.[78]

The ship had been abandoned prematurely, based on an inaccurate assessment of the damage and its implications. *Ardent* could probably have been saved by co-ordinated and determined damage control efforts and good leadership. A full search for survivors was not conducted, so there was no certainty that survivors were not left behind in the damaged areas.

* * *

Those decorated for bravery in *Ardent* (see Appendix) were Lieutenant Commander John Sephton, Distinguished Service Cross (posthumous) for extreme valour and self-sacrifice in directing and manning small arms in a desperate last-ditch attempt to down the Skyhawk which bombed the ship; Commander Alan West, Distinguished Service Cross for his calm courage and direction; Able Seaman John Dillon, George Medal for his bravery and selfless disregard for his personal safety; Marine Engineering Artificer Ken Enticknapp, Queen's Gallantry Medal for showing dedication to duty under constant enemy attack in placing the safety of other lives above his own, despite his own serious injuries; Petty Officer John Leake, Distinguished Service Medal, for his courage, steadfastness and total disregard for his own safety, as a machine gunner; Sub-Lieutenant Richie Barker and Marine Engineering Mechanic Dave Serrell, Mentioned in Despatches.[79]

Surgeon Commander Rick Jolly was decorated by both the British and Argentinian governments for his distinguished conduct during the conflict, treating casualties from both sides: he received the OBE (Order of the British Empire) and the *Oficial Orden de Mayo* (Order of May, one of Argentina's highest decorations), and was the only participant in the conflict to be honoured by both sides.

Commander Alan West, speaking of his continued involvement as president of the HMS *Ardent* Association, has said, 'When you lose a ship like that you keep in touch forever,' adding that the families of some of the deceased send him Christmas cards every year, and seek his advice on family matters: 'It is really quite touching.'[80]

Ardent's bell was salvaged and was placed in St Nicholas' church, HMS *Drake*, Plymouth, where a memorial service commemorating the loss of *Ardent* and *Antelope* is held each year in May. Many of

Ardent's survivors' children have been baptized in the bell, adhering to a tradition in the Royal Navy for members of ships' companies to have their children baptized in this way.[81]

* * *

Ardent was not well equipped for defence against a determined attack from the air, being primarily intended for anti-submarine work. Her main anti-aircraft weapon, Seacat, was notoriously ineffective, and her 4.5-inch gun had minimal capability in the emergency mode that had to be employed. Like other ships, she suffered from her radar's inability to pick up fast-moving aircraft in the proximity of land. Commander 'Sharkey' Ward alleged that the Skyhawks could have been fought off if the Sea Harriers involved in the final attack had been flying low, and if so the bombing would have been averted. After being bombed, there was a noticeable lack of leadership in *Ardent*, leading to a complete breakdown in the damage control efforts. Furthermore, the ship was abandoned prematurely and probably unnecessarily, because of exaggerated reports regarding the damage to the ship and its possible consequences. The erroneous assessment that the ship might soon plunge was made by the marine engineering officer and the first lieutenant, and was not adequately questioned by Commander West. *Ardent* could probably have been saved by co-ordinated and determined damage control efforts and good leadership. It was particularly unfortunate that, in the haste to abandon ship, a full search for survivors was not conducted, with ambiguous information transmitted to the captain, so there was no certainty that survivors had not been left behind in the damaged areas.

Commodore Clapp needed to replace *Ardent* on her station to carry out gunfire support and air defence of the amphibious landings, and, fortuitously for him, HMS *Antelope* arrived in Falkland Sound to fill the gap. Her experience is related in the next chapter.

5

The Loss of HMS *Antelope*

HMS *Antelope* had a short war. After heading south from Devonport she did not speed down with the carrier group to join the fray in the Falklands. Instead, she escorted the slower moving amphibious group and was also used for guardship duties at Ascension Island. When she finally entered the total exclusion zone (TEZ) she received the order to escort transports into the amphibious operating area and found herself in an intense battle zone with no chance to acclimatize to such conditions. Barely four hours after entering San Carlos Water she was bombed, and later the same day had to be abandoned, less than 48 hours after entering the TEZ.

Antelope, a sister ship of *Ardent*, was the second Type 21 frigate of the Royal Navy and entered service on 19 July 1975. She was built by Vosper Thornycroft Ltd, Woolston, Southampton, where she was launched by Lady Kirk, the wife of the Under Secretary of State for the Navy, on 16 March 1972. She was the only unit of her class not fitted to launch Exocet missiles. In other respects, her vital statistics and sensors were the same as *Ardent*. A modernization scheme to improve the Type 21's air defence capability by replacing the Seacat with a Sea Wolf missile system and to fit a towed array sonar was considered in about 1978, but was not implemented because the freeboard to 2 deck (the highest watertight deck) was inadequate.[1] *Antelope* had a nominal complement of 13 officers and 162 ratings. Her motto was *audax et vigilans* – daring and watchful.

Commander Nick Tobin was appointed in command of *Antelope* in early 1981. Brought up and educated in Kenya, he had graduated from Britannia Royal Naval College, Dartmouth in 1963, joining the minesweeper *Glasserton*. He then trained as a fighter controller and served in the aircraft carrier *Victorious* and the destroyer *Aisne* from 1964 to 1968. After completing the Long Direction (Air Warfare) Course, he was appointed to the guided missile destroyer *London* in 1970, and then served ashore in HMS *Dryad* and the Admiralty Surface Weapons Establishment until 1974. Consecutive commands of the patrol vessels *Beachampton* and *Wolverton* in Hong Kong followed until 1976, when he returned to the UK for staff training before appointment as the deputy direction officer in the aircraft carrier *Ark Royal*. Promoted to commander in 1978, he taught at the Royal Naval Staff College at Greenwich.[2]

Antelope had spent three months on deployment to the West Indies between May and August 1981. She had last completed Basic Operational Sea Training* (BOST) at Portland in May 1980, and Continuation Operational Sea Training (COST) was planned for May 1981, but was reduced to four days because a diesel generator needed unscheduled replacement before the West Indies deployment. Whilst in the West Indies two exercises were engaged in, with the ship arriving back in Devonport on 20 August. In October and November there was navigation training, weapon training with *Brilliant*, Exercise *Mad Hatter* (a major exercise) and a visit to La Pallice, France. Throughout 1981 there were concerns about the ship's weapon standards and training in the use of the gun and missile system, which fell below fleet standards. The WSA4 fire control system had had a history of unsatisfactory performance since the ship's refit in 1980. The Type 992 radar had

---

* Basic Operational Sea Training was an intensive programme of training and assessment, based at Portland and usually lasting six weeks, which was intended to bring ships newly out of refit, reserve or the builder's yard up to full operational efficiency and effectiveness prior to deployment. Continuation Operational Sea Training was an intermediate version of this, also at Portland and usually shorter in duration, for ships which were mid-deployment and needed to be brought up to a higher standard of performance.

also been troublesome and was modified in September 1981, but the operators reported unanimously that they were not content with the modification because they were unfamiliar with it. Three Seacat firings attempted in 1981 were unsuccessful. The 4.5-inch gun had a succession of defects throughout 1981, the loading system being particularly problematic, and only five firings had been completed. After the La Pallice visit the ship underwent a maintenance period, coinciding with Christmas and New Year leave, and carried out post docking trials in February and March 1982. These were completed satisfactorily except for WSA4 performance, which was still below standard because satisfactory aircraft acquisitions could not be obtained.[3]

The problems with the two major weapon systems (the 4.5-inch gun and Seacat) had lowered the morale of the users and maintainers, and of the ship's company generally, and for nearly two years the ship had never been fully operational. The chief weapon engineering artificer, M. E. Porter, commented in August 1981, 'Already in the fleet [*Antelope's*] gunnery is regarded as something of a joke when talking of defending oneself against the enemy. If this situation carries on getting worse... the enemy will not have to fight us. We'll defeat ourselves!'. In January 1982 Captain H. M. White, the captain of the 4th Frigate Squadron (which *Antelope* had joined on 1 April 1981), reported, 'The original defect on the 4.5 Mk 8 loading system was never satisfactorily rectified and has been the root cause of the gun's unreliability since refit.' He added, though, that the problems with Seacat firing in auto mode were no more than already prevalently expressed in all ships fitted with the same fire control system, but the decision to allow *Antelope* to proceed to BOST in May 1980 after her refit without completing her sea weapon acceptance trials was a mistake.[4]

Captain White proposed that a BOST programme be carried out to replace a planned COST, but for operational reasons this was not possible. Instead the COST, which was intended to have a particular emphasis on weapons training, started at Portland on 22 March 1982 but was terminated early, on 2 April, when the ship was assigned to Operation *Corporate*, the Falklands task force.

During this COST no Seacat or gun firing was achieved because of equipment and clear range problems. Representations were made by Flag Officer 2nd Flotilla and Flag Officer Sea Training to the staff of the commander-in-chief, fleet, that the COST should be allowed to be completed, but for urgent operational reasons this was deemed infeasible. The ship had tried to remedy shortcomings by the use of passage time and limited weapon training periods, but the virtual absence of COST in spring 1981, which would have provided an essential benchmark in training standards for the newly joined captain, executive officer, principal warfare officer and navigating officer, contributed to reduced performance. Deployment to the West Indies had provided few opportunities to compensate for the organized training and facilities of Portland. Some key officers and ratings in *Antelope* lacked recent frigate experience, which, in conjunction with their new and joint arrival in the ship, hindered achievement of wholly satisfactory operational performance without the benefit of COST/BOST.[5] Nevertheless, Captain H. M. White contended in January 1982 that there had been a tendency for the ship not to make best use of opportunities within the fleet operations programme for weapon proving.[6]

Antelope arrived at Devonport at 16.00 on 2 April and started storing for the South Atlantic deployment, which was completed early the next day. She was placed under the operational control of Commodore Mike Clapp, commander of the amphibious task group. At 07.00 on 5 April the ship sailed from Devonport in company with her sister ship *Alacrity*; later that day they met up with the LSLs *Sir Galahad*, *Sir Geraint*, *Sir Lancelot* and *Sir Percival* to escort them towards Ascension Island. They joined up with the *Hermes* group for two days before joining the *Fearless* group.[7]

During the passage south, *Antelope* made Seacat and naval gunfire support the priorities for training, bearing in mind the reduced COST and the assessment of threat priorities as determined by Commodore Mike Clapp, commanding the amphibious forces, who believed the main threat was Exocet. The ship detached from the *Hermes* group on 8 April and loitered off Madeira to await the arrival of the amphibious group; this came early on 11 April and consisted of *Fearless*, five LSLs (*Sir Tristram* having joined from Belize) and the RFAs *Pearleaf* and *Stromness*.[8]

After conducting an exercise at sea with *Fearless* on that day, *Antelope* assumed command of the LSLs, with *Fearless* detaching for Ascension Island. On passage *Antelope* worked up the LSLs in station keeping, communications, gun firing and emissions control. On 19 April *Antelope* passed Ascension and detached the LSLs *Sir Lancelot*, *Sir Geraint* and *Sir Percival*. She continued south to rendezvous with RFA *Olmeda* to refuel and arrived at Ascension Island on 21 April. There she assumed the role of guardship. Against a supposed threat of attack by 'chariot'-borne underwater swimmers off Ascension, the ship anchored during the day and remained at sea at night, undertaking a sonar search. Argentina was known to have purchased French four-man chariot submersibles and Italian two-man chariots, and *Fearless* had reported underwater noises in the anchorage. *Antelope* carried out gunnery training at sea on 23 April: as well as anti-aircraft and naval gunfire support firings of the 4.5-inch gun, two Seacat firings were achieved, one in auto which was unsatisfactory and one in manual which was successful. This restored some confidence in Seacat, albeit not in its primary (automatic) mode, and was the first successful firing for 18 months. Small arms, 20mm Oerlikon and 3-inch rocket launcher firings were all practised.

Two days later, *Antelope* was ordered to shadow the Argentinian government-owned freighter *Rio de la Plata*, which had been sighted by Nimrod aircraft approaching within 4 miles of Ascension Island and may have been associated with the underwater chariot threat. On 29 April *Antelope* escorted another Argentinian freighter out to a distance of 100 miles to make sure it did not turn back. On 30 April she returned to Ascension Island for attention following a vibration problem, which required the removal of eddy plates by divers.

On 1 May she was ordered to proceed south to the holding area to the east of the great circle route to the Falklands, escorting the five LSLs and the tanker *Pearleaf*. After the sinking of *Sheffield* on

4 May, the ship spent a lot of time practising anti-Exocet drills including firings. On 7 May, *Antelope* was ordered to rendezvous with *Antrim* and escort RFA *Tidespring* to Ascension Island with 180 Argentinian prisoners of war in *Tidespring*, these POWs having been captured at South Georgia; *Antelope* provided 12 guards in the RFA. One officer prisoner of war (Lieutenant Commander Alfredo Astiz, of the Argentinian marines, who had also been captured in South Georgia) and 18 members of the British Antarctic Survey (BAS) who had been stationed in South Georgia were transferred from *Antrim* to *Antelope*. The two ships reached Ascension on 13 May and disembarked the prisoners and BAS personnel. Meanwhile *Antrim* took over duties with the southbound LSLs, as it was felt necessary to provide a stronger escort. On 14 May *Antelope* headed south from Ascension with her sister ship *Ambuscade* and *Tidespring*.[9]

An NBCD (nuclear, biological and chemical defence and damage control) team embarked from *Fearless* to provide advice and conduct training exercises. Paint and some other flammable materials were ditched and the fire main was isolated into three parts. However, fuel was not removed from ship's boats and the significant removal of fire hazardous material from ship accommodation spaces was not attempted. Some *Sheffield* survivors came aboard to debrief their experiences. On 18 May *Antelope* fuelled to 60 per cent from the BP tanker *British Esk*, there being insufficient for a complete fuelling. In the event this nearly prevented *Antelope* from reaching the total exclusion zone (TEZ), because although a rendezvous with RFA *Plumleaf* for further fuel was made the following day, it was unsuccessful due to bad weather. *Antelope* had less than 37 per cent fuel at this point, which was below the safe minimum in icing conditions, and caused concern about ship stability. At 19.00 (Falklands Standard Time) on 21 May she entered the TEZ, a week after sailing from Ascension.[10]

The senior weapons engineer officer (SWEO) of the 4th Frigate Squadron was embarked on 22 May to brief the ship on lessons learnt from the 21 May anti-aircraft battle, in which *Ardent* was attacked and disabled. He advised them that all aircraft should be treated as hostile; the 3-inch rocket launchers should be used as an anti-aircraft weapon; Seacat should always be in emergency mode, manually controlled from the pedestal site on the hangar top; the 4.5-inch gun should be used in emergency 'rifle' mode; 20mm guns should be permanently loaded when close to shore; and an officer should be on the gun direction platform with authority to open fire. He was impressed by the material preparations *Antelope* had made since he had last been aboard at Ascension and considered that real progress had been made. However, exercising both Seacat and the 4.5-inch gun in emergency mode had not been given the attention it deserved, and its importance was only fully appreciated after learning about the events of 21 May and the SWEO's briefing. During this visit *Antelope* was ordered by Admiral Woodward's staff to escort the first re-supply convoy, consisting of the merchant ships *Norland* and *Europic Ferry* and RFA *Stromness*, into the amphibious operating area. The ship had been six weeks on passage to the TEZ.[11]

At 21.00 on 22 May *Antelope* entered Falkland Sound, and sailed into San Carlos Water about 30 minutes later. Both *Antelope* and *Ardent* had been with Commodore Mike Clapp during the winter exercises in Norway, and he considered them to be the only two escorts specifically worked up for amphibious operations. Now *Antelope's* role was to replace the lost *Ardent* in gunfire support and carry out air defence of the amphibious landings, positioned at the entrance to Port San Carlos, south of Fanning Island and Rabbit Island. Her station was at the junction of two valleys, which exposed her to attack from most directions; she assessed the main threat to be from the west. She headed west north-west in the vicinity of her station, in good visibility with the wind west north-west 12 knots. Commander Tobin was in the operations room, but the air warning radar picture was seriously degraded because of the proximity of land. Tobin was aware that they could monitor the anti-air warfare control network, but the primary (automatic) modes of the main weapon systems were severely limited, if not totally ineffective, with the ship positioned as it was. Use of the 4.5-inch gun in emergency mode was known to be a last-ditch method with little chance of success. The ship was unaware of the positions of shore-based Rapier and Blowpipe missile batteries. Enemy aircraft activity was quiet during the morning and the air raid warning status remained at Yellow.[12]

At 12.00 on Sunday 23 May the ship's Lynx helicopter was launched to observe the Argentinian stores ship *Río Carcaraña*, which it had attacked earlier with two Sea Skua missiles, both of which had hit. The ship was found to be sinking and the Lynx returned to the Sound. At 12.40 *Antelope* was overflown by four Argentinian Skyhawk A4Bs going in the same direction and the Lynx pilot broadcast an urgent warning of the raid, having first detected the radar emissions of the aircraft on his ESM* sensor. At the same time the air raid warning from *Broadsword* (which was stationed a little further south, off the land between Hospital Point and Doctor's Head: see Map 6) became Red. The Lynx pilot was fortunate because Captain Pablo Carballo, leading his second strike against the landings, had attempted to shoot down the Lynx, but his Skyhawk's 20mm cannon jammed after the first few rounds. The Lynx positioned itself to the south of Chancho Point in a low hover.[13]

The Skyhawks were seen from *Antelope* flying between Chancho Pont and Fanning Head before they disappeared behind land. The raid singled out the exposed *Antelope* for a co-ordinated attack. Two aircraft flew between Fanning Head and Findlay Rocks, then turned south over Port San Carlos Settlement below the skyline, where they were engaged by shore-based missiles (see aircraft 1 and 2, Map 6). The aircraft disappeared from view, but re-emerged and approached the ship about 50ft above the water and at about 400 knots, along the southern shore of Port San Carlos River. The first aircraft was engaged by Seacat in emergency manual mode from the pedestal above the hangar, and the second was engaged by the 4.5-inch gun in emergency rifle mode. The lead aircraft turned away over the ridge between Hospital Point and Doctor's Head pursued by a Seacat missile, with which a hit was wrongly claimed (though this aircraft was probably damaged on its port wing by

* Electronic support measures.

Map 6: The air attacks on HMS *Antelope*, 23 May

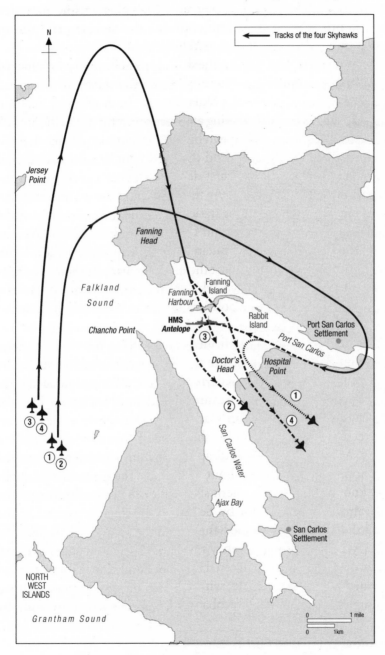

Antelope's Seacat missile exploding beneath it, and was nursed back to Río Gallegos by its pilot, Carballo). The second aircraft continued to attack from the port quarter and was unsuccessfully engaged by the 4.5-inch gun, which fired 14 rounds before stopping because of a control problem due to a 'phantom round', the breach having closed on an empty gun. The Skyhawk released a 1,000lb bomb that entered the ship in the petty officers' mess, where it failed to explode. The port light machine gun engaged the Skyhawk, but no hits were observed. Olympus exhaust gases obscured the aircraft from the port 20mm gun until almost overhead, and this gun did not open fire.[14]

When the bomb entered the petty officers' mess, Steward Mark Stephens received fatal head injuries, Leading Stores Accountant Paul Ridge received a serious head injury and Supply Assistant R. J. Carr sustained wood splinters in his eye and the side of his face and bruising to his arm. Leading Medical Assistant Andrew Till and Petty Officer Bob Hutton were unhurt. Till and Hutton transported Stephens to the after first aid post on a stretcher, where he was examined by the medical officer, who assessed that his life could not be saved: Mark Stephens died about five minutes later. Ridge was seen in the petty officers' mess by the medical officer: he was conscious but concussed and 'very irritable', and showed signs of a fractured base of the skull. He was given antibiotics and was later taken by helicopter at 15.15 to the field hospital at Ajax Bay.[15]

Simultaneously, the other two aircraft approached the ship from the north-west, contour flying down the hill across Fanning Harbour (see aircraft 3 and 4, Map 6). The right-hand aircraft climbed, passing astern of the ship, but the other attacked at low level. It was engaged with the starboard light machine gun and the starboard 20mm gun (manned by Leading Seaman Jeffrey 'Bunny' Warren) when within range, and hits by the latter were observed, causing the aircraft to hit the main mast, disintegrate and crash into the sea, together with *Antelope's* HF/DF aerial. The Skyhawk, practically beyond doubt, was also hit almost simultaneously by *Broadsword's* Sea Wolf and a land-based Rapier missile; the pilot, Lieutenant Luciano Guadagnini, was killed.[16]

Warren recalled that, as the first aircraft approached, his first thought was:

'We are at war and are going to kill or be killed.' The hairs on the back of my neck stood up and the sudden flow of adrenalin to the system made me feel sick inside... I turned to see an aircraft wave-hopping across Fanning Island literally feet above the waves. I opened fire... hitting the aircraft in the starboard wing and fuselage. It lurched and climbed, at the same time dropping its two 1,000lb bombs... [before hitting] the after-pole mast and disintegrating in a huge ball of flame, showering the immediate area with shrapnel.[17]

During this attack one or possibly two bombs were released; the first bounced off the water and entered the ship amidships in the load centre, passing onwards into the air conditioning machinery room, but did not explode; the other bomb, if it existed (as reported by Warren), passed harmlessly between the masts. The aircraft was not engaged by the 4.5-inch gun or Seacat. By the time the gun had been slewed around, the aircraft was in its blind arc. The Seacat firing sequence was initiated, but the missile did not fire because the launcher was in blind arcs for elevation and the operator did not follow the procedure to correct this. Moments later a Skyhawk reapproached the ship from the direction of Port San Carlos, but no bombs were seen to be dropped. It was engaged by the port 20mm gun, which jammed after just one round, and by the 4.5-inch gun with four rounds, as it was opening towards Fanning Head. This may have been Carballo's aircraft, as he tried to establish if the Skyhawk was fit to fly. *Antelope*'s Seacat was ready to fire but, because of a misunderstanding of safety orders, fire was checked, as it was considered that *Broadsword* might have been endangered.[18] The general purpose machine gun was fired from the flight deck after jamming initially. The port and starboard light machine guns were fired from the gun direction platform in each attack.[19]

There were several more air raids on San Carlos Water later that day, but *Antelope* was not directly attacked. In one of the raids, the starboard 20mm gun opened fire at an aircraft but was stopped by toppled rounds.[20]

The second bomb came to rest in the air conditioning compartment but caused no casualties. The bomb damaged the heat exchanger and caused an escape of refrigerant gas: eight men involved in damage control and first aid duties were affected by the gas and experienced hypoxia, but only two (Supply Assistant R. J. Carr and Steward J. G. Sim) sought medical advice; recovery in all cases was rapid on return to fresh air. The medical officer, knowing of the unexploded bomb aft, moved the sick bay forward into the wardroom together with the two patients, Carr and Sim. This was moving closer to the forward bomb. The medical officer was later to tell the board of inquiry that he had had no training in combat casualty care or in the medical organization of a ship for war.[21]

Damage control parties were soon in action aboard *Antelope*, and a host of repairs and emergency fixes were necessary. Some important electrical cables were damaged in the action, resulting in loss of power supplies to the forward auxiliary machinery room and aft engine room fire pumps, gyro stabilization to all positions, and interruptions to external and internal communications. Emergency cables were run to both fire pumps and supplies were restored quickly. The forward damage control repair party isolated the branch of the fire main, which had breached in the petty officers' cabin space, and stopped water leaking into the area. Field telephones were run from the forward section base to the ship control centre and from the 4.5-inch gun power room to the ops room. The bomb in the forward section was found after 30 minutes of searching by Petty Officer Effemey: some 6 inches of a grey cylinder was visible under a pile of debris as it lay in the middle bunk of No 7 cabin – his bunk! Marine Engineer Mechanic J. J. Taylor had volunteered to clear away the debris in the search for the bomb. In the aft section, the mobile repair party found the bomb in the starboard air conditioning unit compartment almost immediately and wedged it to prevent it rolling across the deck as the ship heeled.[22]

An explosive ordnance disposal team was requested at 13.30. At 14.10 the ship proceeded slowly to anchor, remaining at action stations with NBCD at the highest state, and a helicopter was requested for casualty evacuation. During this passage the executive officer and the marine engineer officer identified a vent route for the egress of gases within the midships section, in case the bomb in this area exploded. The executive officer gave instructions to Chief Petty Officer Smith to open the hatch to a cross passage and both outer superstructure doors. The instructions were misinterpreted: Smith thought the route was for venting diesel fumes. Consequently, the hatch and doors were not lashed open or marked with 'May be Left Open' notices. They were closed 15 minutes later when Smith thought the fumes had dispersed. A vent route for the bomb in the forward section was not considered. The salt-water system for the fire main was isolated into three separate sections and electrical power distribution arrangements were made, both consistent with the highest damage control state. Fire hoses were flaked out in the junior ratings' dining hall and the ship control centre flat. At 15.05 *Antelope* anchored in Ajax Bay close to the frigate *Argonaut*, which by now also had an unexploded bomb aboard – in her boiler room. On advice from the explosive disposal team, Commander Tobin instructed the executive officer to clear personnel to the forecastle and the flight deck before the process of rendering the bombs safe began. Unwittingly this dispersed the damage control parties and no attempt was made to retain their operational organization. Skeleton crews remained on the bridge, in the ops room, on the gun direction platform, on the Seacat pedestal sight, in the ship control centre (where the marine engineer officer based himself with the explosive disposal team) and in the machinery control office. Damage control responsibility was assumed by the captain to remain with the marine engineer officer.[23]

Antelope's Lynx re-embarked at about 14.45, having previously landed on *Broadsword* to load extra Sea Skua missiles during a lull between air attacks. Subsequently it launched for the field dressing post in Ajax Bay with the seriously injured Ridge. It remained at this post while the bomb disposal process took place.[24]

The bomb disposal team sent to *Antelope* consisted of Warrant Officer John Phillips and Staff Sergeant James Prescott, of the Royal

Engineers. On arrival they met the executive officer and the marine engineer officer, then inspected both bombs in the company of two senior rates. Prescott had already rendered safe the bomb in *Argonaut*'s boiler room. The bomb in the air-conditioning unit was assessed as a British 1,000lb bomb, manufactured in 1971. The front fuse pocket was empty except for debris and the after fuse pocket contained what was thought to be a British Mk 78 pistol. The pistol body was damaged and the arming fork was missing. The team considered that this bomb was armed. The tail was not sighted. Prescott partially sighted the forward bomb in the petty officers' cabin and considered it similar to the other bomb. Because of debris he did not inspect the bomb closely and did not sight the pistol. The team returned to the ship control centre and met the captain. They informed him that they were content to attempt to defuse both bombs, starting with the after bomb as this was armed and more accessible than the forward bomb. They advised that the ship should be cleared of non-essential personnel. Lieutenant Commander R. F. Goodfellow and Mechanician H. B. Porter remained in the ship control centre to liaise between the disposal team and the command.[25]

The first attempt to defuse the bomb started at about 17.00. A rocket wrench was attached to the pistol but was not tightened hard because of the damaged body. (A rocket wrench is a robust high torque wrench, developed to unscrew fuses from explosive devices at a safe distance, and initiated by electrically initiated power cartridges.) The team retired to the firing point at the after end of the ship control centre flat, closing and clipping all doors. Following command approval, the rocket wrench was fired. On inspection, the pistol had been slightly unscrewed and the wrench had come off. A second attempt produced similar results, except that the pistol came out about a quarter inch. The firing point was moved into the junior rates' dining hall as an extra precaution, as anxiety about progress mounted. For the third attempt the wrench was secured very tightly to the pistol, but on firing the result was similar. The bomb disposal team became very anxious that the procedure for rendering the bomb safe was not proceeding smoothly. Warrant Officer Phillips considered cutting a hole in the ship's side and rolling the bomb out.

However, neither this consideration nor his concern was discussed with the command; indeed, the team led the command to believe that they were confident of eventual success.[26]

Phillips decided to discard the rocket wrench and use a de-armer. (This device shoots steel slugs at high velocity into the fuses or pistols of the bomb.) The ship was informed that a different method was to be attempted, but before this was done those personnel on the upper deck were moved into the hangar because they were getting cold in the biting wind. The de-armer was placed in a cardboard box alongside the pistol. Because the pistol was in the rear of the bomb, achievement of the correct angle of attack was difficult, but the team was satisfied that the de-armer was set up properly. Having withdrawn to the firing point, closing and clipping all doors behind them, the team obtained approval from the command to fire. The de-armer was heard to fire, and after a short pause, the bomb disposal team and the ship control centre crew moved forward from the dining hall into the ship control centre flat. But approximately 45 seconds after the de-armer fired, the bomb exploded. Staff Sergeant Prescott was killed instantly and Warrant Officer Phillips' left arm was badly injured. He was treated using first aid kits from the hangar before being taken by landing craft to the Ajax Bay field hospital where his arm was amputated, and he was then moved to the hospital ship *Uganda*. The two Antelopes sustained only minor injuries, although they were little more than 30 feet from the seat of the blast. Leading Seaman M. J. Hancox was thrown from a ladder and sustained minor knee injuries.[27]

Argentina had bought four different types of detonators for use with the British Mk 78 pistol, including one type that had a 25–30-second delay to allow low flying aircraft to clear the area before the explosion. This would explain the delay that occurred between the time when the bomb disposal team fired the de-armer and the explosion.[28]

A hole 35ft wide was blown in the ship's side from the boot-topping to the upper deck, and heavy damage was inflicted in both engine rooms and to about five adjacent compartments.[29] At the time of the blast, most of the ship's company were in the hangar:

many were thrown to the deck and disorientated by the shock of the explosion. A wooden air conditioning door from the lower aircraft workshop was blown into the hangar, striking two ratings but not significantly injuring them. Blast gases and a bright flash were seen at the forward end of the hangar, and all personnel moved quickly towards the after end of the flight deck, causing confusion; it took several minutes to bring order. The steel bulkheads adjacent to the air conditioning machinery spaces were probably totally destroyed and damage spread across the ship to at least the port side of the centre passageway, down to the two engine rooms and upwards through the starboard side offices. All of the ship's systems in these areas would have been severed.

Shortly after the blast the executive officer arrived on the flight deck, ordered Lieutenant Govan to take control of personnel and instructed the deputy marine engineer officer to take charge of firefighting. This control came after the initial individual attempts to fight the fire on the starboard side of the upper deck had been abandoned because of smoke and the lack of pressure in the fire main. Despite determined attempts by a number of personnel, including Lieutenant Commander David Highett, Chief Petty Officer Meechan, Marine Engineering Mechanics Parker, Taylor and Clarke, Leading Seaman Warren and Weapons Engineering Mechanic Jennings, the firefighting efforts continued to be frustrated by the lack of water pressure. Both the forward and midships fire-main sections lost all pressure immediately after the blast. The after section was at reduced pressure for a few minutes before failing completely. A fire-main fracture followed by a power supply failure to the aft auxiliary machine room fire pump probably caused the losses of pressure.[30]

Leading Seaman Jeffrey 'Bunny' Warren recalled that he had been picked up and thrown onto the flight deck by the explosion. Once on his feet he could see flames emerging from a hole forward. Moving forward, he started rigging hoses with Marine Engineer Mechanic Vince Parker and supply officer Lieutenant David Highett, and they directed water through the hole. Parker leant over the side to reach inside with the hose. But the fuel on board started to burn, creating noxious black smoke which got so thick that they could get no air:

> I slapped Parker on the back and said, 'It's time to go'. Upon reaching the flight deck, eyes streaming and throat still burning from lack of air, I realised that Parker was still back at the hole... Taking a deep breath, I lunged back into the smoke and went forward... and found Vince semi-conscious, half in, half out of the hole... I grabbed hold of him and slung him over my shoulder... as a sheet of flame erupted from where Vince had just been, making Vince's overalls smoke and singeing my face and hands.[31]

With his throat feeling as though it was on fire, Warren staggered back and laid Parker on flight deck, whilst shouting for first aid to see to him. Warren resumed his firefighting efforts from the starboard side forward where the smoke was thinner, but all of the hydrants his party tried had no water at all.

A landing craft, utility (LCU) from *Fearless* had a Rover gas turbine fire pump on board and Lieutenant Govan directed it to the starboard side to fight the fire through the ship's side, but the attempt was unsuccessful because the hose was incorrectly rigged and aqueous firefighting foam was neither available in the LCU nor supplied from the ship. One member of the LCU crew tried unsuccessfully to obtain supplies from the flight deck, but the noise from helicopters hovering overhead drowned out his voice. The ship did not request further firefighting assets from outside units though communications were available.[32]

The weapons engineering officer attempted to set up an emergency damage control headquarters at the port after side of the hangar. Poor communication caused by damage, fire and loss of power supplies together with a lack of good information made this attempt ineffective. The captain remained in the bridge and many attempts were made to pass information to him. It was apparent from patrols that the forward half of the ship was tenable and that some power supplies remained there. However, no attempt was made to deploy hands forward to use the equipment in the forward damage control base, which included portable pumps and breathing apparatus. Despite the availability of power, with at least one generator continuing to function, no attempt was made to restore supplies to hull and fire pumps or to portable pumps. The initial attempt to remove the Rover gas turbine portable pump from the starboard access was thwarted by smoke. It was later removed, with difficulty, by personnel using diving equipment (breathing apparatus was not available) but had not been prepared for running before the order to abandon ship was given.[33]

Spray systems in the magazines (at least one of which was automatic) did not operate and apparently no attempt was made to operate them manually. The only exception was the starboard shipborne torpedo weapon system spraying system, which the weapons engineering officer successfully operated shortly after the explosion as a precaution against the burning debris falling on the starboard side of the ship. There was no evidence that the aluminium superstructure automatic spray system operated. The manually operated machinery space CO_2 drenching system was not operated, not least because all operating positions were in the area of explosion damage. The lack of fire-main pressure was no doubt a significant contributory factor in these cases, since the only area where pressure was maintained for a period was the after section, and there only for a few minutes.[34]

Mechanics Clarke and Taylor, dressed in fearnought firesuits and breathing apparatus, entered the ship aft through the flight deck hatch to establish what damage had been caused and, if possible, to attempt to fight the fire; Petty Officer Effemey acted as their controller. The two men passed through the junior rates' dining hall to just aft of the bulkhead into the ship control centre. They used flaked-out hoses as guidelines but did not attempt to test for fire-main pressure. Visibility was reduced by smoke, but they saw a red glow of a fire and felt direct heat through the door from the ship control centre. However, Effemey mistakenly instructed the two mechanics to return in the belief that the order to abandon ship had been given. Lieutenant Mugridge and Chief Petty Officer Meechan were instructed by the captain to go below in the forward section to ensure the ship was watertight and secured. They collected hoses and nozzles from the forward damage control base, inspected all spaces, noting that lighting was normal throughout, and ordered all personnel to proceed to the upper deck.[35]

Fanned by near gale-force winds, the fire increased in intensity quickly and flames began to break through the superstructure in and around the funnel area. It became evident to the captain that the ship might need to be abandoned, but before the fire developed across the ship on the port side he ordered the executive officer aft to continue all attempts at firefighting commensurate with personal safety. The captain called for boats and landing craft to stand by close to the ship. Then, some 30 minutes after the explosion, when fire broke out on the port side at 17.55, the captain and the executive officer simultaneously ordered their sections to abandon ship. The fire was advancing aft, threatening the Seacat, ready-use, torpedo and Sea Skua magazines; there was no fire-main pressure and a 1,000lb unexploded bomb remained forward.[36]

In response to a radio message from *Antelope* to *Fearless*, rescue of the survivors and casualties was carried out rapidly by landing craft from *Fearless* and the whaler from *Argonaut*. Those on the flight deck were able to step into the rescue craft. Those forward of the fire could not reach the flight deck and climbed down the Gemini davit and across the canopy of a life raft into a landing craft. Casualties, apart from Leading Stores Accountant Ridge, who had been evacuated by air earlier with a fractured skull, were taken to the field hospital at Ajax Bay by landing craft. Three helicopters hovered over the flight deck from shortly after the explosion until the ship was abandoned. They provided light and the downdraft helped to disperse the smoke, but the noise made communication on the flight deck very difficult.[37]

Commander Tobin was the last person to leave the ship, at about 18.10. Pale bluish flames were issuing from the ship's funnel and burning debris was showering the flight deck. Twenty minutes after evacuation of the ship was completed there was a major explosion, thought to have been a magazine.[38]

The ship continued to burn during the night and a number of explosions were heard, which were thought to have been in the torpedo body room. There was no evidence to suggest that the forward bomb detonated. At daybreak the ship was still afloat but her back was broken and at noon a further explosion was heard. At about 08.15 on 24 May the ship sank in 20 metres of water in position 51°33'38 south, 59°03'72 west in San Carlos Water.[39] Commander Tobin's report observed that the ship's 'bow and stern remained just proud of the water in a final V gesture of defiance'.[40] Nothing was salvaged from the ship except the contents of the captain's safe. *Antelope's* Lynx helicopter survived and was transferred to HMS *Fearless*.[41]

* * *

Commander Tobin had been desperate to join the action, but this catastrophe had occurred on his first day. Mike Clapp recalled, 'That evening I gave Nick my bunk and a whisky and when she finally sank after midnight I took him quietly up on deck and we shed a tear together.' Speaking of the Antelopes, Clapp said, 'They were a superbly motivated and gallant crew; the final sight of them disembarking for the trip home with their chins high was a stirring sight and a reminder to me of just how good a properly led and disciplined ship can be. I felt very proud of *Antelope*, Nick and his ship's company.'[42]

Those who lost their lives were Steward Mark Stephens, who died of head injuries when the bomb entered the petty officers' mess, and Staff Sergeant James Prescott, who died when the bomb exploded. The seriously injured were Leading Stores Accountant Paul Ridge, who suffered a cracked skull when the bomb entered the mess, and Warrant Officer John Phillips, who suffered severe blast injuries to his left arm. The injured were Supply Assistant R. J. Carr, who sustained lacerations to his face and multiple bruising when the bomb entered the mess; Leading Seaman M. J. Hancox, who suffered mild shock and a bruised leg from the bomb explosion; and Lieutenant Commander R. F. Goodfellow, who received multiple bruises from the blast during the bomb explosion.[43]

Decorations were awarded to Commander Nick Tobin, Distinguished Service Cross, for his exemplary leadership, courage and foresight; and Leading Seaman Jeffrey Warren, Distinguished Service Medal, for his bravery in firefighting and his action manning a 20mm gun, scoring a hit on a Skyhawk. Staff Sergeant James Prescott was posthumously awarded the Conspicuous Gallantry Medal, whilst Warrant Officer John Phillips received the Distinguished Service Cross, both for their bravery in the bomb disposal team. Two Royal Marines from *Fearless*, Colour Sergeant Michael Francis, coxswain of LCU F1, and Colour Sergeant Brian Johnston, coxswain of LCU F4, received the Distinguished Service Medal and Queen's Gallantry Medal* respectively for their bravery in the evacuation of *Antelope* (see Appendix).[44]

* * *

A board of inquiry was convened at HMS *Drake*, Plymouth, and comprised Captain G. A. Eades (president), Commander D. R. Price, Surgeon Commander C. W. Evans, Commander R. W. White and Lieutenant Commander T. H. Boycott. Their report was presented to the commander-in-chief, fleet, on 11 August 1982.[45]

The board considered the preparedness of *Antelope* and her crew for warfare in the Falklands area. It reported that morale had fallen during the periods escorting prisoners of war and waiting at

---

* On 8 June, LCU F4 was attacked by enemy aircraft in Choiseul Sound. During this action Colour Sergeant Johnston and five of his crew were killed. Colour Sergeant Johnston's selfless bravery in the face of extreme danger was in the highest traditions of the Corps.

Ascension. *Antelope* finally entered the amphibious operating area at short notice without a full briefing to carry out a task she had neither anticipated nor exercised, and without any introductory combat experience. The ship's company was not mentally prepared for its role in San Carlos Water.[46]

For some operations in the Falklands, escorts had to exhibit a high degree of skill in capabilities that did not receive priority for training in peace. In this case, *Antelope* was required to contribute to the defence of an amphibious anchorage against air attack. Early warning of direct enemy attack was limited, and insufficient air cover was available to provide assured defence in depth. She operated in close proximity to, and almost surrounded by, high ground, which made her own air warning radar ineffective and severely reduced her anti-air warfare capability to visual and emergency means and to secondary armament. Seacat in emergency mode and the 20mm guns were the only weapons that had a chance of success in the circumstances *Antelope* was in.[47]

Antelope had no opportunity to be 'blooded' before being singled out for the large and co-ordinated air attack that was her first taste of action. The ship had received scant information earlier on what her task was to be and what to expect. The senior weapons engineer officer of the 4th Frigate Squadron had advised that the command should be stationed on the bridge with a principal warfare officer on the gun direction platform. This advice was not put into effect, perhaps because time prevented reorganization (and in some cases retraining), and there was persistent confidence in the Type 992 radar and the ship's ability to fight in primary weapon control. Despite the advice, the ship's principal warfare officer (air) thought from his limited experience that the 992 radar with its moving target indication facility would perform satisfactorily and that weapons could be used in the primary (auto) mode, and advised accordingly, which the captain accepted, both content in the knowledge that switching to emergency/visual control incurred only a moment's delay. The gun direction platform remained at normal manning and was not reinforced by a principal warfare officer, which might have improved the effectiveness of visual control. The inquiry considered that failure to make these changes was an error of judgement on the part of the principal warfare officer (air) and Commander Tobin due to their inexperience of operations in a land-locked environment.

As the first attack developed, Seacat and the 4.5-inch gun were put into emergency visual control, because the primary methods of weapon control (through radar detection of aircraft) could not be used due to the radar performance being severely degraded by the surrounding land. As a result, the captain and the principal warfare officer (air) in the ops room effectively took little part in the action. The chief petty officer (operations) was stationed on the gun direction platform as missile gun director (visual) and was also manning the starboard light machine gun. The command safety officer, Lieutenant Frankland, was manning the port light machine gun. All weapons operators were authorized to engage hostile aircraft by a captain's temporary memorandum, but no control orders were passed to the 20mm guns and the only instruction to the Seacat was not to engage aircraft attacking from the direction of friendly ships. The pedestal site Seacat operator had received no safety brief and was confused as to his responsibilities. He did not know how to overcome the problem when on one occasion aircraft were low and Seacat was depressed into elevation blind arcs interrupting the firing sequence. Also, he had not been clearly briefed on missile direction safety orders: once launched, the missile whose firing was aborted in the second attack could have been fired and controlled to miss *Broadsword* if it had not hit the aircraft. The board concluded that the captain was not best placed to fight the ship in the prevailing conditions, whilst the principal warfare officer (air) remained in the ops room and did not consider how to improve the ship's fighting effectiveness. Also, the ship had been placed in the front line without having a period of acclimatization in the war zone.[48]

To summarize, the 4.5-inch gun was fired in emergency mode with little if any chance of success. One Seacat was launched and controlled manually by the pedestal operator, and damaged an aircraft. The starboard 20mm gun scored hits on a second aircraft, which was downed with assistance from *Broadsword*'s Sea Wolf missile and a land-based Rapier missile. This modest achievement, the board said, was a result of problems with Seacat, which had a history of unsatisfactory performance, failures of guns, and the inability of the Type 992 radar to cope with the proximity to land. Maintainers and operators did not have confidence in the 992 radar modification. Seacat had not been fired successfully in its primary (automatic) mode since the refit in 1980. The ship had had only eight days' operational sea training during the previous two years because COST periods in May 1981 and April 1982 were each reduced to four days.

In evidence to the inquiry, it was clear that the captain, executive officer, and marine engineer officer gave no more than passing consideration that the bombs lodged in the ship might explode and did not appreciate the extent of damage this would cause to the ship's structure and systems. This was reflected in the absence of any discussion between these officers. They did not confer to evaluate the situation and decide on the best method of dealing with a possible bomb explosion and how to maintain the ship's damage control organization and services, or make arrangements to rapidly bring into action alternative or emergency facilities. The dispersal of the damage control parties immediately before the start of bomb disposal work reduced the ability to take countermeasures should there be an explosion, and there was no evidence that any officer or senior rating attempted to maintain the damage control organization structure. The isolation of the salt-water system into three sections did not take into account the possibility of damage from explosion, which would likely destroy one or two isolation points and put at risk the entire structure. The board considered that the marine engineer officer, Lieutenant Commander Goodfellow, failed both to appreciate fully the implications of an explosion and to make the appropriate and adequate material and system preparations, and did not provide advice to the executive officer or captain accordingly. Stationing the marine engineer officer in the ship control centre for communications between the explosions disposal team and the command precluded his use as action damage control officer in the event of an explosion. However, the decision to remove all but skeleton staff to the upper deck prevented any loss of life or serious injury.[49]

In fact, the board pointed out that the executive officer was charged with co-ordinating ship arrangements for making safe an unexploded bomb, something that the captain was unaware of. The executive officer had completed a one-day explosive safety course at HMS *Collingwood* on 25 February 1981 as part of his executive officer (designate) courses and was aware of his responsibilities. He had briefly met the bomb disposal team when they arrived on board, but the marine engineer officer was left to liaise with the team. The executive officer was busy elsewhere. Because the Army bomb disposal team were inexperienced in dealing with unexploded bombs in ships, the board considered that the staff mine clearance and disposal officer should have accompanied the team to *Antelope*, but he had been busy throughout the day in *Argonaut*. His presence in *Antelope* might have prompted discussions on preparing the ship prior to the defusing attempts.[50]

The bomb disposal team had considered the rocket wrench to be the best method of defusing the after bomb. The rocket wrench probably came off the pistol because the body was damaged, and the wrench could not be tightened sufficiently. Once this failed, other methods, including the de-armer and physical removal of the bomb, were considered. The after bomb was chocked up by ship's staff soon after the attack. If the disposal team had been aware that the bomb had previously been rolling around the deck, they may have considered more carefully removing it physically without attempting to defuse it. The board noted that no render safe procedure was laid down for British-made bombs, and the bomb disposal team was unaware that communications with the UK were available to discuss ordnance disposal.[51]

The board considered that when *Antelope* emerged from this, her first battle, in which members of the ship's company were killed or injured, it was likely that many were suffering from 'mild battle shock' that could have impaired the judgement of those responsible for decisions. During the passage to Ajax Bay, the ship was still an effective fighting unit and rightly the captain's main concern was to provide air defence. The bomb disposal team arrived as the threat of air attack receded, but the prospect of renewed fighting the next day became dominant in the captain's mind, and precautions that might have helped the ship to survive explosion of the bomb were forgotten. *Antelope* had been tasked with taking a Special Boat Service patrol that night onto Weddell Island to watch the airstrip, and a 3 Para patrol onto Great Island to watch for shipping, but these had to be postponed. The inquiry concluded that the captain had not ensured adequate preparations for bomb disposal were made, had not appreciated the extent of damage likely to be caused in the event of premature explosion, and did not liaise closely with the bomb disposal team.[52]

No plan had been made to re-establish alternative damage and NBCD control positions in the event of an explosion. Hence it was impossible to take co-ordinated action quickly after the bomb detonated, and firefighting efforts were severely limited. Even if full, considered preparations had been made, it is not known if the fires and damage caused could have been contained. As it was, the ship was abandoned and further loss of life was prevented. The board considered that a determined approach to firefighting from an alongside vessel well equipped for firefighting directly into the damaged area might have made a significant impact on the fire. However, no firefighting equipped tug was present in the anchorage, so any such effort would have needed to come from another warship.[53]

The board said that the executive officer had acted negligently by ordering the evacuation of the ship's company to the upper deck without making alternative arrangements to maintain the ship's damage control capability. Also, he did not make a full and proper consideration of the consequences of an explosion or consult with others to organize appropriate damage control measures. The marine engineer officer had acted negligently in failing to consider the consequences of damage in the event of an explosion and did not initiate action to limit these effects by system isolation or advise the captain and executive officer of the possible damage to the ship's structure and systems. The captain was also considered negligent. He had approved the move of the ship's company to the upper deck without considering the effect this would have on the damage control capability. He did not enquire about precautionary measures necessary when dealing with unexploded bombs, nor ensure that these had been implemented. Similarly, the captain and executive officer were criticized for failing to seek advice on explosive ordnance disposal from appropriate authorities and officers, including the staff mine clearance disposal officer, and failure to co-ordinate and ensure proper measures for the bomb disposal. The staff mine clearance disposal officer should have accompanied the disposal team to *Antelope*; that he did not was an error of judgement on his part.[54]

In mitigation, the board considered that stress in action may have impaired the judgement of the captain, executive officer and marine engineering officer. Battle stress causes concentration on a perceived main task, and the captain's preoccupation was the threat of further air raids and the requirement, urgent in his mind, to sail for the tasks of the following day. The executive officer had been involved with immediate matters, including dead and injured ratings, anchoring, and ensuring that the ship was operational, and did not consider the possibility of bomb explosion. The marine engineering officer was concerned initially with action damage repairs and then with liaising between the bomb disposal team and the command. The ship's officers were totally inexperienced in bomb disposal procedures and the bomb disposal team had inspired complete confidence because they had dealt with a similar bomb the day before in *Argonaut* and throughout the operation they gave every indication of a successful outcome (it was said that although they became anxious they had not communicated their concerns to ship's officers). The information available in HM ships about bomb disposal was limited. It was not a subject which received prominence in training afloat or ashore; therefore, in the minds of the inexperienced, it was a matter left to experts. All these factors were strong grounds for mitigation and had a significant effect on the culpability of the ship's officers. None of the officers had acted wilfully and their negligence was unintentional.[55]

The inquiry analysed the possible reasons for the bomb not exploding on impact. The British Mk 78 pistol would not function if dropped from less than 60ft in a straight drop, but this distance would be reduced considerably if dropped from an aircraft giving it forward momentum. It was possible that the deceleration of the bomb on striking the ship was insufficient to activate the pistol. The after bomb bounced before hitting the ship. It may have flipped and entered tail first, damaging the pistol and shearing off the arming fork, but remaining unarmed.[56]

Amongst the main conclusions of the inquiry were that *Antelope* was unprepared for her task; the inadequate operational sea training had meant that key personnel were inexperienced in operating some aspects of the ship. *Antelope* had received only 12 hours' warning of her task; she was neither briefed for nor practised in that role. The ship's armament was inadequate for the task allocated to her. Adequate precautions were not taken to minimize the effects of damage in the event of an explosion of the unexploded bombs.

The board's main recommendations included that the priority accorded to the satisfactory completion of operational sea training should be reviewed; that improvements should be made to the emergency fire control arrangements of the 4.5-inch gun and Seacat against low-level aircraft; that improvements should be made to the range, firepower and destructive capability of the secondary armament fitted in Type 21 frigates; that render safe procedures for UK ordnance should be authorized and promulgated; and that improvements should be made to the fixed and portable firefighting arrangements in Type 21s.[57]

The board of inquiry considered that the initiative and actions of Lieutenant Commander Highett, Chief Petty Officer Meechan,

Petty Officer Parker, Leading Seaman Warren, Weapons Engineering Mechanic Jennings, and Marine Engineering Mechanics Clarke and Taylor in firefighting activities were noteworthy. Furthermore, the removal of personnel to the flight deck during the defusing attempts prevented severe loss of life, and the rescue of personnel was conducted swiftly and efficiently.[58]

* * *

To conclude, it has been seen that *Antelope* suffered similar problems to *Ardent* with the fire control system for the 4.5-inch gun and Seacat, the emergency (manual) mode having to be used in inshore locations, rather than the radar controlled automatic mode. This contributed to her inability to ward off attackers in the confined waters of Falkland Sound, not helped by the persistent unreliability of her 4.5-inch Mk 8 gun and the well-known ineffectiveness of Seacat. She was thus ill-suited to the air defence role that she had been given, and the earlier inadequacies of her operational sea training meant that the ship was not well prepared for the hostile environment she entered. But other shortcomings contributed to her loss. The captain and principal warfare officer (air), who had been advised to station themselves on the bridge and the gun direction platform respectively when under attack in confined waters, failed to do so: remaining in the operations room, they took little part in the action. The operation to defuse the unexploded bombs was plagued with problems: both the captain and executive officer failed both to seek external advice on the procedure and to liaise with the bomb disposal team, who also did not seek external advice on how to deal with a bomb with which they were unfamiliar. The captain, executive officer and marine engineering officer also failed to prepare the ship for the possibility of a bomb exploding, and consequently damage control organization was poor. If a determined and well-organized firefighting operation had been mounted, with the assistance of another warship, the ship might have been saved. Battle stress and competing priorities were amongst the mitigating factors when the negligence of the captain and marine engineering officer was considered, and they escaped official reprimand.

There was to be no respite for the ships of the task force, for on the day after *Antelope* sank, two more British ships, *Coventry* and *Atlantic Conveyor*, were to fall victim to Argentinian air attacks.

6

The Sinking of HMS *Coventry*

The date 25 May was Argentina's national day, and the task force expected that the enemy would make things uncomfortable for them by launching even more air raids than usual. That day found the destroyer *Coventry* and frigate *Broadsword* together in an exposed position, 7½ miles north of Government Island (which is off the north-western tip of Pebble Island), protecting the amphibious landings that were still under way. Their position became known to the Argentines, who directed two successive groups of Skyhawks towards them, and *Coventry* fell victim to the bombs of the second attack of the day. Quickly the ship began to capsize, and her men had to take to the water and swim towards life rafts that had been released from the ship and inflated.

HMS *Coventry*, the fourth Type 42 destroyer, was launched at Cammell Laird's Birkenhead yard on 21 June 1974. She was accepted into service at Portsmouth in October 1978 and commissioned on 10 November 1978. Sea trials lasted some ten months and the ship became operational on 17 August 1979. She had a standard Type 42 weapon fit, with one 4.5-inch Mk 8 gun, a twin Sea Dart medium-range anti-air missile launcher (and 22 missiles), STWS (shipborne torpedo weapon system) firing the Stingray anti-submarine torpedo for self-defence, two 20mm Oerlikon guns, and a Lynx Mk 2 helicopter equipped with Sea Skua short-range anti-ship missiles and Mk 46 homing torpedoes. Her radar fit included one Type 965R for long-range air search, one

Type 992Q for medium-range surveillance and target indication, two Type 909s for Sea Dart target tracking and fire control, and one Type 1006 for navigation and helicopter control. She also mounted a Type 184M sonar for underwater target detection. *Coventry* was powered by four Rolls-Royce gas turbines (in the same format as *Sheffield*), which gave her a top speed of 29 knots and a range of 4,000 miles at 18 knots. The ship displaced 3,500 tons at standard load or 4,100 tons at full load. Her nominal complement was 21 officers and 249 ratings,[1] but at the time of this action it comprised 28 officers and 271 ratings plus the captain, a total of 300.[2]

The fire control system was the computerized ADAWS 4 (Action Data Automated Weapons System Mk 4), which provided data and calculations to control the 4.5-inch gun and Sea Dart missiles. The Sea Dart missile was powered by a Rolls-Royce ramjet motor to give it a high sustained speed. It used semi-active radar homing, via aerials on the nose cone, to ride on the beam of one of the 909 radars that illuminated the target, and the missile would then home in on it. With two missiles on the launcher, two targets could be engaged in quick succession. The range was up to 40 nautical miles.[3] The weakness of the system was the inability of the Type 965 radar to deal with low-level targets, which became lost in radar clutter from land or the surface of the sea, partly because it lacked moving target indication. This resulted in Sea Dart being unable to lock onto fast-moving low-level targets.

After the ship was commissioned, work-up and sea training followed at Portland between September and November 1979. The early months of 1980 were spent in a series of trials, minor exercises and weapon training periods, and the ship deployed to the Middle and Far East with a task group in mid-May 1980. After several exercises in the Indian Ocean and an assisted maintenance period in Hong Kong in early August, *Coventry* visited Shanghai and Tokyo in company with other ships of the task group. Alongside *Antrim* and *Alacrity*, she was the first British warship to visit the People's Republic of China in 30 years. *En route* back to the UK, *Coventry* was diverted to the Persian Gulf following the outbreak of the Iran–Iraq War, where the ship remained on the Armilla Patrol in the Gulf of Oman for four weeks.[4] She returned to the task group early in November for the homeward passage, reaching Portsmouth on 9 December. The first four months of 1981 were spent in maintenance at Portsmouth and sea trials, followed by two weeks' work-up and sea training at Portland in May. Continuing defects with the 909 radars, 4.5-inch gun and the UAA1 radar sensor caused considerable frustration. On departure from Portland *Coventry* had achieved a satisfactory standard, but it was noted that much effort would be required to get the 909s and UAA1 fully operational, and anti-air warfare remained a weak area. The ship took part in the two-week Exercise *Roebuck* and then returned to Portsmouth for a six-week assisted maintenance and leave period there, which began in late June.

Captain David Hart Dyke took command of *Coventry* on 30 June 1981. Born on 3 October 1938, he was educated at St Lawrence College, Ramsgate. His father had served as a commander in the Royal Navy before being ordained in 1953. David was conscripted for national service in 1959, and served as a midshipman in the Royal Naval Volunteer Reserve before joining the regular service for officer training at Dartmouth, serving aboard the frigate *Eastbourne* east of Suez. He was commissioned as a sub-lieutenant on 1 September 1961 and was promoted to lieutenant on 1 January 1962, commanding a fast patrol boat used as a target towing launch at Plymouth. After service in the minesweeper *Lanton* during the Indonesian Confrontation in 1963, he was navigating officer aboard the frigates *Palliser*, *Gurkha* and *Tenby* in turn between 1963 and 1968. He was appointed an instructor at the Royal Naval College, Dartmouth, and promoted to lieutenant commander on 1 January 1970. In 1967 he married Diana Luce. Promoted to commander on 30 June 1974, he was appointed first lieutenant and executive officer in the guided missile destroyer *Hampshire*. From 1976 he served on the staff of the Royal Naval Staff College again, then from 1978 as commander in the Royal Yacht *Britannia*. On 31 December 1980 Hart Dyke was promoted to captain.[5]

Coventry sailed for various trials and a shakedown before leaving for a planned 3½ months away from her base port. Exercise *Ocean Venture*, which followed, provided many good training opportunities, thereby preparing the ship for joining NATO's Standing Force North Atlantic on 1 September 1981 and launching immediately into Exercise *Magic Sword North*. This exercise gave *Coventry* some valuable experience in offshore barrier operations near the Norwegian coast when 'enemy' patrol boats attacked carrier forces. Weather conditions encountered were similar to those the ship was to meet some six months later in the South Atlantic. In early November, another exercise provided a testing opportunity for *Coventry* in which considerable air defence training was undertaken, again in South Atlantic style weather conditions. The ship returned to Portsmouth on 8 December for leave and maintenance.

The year 1982 began with a short period of 909 radar trials in the Portsmouth area and three weeks of training in the Portland area. A period of shore-based command team training followed in February and early March for the team that had joined the ship at Christmas, and the standard achieved was said to be most satisfactory, with a well-motivated team able to fight the ship. *Coventry* sailed from the UK for the last time on 17 March 1982 to take part in Exercise *Springtrain 82* off Gibraltar. Air defence was high on the agenda and the captain described his steadily growing confidence in his operations team, which was now soundly trained and extensively practised. However, high seas firings at the end of March were disappointing as two out of the three Sea Dart rounds fired appeared to be rogue. In general, therefore, the ship was well prepared for war, although low-level air strikes coming off the land, as were to be experienced off the Falklands, were never a high priority in the operational training, and 909 radar acquisitions in these circumstances had never been practised. Once *Springtrain 82* was complete, *Coventry* was scheduled to return to the UK prior to a deployment on an intelligence-gathering mission against Soviet naval forces in the Barents Sea, for which the ship had been fitted with special communications monitoring equipment.[6]

On 2 April 1982, after receiving news of the Falklands invasion, *Coventry*, in company with *Antrim, Glamorgan, Sheffield, Glasgow, Arrow, Brilliant, Plymouth* and RFA *Olmeda*, was ordered to proceed to Ascension Island. *Antrim* was the flagship of the First Flotilla, commanded by Rear Admiral J. F. 'Sandy' Woodward, who would soon take command of the carrier battle group, flying his flag in *Hermes*. During this nine-day voyage, preparations for war began in earnest. For the first 24 hours the southbound ships paired off with those who were homeward bound and topped up with all possible items of ammunition, stores and spares. *Coventry* was allocated *Aurora*, but at the end of lengthy transfers there were still significant deficiencies – Sea Dart missiles and 4.5-inch rounds, for example, which did not become available until later. In this early phase there was also a full and intensive practice programme, but without carrier support it was very difficult to exercise any realistic air defence drills. However, it was felt that the earlier exercises had put the ship in good stead. Heavy emphasis was placed on drills against the perceived surface threat from the five Argentinian Exocet-armed destroyers that *Jane's Fighting Ships* listed.[7] At Ascension more storing took place, the ship was painted in her war colours, and further practices and exercises were conducted. Before storing was fully completed, *Coventry* was ordered on 15 April to proceed south with despatch in company, as part of a task unit which also included *Brilliant*, *Sheffield*, *Glasgow*, *Arrow* and RFA *Appleleaf*, to enforce the total exclusion zone that was to come into force around the Falkland Islands on 1 May. *Coventry* thus left Ascension still short of spares for weapon systems and was concerned that these should be obtained before action was joined.

Coventry's main role would be to take the action to the Argentinian air forces with the ship's Sea Dart missiles, and to direct the Sea Harriers to incoming enemy aircraft detected by the ship's long-range surveillance radar. In addition, she could be used for naval gunfire support of the troops when they got ashore, though this role would not be dominant because it could also be performed by the Type 12 and Type 21 frigates and the County-class destroyers, which did not have *Coventry's* air defence capabilities.

The second stage of the passage south also included more practice drills and gunfire practice, and the task unit reached a waiting position equidistant about 1,000 nautical miles from South Georgia, the Falklands and Buenos Aires, where the ships remained for several days, awaiting the arrival of the carrier group. Each ship was visited by Admiral Woodward, who addressed the ship's company. In *Coventry* he reportedly said, 'We're going to war, we will get fired at... some of you may not be returning home, some of you will die.' Petty Officer Sam MacFarlane, a radio communications supervisor, recalled, 'I think he intended to give a pep talk, but singularly failed in that... Everybody's chin was hitting the deck afterwards... we all thought we were going to die.'[8] After the conflict was over Admiral Woodward reflected that although he wanted to prepare them for war, both mentally and physically, perhaps he had overdone 'the realism'.[9] Nevertheless, *Coventry* was said to be well prepared for war despite there being some outstanding mechanical defects, Sea Dart remaining unproven, and the ship having little experience of inshore anti-air warfare.

On 1 May the task group entered the 200-mile total exclusion zone, where it met strong opposition from the Argentine Air Force. Hostile aircraft were held at arm's length by Sea Harriers, and *Coventry* took a key and successful part in directing the Sea Harriers into positions to attack Skyhawk and Mirage raids. At this stage, and for the next few days, the ship was some 20 miles west of the carrier group, which itself was about 80 miles east of Port Stanley. During these early days many Sea Harrier patrol engagements took place well to the west of the force, often over land on the Falklands. Whilst enemy aircraft remained at high altitude the land posed little problem to the task group's radars; however, many of the enemy jets flew low over the islands and the resultant loss of radar contact in the ships served to heighten apprehension that air attack on the task group was imminent. Air-launched Exocet was now seen as a prime threat and there was early use of chaff by most ships.

Following the sinking of *General Belgrano* on 2 May, Captain Hart Dyke, who spent most of his time in the operations room, told his ship's company, 'We can expect the enemy to hit back... we need to be at our very best and ever alert.'[10] During the night of 2/3 May a surface contact was detected by a patrolling Sea King helicopter about 50 miles north of the force and, being in the nearest ship to it, *Coventry's* Lynx helicopter, armed with Sea Skua missiles (which had been hastily embarked off Ascension), was despatched to investigate. In the action that followed, the contact was identified as a hostile patrol boat, *Comodoro Somellara*, and was attacked with two Sea Skua missiles, blowing up and sinking. This historic engagement marked the first firing of Sea Skua in anger, and that in a highly successful operation. The Lynx flight commander Lieutenant Commander Alvin Rich and pilot Lieutenant Hubert Ledingham were congratulated by Captain Hart Dyke on their return to the ship, and he later said: 'Both were shocked and shaking, no doubt with relief at their safe return but also with the realization of what they had done. They were now getting used to being at war.'[11]

Task force operations took a more hostile turn during early May when ships began night-time bombardments of Argentinian positions in the vicinity of Port Stanley. When *Coventry's* first turn at naval gunfire support came on 6 May, she was paired with *Broadsword*, who was to provide point air defence cover and anti-submarine support, and bombardment took place on a gun emplacement to the south of Cape Pembroke (just east of Stanley). Difficulties were experienced with *Coventry's* 4.5-inch gun mounting and this caused the action to be terminated prematurely.[12] This pairing was the precursor of the idea to operate a Type 42 destroyer in combination with a Type 22 frigate.

Another shore bombardment operation, again with *Broadsword*, took place two nights later. Although the mechanical defect in the gun mounting had been rectified on the intervening day, there was a recurrence of the same problem, but the ship's engineers were able to effect a full repair, and the gun was to give no further problems. In addition to the overnight naval gunfire operation, the two ships were ordered to remain by day in the area south of Stanley and to attack Argentinian aircraft that were attempting to drop supplies to their beleaguered garrison. The aim was clearly expressed by Admiral Woodward when he instructed *Coventry* to act as a 'missile trap', letting enemy supply aircraft approach Stanley so that they could be shot down, rather than driving them away with Sea Harrier combat air patrols. The likely targets, believed to be Hercules supply aircraft with Skyhawk or Mirage escort, were known to be transiting from the west, crossing West Falkland and coming down to approach Stanley.[13]

On this occasion (9 May), *Coventry* held long-range 965 radar contact on a group of aircraft approaching from the west at 120 miles; there were also voice communications intercepts that indicated a Hercules C130 and Skyhawk mix. Two aircraft peeled off, presumably to create a diversion, but the remaining three were successfully acquired on both 909 radars at some 60 miles' range. The first missile was fired at 38 miles and was seen to pass through the 909 range gate but missed its target. The Hercules took evasive action, having seen that first missile pass very close. The second missile was fired at 35 miles, and the third when the previous shot was reported to have missed. These were long shots taken at the earliest opportunity for fear that the targets might detect that they had been illuminated by radar and then turn away. Although it appeared that all three Sea Darts missed their targets, it was later discovered from a communications intercept and a report from *Broadsword* (who had been watching on her radar) that two of the Skyhawks had collided and crashed whilst trying to avoid one of the missiles, with both pilots losing their lives.[14]

Later that day, *Broadsword* detected a slow-moving aircraft flying south-west over land in the vicinity of Port Harriet. *Coventry* acquired the contact firmly when it came clear of the land near Port Fitzroy and fired a single Sea Dart, hitting an Argentinian Puma helicopter that exploded in a spectacular manner. It had been a difficult target: flying low against a land background. These were the first Sea Darts fired in anger and the first to claim a 'kill'. For *Coventry* this was a good morale booster and a welcome confidence builder after a disappointing period of difficulties with the gun and worrying about Sea Dart performance.[15]

The significance of these two engagements when considering later events is that both were markedly affected by the proximity of land. In the case of the Hercules/Skyhawk, the moment of incidence may even have been over the land, although the target height was presumably sufficient to allow the 909 radars to acquire at longer range. The causes of the failure on this occasion (ignoring the fortuitous collision) are believed to have been that the targets were at the limit of Sea Dart's range, and the effects of any evasive manoeuvres they may have made. There was also evidence to suggest that the 909s were searching between the targets, which were in close formation, and this may have affected the accuracy of the shots.[16] Admiral Woodward considered that *Coventry* had launched the missiles too soon and signalled Hart Dyke, advising him, 'Don't fire until you can see the whites of their eyes.' Hart Dyke has recalled, 'He was quite right; I had been too eager and should have waited for just a few seconds before engaging.' The successful Puma engagement masked the potential difficulty that would eventually be encountered operating a Type 42 destroyer in air defence role so close to land. Here, *Coventry* had hit a low altitude target, albeit slow moving, at close range and whilst it was skirting along a rocky and prominent coast. After 'splashing' the helicopter, Hart Dyke had signalled Woodward, 'You will be pleased to know the Argentinians do have whites to their eyes!'[17]

Coventry took no further part in the naval gunfire operations off Stanley and returned to her more usual air defence role in support of the carrier group operating well to the east. Hart Dyke was concerned that Sea Dart was not being given the opportunity to prove itself in anything like its designed role (which was in the open ocean of the Cold War North Atlantic). In the east no feasible targets presented themselves, and further west the system had often been hamstrung by land. The most fertile ground seemed to him to be to the west of West Falkland, on the enemy's over-sea flight path. He suggested this, but it was not taken up in the task force's immediate plans.[18] However, when defending the amphibious operations on 21 May it became clear that *Broadsword* operating in confined waters could not provide effective cover. Sea Wolf was virtually useless in these circumstances, with enemy aircraft using contour flying techniques to great effect to achieve maximum surprise. *Broadsword*'s captain, Bill Canning, suggested that a

Type 22 and Type 42 combination could be effectively employed in taking the fight to the enemy by intercepting their attacks as they closed from the west rather than waiting for them to reach their target. The Type 42 destroyer, equipped with Sea Dart for medium-range anti-air warfare, would work in combination with a Type 22 frigate as the 'goalkeeper' to provide close point defence using its Sea Wolf. As noted above, *Coventry* and *Broadsword*, when operating together south of Stanley, had developed stationing and manoeuvring drills that kept the two ships in close station, with *Broadsword* up-threat of *Coventry*.[19]

This idea was embraced by Admiral Woodward and resulted in an aggressive and offensive plan that saw *Broadsword* and *Coventry* being detached from the carrier battle group by Rear Admiral Woodward on 22 May and embarking on an anti-air patrol to the north of West Falkland, with Sea Harriers in support, with the object of protecting the amphibious operations area from the more northerly raids. *Coventry* looked forward to better opportunities to harass incoming enemy air raids with Sea Dart. In a secure voice circuit briefing by the admiral, Hart Dyke freely expressed his belief that Sea Dart must be given the opportunity to fire at suitable targets on its own terms, but was apprised by Woodward of the problems facing amphibious forces in Falkland Sound and the need for a 'missile trap' to the north of West Falkland to counter the more northerly raids, inbound or outbound. The admiral's term 'missile trap' left *Coventry* in no doubt that the aim was to carry out aggressive anti-air warfare operations with Sea Dart as the prime offensive weapon system.[20]

Whilst on passage to the new patrol line, *Coventry* acquired on 909 radar what was believed to be an Argentinian 707 reconnaissance aircraft and a missile launch was attempted, but it failed because the flash doors through which the missile passed onto the launcher had temporarily jammed shut and as a result the whole system had shut down. David Hart Dyke felt sick with anger and frustration, having missed a golden opportunity to deliver a massive blow to the enemy's surveillance capability and probably to President Galtieri himself, whose personal aeroplane he believed it was. The problem was solved by a sailor going onto the upper deck to break away accumulations of salt and straighten out the hatch, which had been damaged by buffeting from heavy seas.[21] By the time this was cleared the 707 was out of range, to the frustration of all involved on the ship. Once on the patrol line no targets were available, since the raids were closing in from the west. *Coventry* and *Broadsword* planned to move further west overnight on 22 May, but were ordered to rejoin the carrier group because a major air-launched Exocet offensive was thought possible on the following day.

On 23 May *Coventry* again detached from the carrier group to conduct an anti-air patrol with *Broadsword* the following day, some 10–15 miles north of the northern entrance to Falkland Sound, to protect the amphibious forces. Again, Hart Dyke was personally briefed by the admiral on secure speech before departing, and in response to his expression of concern about the choice of operating area was told to discuss his requirements with Captain Bill Canning of *Broadsword*. Admiral Woodward made it clear to Captain Hart Dyke that although Sea Dart might be hampered by the close proximity of land there was a pressing need for a co-ordinated anti-air warfare picture to be compiled and given to the amphibious forces in San Carlos Water, who were subject to repeated and heavy air attack. This verbal brief was followed up by signalled outline instructions from Woodward to *Broadsword*.[22]

On meeting with *Broadsword* in the early hours of Wednesday 24 May, Hart Dyke discussed the question of positioning for the day's patrol. To provide protection for *Coventry* with her Sea Wolf missiles, *Broadsword* would try to position herself close to *Coventry* and between her and the attacking aircraft, i.e. up threat. Hart Dyke considered it would be hard enough to manoeuvre in close company in the frantic moments of an air attack from one direction, but even harder if they were under attack from two directions. The two ships were going to have to manoeuvre with split-second timing to have any chance of bringing their very different weapon systems to bear. Canning and Hart Dyke agreed that *Coventry* should be free to manoeuvre as required to fire Sea Dart, but would not increase speed. This would make it easier for *Broadsword* to use her speed advantage to position herself to give Sea Wolf a clear view of any approaching aircraft. 'Don't worry, David, you manoeuvre as you wish and I will keep out of your way,' said Bill Canning.[23]

The day dawned at about 06.30 with clear, fine and cold conditions, and the enemy took advantage of the weather to press home repeated attacks on shipping and ground forces in the vicinity of San Carlos Water. The Argentines planned to change direction, with the majority of the aircraft coming in from the south-east over land and straight down the narrow bay to the anchorage. It was very much a Sea Harrier day, with *Coventry* and *Broadsword* controlling their combat air patrols with significant success. No attempt was made by the enemy to attack the two ships on their patrol line and all potential Sea Dart targets were either downed or dispersed by a combination of Sea Harriers and fire from both shore and ships in the Sound: three Dagger As (Israeli-built versions of the Mirage) were downed, all by Sidewinder missiles from Sea Harriers directed by Sub-Lieutenant Andy Moll, *Coventry*'s fighter controller.[24] Air picture compilation worked well, with *Coventry* commenting on the effectiveness of *Broadsword*'s Doppler radar in holding air tracks over land and passing them on. The fearless, almost suicidal, flying of the enemy pilots continued to surprise *Coventry*, but there was a general feeling that the air battle was being won. *Coventry*'s command team again pressed for a move to more open water and away from their current position, which would have become known to the enemy in the clear weather conditions that prevailed. After consultation with *Broadsword*, a patrol line for the following day was agreed slightly further to the north-west to allow *Coventry* a clearer look over the sea towards any threat developing from the west. *Broadsword* retired to refuel during the night and *Coventry* conducted an anti-submarine patrol in the northern approaches to the Sound.[25]

First light on Thursday 25 May was at about 06.30 and the day was again cold and clear, with very little cloud and light south-westerly winds. The date was ominous, being Argentina's national day (after which the aircraft carrier *Veinticinco de Mayo* was named), and a big Argentinian attack was anticipated by the British ships;

The Argentinian cruiser ARA *General Belgrano* was formerly USS *Phoenix*, the Brooklyn-class cruiser which survived the Japanese attack on Pearl Harbor in December 1941. She was sold to Argentina in 1951 and is shown here in that navy's service. Her main armament was 15 6-inch guns, arranged in five triple turrets. (Wikipedia, public domain)

The death throes of *General Belgrano* after being torpedoed by the submarine HMS *Conqueror* on 2 May. A total of 323 men perished, from a ship's company of 1,093, the biggest loss of life in any incident in the Falklands conflict. (*La Nación*/Wikipedia, public domain)

The memorial at Ushuaia, on the Beagle Channel, to those lost in *General Belgrano*.
It was from Ushuaia that the ship sailed on her final, fatal voyage. (Paul Brown)

The nuclear-powered submarine HMS *Conqueror*, which successfully attacked *General Belgrano*, scoring two hits with Mk 8 torpedoes. She is seen entering Portsmouth harbour on 27 October 1982. (© Michael Lennon)

HMS *Sheffield* was a Type 42 destroyer, completed in 1975, and is seen here leaving Portsmouth on 26 March 1980. Her main armament, which can be seen forward of the bridge, consisted of one 4.5-inch Mk 8 gun and a twin Sea Dart medium-range anti-air missile launcher for which 22 missiles were carried. (Crown Copyright – Open Government Licence)

On 4 May *Sheffield* was struck by an Exocet missile fired by an Argentinian Super Étendard jet. The missile's impact left a 15ft-by-4ft hole in the ship's starboard side and caused widespread minor shock damage. Large fires broke out immediately in the forward engine room and auxiliary engine room area. (The National Archives, ref. DEFE25/555)

An Argentine Navy Super Étendard, two of which attacked *Sheffield*, with each launching an Exocet missile, one of which hit the ship. (Don Montgomery/US Defense Imagery DN-SC-91-02304)

The firefighting efforts in *Sheffield* lacked cohesion and the fire spread uncontrollably. The abandoned *Sheffield*, seen here, was eventually taken in tow by the frigate HMS *Yarmouth*. However, she rolled over and sank on 10 May. (The National Archives, ref. DEFE25/555)

There was a very rapid spread of acrid black smoke through the centre section of *Sheffield*, and upwards to the bridge. The frigate HMS *Arrow* came alongside on the port side and assisted with the firefighting efforts, providing boundary cooling to *Sheffield*. (The National Archives, ref. DEFE25/555)

Two Sea Harriers of the Royal Navy, in the low-visibility paint livery used during the Falklands conflict. The combat air patrols of Sea Harriers destroyed 23 enemy aircraft in air-to-air combat for the loss of none of their own number, but they were never available in sufficient numbers at any one time to achieve air superiority. (US Defense Imagery, DN-SC-87-05770)

A Douglas A4 Skyhawk of the Argentine Navy, on display at the Argentine Naval Headquarters in Buenos Aires. A total of 48 of these aircraft were deployed by the Argentine Navy and the Argentine Air Force during the Falklands conflict, and were responsible for the attacks which led to the loss of HMS *Ardent*, HMS *Antelope*, HMS *Coventry* and RFA *Sir Galahad*. (aeroprints.com/ Wikimedia Commons, public domain)

HMS *Ardent* was a Type 21 frigate, completed in 1977. Her top speed was 32 knots, with a burst speed of 37 knots. Forward of the bridge can be seen her Exocet launchers and 4.5-inch gun. (Crown Copyright – Open Government Licence)

The abandoned HMS *Ardent* in San Carlos Water after the final two Argentinian air attacks. HMS *Yarmouth* (left) pulls away from *Ardent* after taking off her crew. Note that the 992 radar aerial atop *Ardent*'s foremast has been bent by an attacking Skyhawk flying low over her. (© IWM FKD 144)

The fire rages aft in *Ardent*. She was abandoned because it was thought that the ship was in a terminal state and about to plunge below the waves. (© IWM FKD 146)

HMS *Antelope* was a Type 21 frigate, completed in 1975. Her Seacat missile launcher can be seen atop the hangar aft. (Crown Copyright – Open Government Licence)

The explosion of one of the two 1,000lb bombs lodged in the hull of *Antelope* during the night of 23/24 May, following the attack by Argentine Air Force Skyhawks earlier that day. (Photo by Martin Cleaver/Pool/Central Press/Stringer/Getty Images)

HMS *Antelope* afloat at dawn on 24 May 1982. The first explosion was followed by the sympathetic detonation of *Antelope*'s Seacat and torpedo magazines which broke the ship's back and led to her sinking. (© IWM FKD 71)

SS *Atlantic Conveyor* in dry dock at Devonport dockyard, under conversion to an aircraft transport. (The National Archives, ref. DEFE69/1338)

The wreck of *Antelope*, in two halves, barely afloat in Ajax Bay on the morning of 24 May. (© IWM FKD 192)

The abandoned hulk of *Atlantic Conveyor* after the Exocet attack launched by an Argentine Navy Dassault-Breguet Super Étendard jet. A Wessex helicopter can be seen on deck. The presence of cluster bombs in the ship was a significant factor influencing the decision to abandon ship. The bow was later blown away by explosions. (The National Archives, ref. DEFE69/1338)

HMS *Coventry* at sea in about 1981; she was a Type 42 destroyer completed in 1978 and had a complement of 300 men, including her captain, when she sailed in the Falklands task force. The large rectangular radar is the Type 965 for air warning, whilst the two prominent domes house the Type 909 tracker (fire control) radars. (US Defense Imagery DN-SC-87-0584)

Coventry listing to port after being hit by three 1,000lb bombs dropped by Argentine Air Force Skyhawks of the 5th Air Brigade in the afternoon of 25 May, Argentina's national day. (© IWM FKD 1265)

Two Sea King helicopters of No 846 Naval Air Squadron hover over the upturned hull of *Coventry*, searching for survivors. A total of 276 survivors had entered the water and were rescued by HMS *Broadsword*'s boats and helicopters from RFA *Fort Austin*. (© IWM FKD 1274)

The landing ship RFA *Sir Galahad* leaving Devonport for the Falklands on 6 April.
She was accompanied by her sister ship *Sir Geraint* and met up with *Sir Percivale* and *Sir Lancelot*
in the English Channel. (Author's collection)

Ships' boats bring ashore the survivors from *Sir Galahad* after the ship was bombed at Fitzroy.
(© IWM FKD 2126)

Sir Galahad on fire at Fitzroy on 8 June after being bombed by Argentine Air Force Skyhawks. At least three bombs struck, created a blazing inferno, whilst dense black smoke emitted from a ruptured diesel fuel tank. (© IWM FKD 359)

The stern of Sir *Galahad* after the attack. The hulk was later towed out to sea by the tug RMAS *Typhoon* and sunk by the submarine HMS *Onyx*, becoming an official war grave. (The National Archives, ref. DEFE69/920)

RFA *Sir Tristram*, damaged in the air raid at Fitzroy which led to the loss of *Sir Galahad*, seen aboard the heavy lift ship MV *Dan Lifter* for transport to the UK, where she was repaired. (Wikimedia Commons, public domain)

HMS *Broadsword* returns to Plymouth after the Falklands campaign. She was in company with *Coventry* during the final attack on the latter, but could not fire her Sea Wolf missiles because the view was blocked by *Coventry*. (Author's collection)

The monument to the Malvinas conflict on the harbour front at Ushuaia, Argentina.
(Paul Brown)

The Liberation Memorial at Stanley, on East Falkland, to all those who died in the Falklands conflict.
(Alex Petrenko, panoramio/Wikipedia, CC BY-SA 3.0)

indeed, it was to be a tumultuous day. The two ships took up their new patrol line some 10 miles long, stretching east/west, about 7½ miles north of Government Island; this was some 30 miles west of the previous patrol line. *Broadsword* manoeuvred to remain within 1,000 yards up threat of *Coventry*. The threat direction was assessed as being all round and air attack was considered highly probable, particularly with the clear weather. Thus, on what was to be her last day, *Coventry* resumed anti-aircraft operations in support of the amphibious operating area in close company with *Broadsword*.

This new position better suited *Coventry's* Sea Dart requirements and, given that the Argentinian raids on San Carlos were generally routed along the north or south coastlines of West Falkland but remained over land, was deemed most likely to provide target opportunities for both ships' missile systems. For *Coventry* the new position provided a longer look for both 909 radars, to the south-west and south-east over open water. With the exception of attacks from due south, which at this stage had not been observed, the move to the west seemed to solve many of the problems of Sea Dart employment about which *Coventry* had made representations to both Captain Canning in *Broadsword* and Sandy Woodward. Also, the new position was likely to give an additional 30 miles' warning from *Coventry's* 965 radar and thereby improve the air raid warning given to units in Falkland Sound, although the added distance made radio communication (on high frequency) with the ships in the anchorage more difficult. *Plymouth* became their main point of contact, and she radioed the picture to the other ships in the Sound. *Coventry* was in good shape: her fuel and ammunition reserves were high, there were no known serious defects with either sensor or weapon systems, the propulsion machinery was in good order, and morale was assessed as high, with the ship's company quite well rested and generally confident in their ability to deal with enemy attacks.[26]

A Learjet reconnaissance aircraft overflew the amphibious operating area early in the day at very high level, and its photographs revealed the position of the two ships.[27] It was a calm, bright sunny day. However, a small formation of Skyhawks was circling out over the Atlantic to the west, ready to fly in over West Falkland and attack the British anchorage. This was exactly the threat that *Coventry* and *Broadsword* had been positioned to detect (and warn the ships in the anchorage of) and intercept with Sea Dart missiles.

The first hint of action for the Type 42/22 pair came at about 08.30 when *Broadsword* reported two hostile air contacts being tracked over land on 967 Doppler radar, and these were also detected over land by *Coventry*, on 992 radar at about 52 miles, bearing 130°. Contact was held intermittently as the range closed to about 45 miles. The targets, apparently flying in close formation, had meanwhile crossed North Falkland Sound and were heading towards Pebble Island. They were acquired on both 909 radars and the launcher was loaded with two Sea Darts when the range of the target was about 30 miles. However, at this stage *Coventry* altered course to starboard and temporarily placed the missile homing eyes in the bow blind arcs. The target was now seemingly single on the 992 radar. *Coventry* assessed that the two aircraft were flying in close formation and, because of lingering doubt about Sea Dart performance after the Hercules/Skyhawk incident on 9 May, a salvo of two missiles was fired rather than a single shot as soon as the missile homing eyes became clear, at a range of 15 miles, with the target crossing rapidly from left to right. The ship's head was by now approaching south, still turning to starboard with the launcher bearing to port. One of the Skyhawks was shot down, and a parachute was seen to be deployed,[*] whilst the other missile missed and may have hit a rocky islet to the north of Pebble Island.[28]

The turn to starboard was not essential to engage the targets and was probably made in order to present a fine aspect to the potential attacking aircraft, coupled with a feeling that arcs would remain open for longer if the ship altered course to the west. However, this turn made it more difficult for *Broadsword* to get up threat. During

---

[*] However, its pilot, Lieutenant H. A. V. Palaver, was killed: 'Argentine Aircraft Lost', Naval History, www.naval-history.net/F64-Falklands-Argentine_aircraft_lost.htm (retrieved 27 April 2020).

the engagement, *Coventry* intercepted an Argentinian signal from one of the attacking aircraft or a shore position reporting that two British warships were north of Pebble Island. It was thus clear that the ships' positions had been compromised, and this was to colour *Coventry*'s later thinking.

Later in the morning, at about 11.30, ships in the Sound reported enemy activity in their vicinity. *Broadsword* soon detected this raid at some 44 miles' range on Doppler radar and sent the picture to *Coventry* on a data link. *Coventry* gained 992 radar contact at about 36 miles with the target closing through a radar clear gap but still over land, and then acquired it with 909 radar at about 33 miles. Although 992 contact was lost as the target approached the coast and merged with radar returns from high ground on Pebble Island, 909 remained locked on and a single Sea Dart was fired just as the target neared the northern edge of the land. The Skyhawk aircraft was downed over the sea just to the north of Pebble Island, the second to be destroyed by *Coventry* that day. During this engagement *Coventry* again altered course to the south from an easterly heading, for reasons similar to those used in the earlier attack. The Sea Harrier fighters that *Coventry* helped to direct were on patrol during these raids, but Hart Dyke and Canning held them off, assessing that their ships' missiles offered the best and quickest option for attack: this was always a close call and they didn't necessarily get it right.[29]

The 'missile trap' was working well, having been responsible for the downing of five aircraft in the past 24 hours – the three Daggers shot down by Sea Harriers directed from *Coventry* and the two Skyhawks just destroyed. *Coventry* had been quite successful in dealing with the problems caused by the nearness of land, but because of these successes and the likelihood of observation from the shore, the two ships were always aware of their vulnerability inshore.

The final raid was thus to come as no surprise. Shortly after 13.00 *Coventry* received an intelligence report of a possible raid approaching from the west and went to action stations. Six Skyhawks of 5th Air Brigade had taken off from Río Gallegos at 13.00, heading due east to rendezvous with a Hercules tanker to re-fuel, which only four of them successfully achieved: after being detected flying mid-air, the four split into two pairs and headed east for the Sound. A Spanish-speaking officer in *Coventry* tuned in to the Argentines' radio and heard them finalizing their plan to 'get that Type 42 out there' because it was causing so much trouble. Sea Harriers were sent out to meet them, but the intruders dived instantly, spearing up the south coast of West Falkland, and rushed low over the land to appear again on the coast of the Sound. All the ships in the Sound anchorage prepared for the raid, but the aircraft suddenly swerved to head inland over West Falkland.[30]

At 13.40 *Coventry* gained an internal UHF enemy signal intercept that indicated that three or four Argentinian aircraft were active somewhere in the Falklands area. Soon afterwards, at about 13.45, aircraft were detected on 965 radar bearing about 270°, range 160 miles. By their relative movement, at a very slow closing rate, it was assessed that those contacts were the incoming raid refuelling before commencing their attack. Contact was held on 965 radar until about 13.55 when, at some 90 miles' range, it was assumed that they had as usual gone low over the hills for their transit across West Falkland. The two ships were about to be attacked by two pairs of Argentinian Skyhawk aircraft armed with cannon and 1,000lb bombs. Air Raid Warning Red was called and at 14.00 both ships were at action stations, course 090°, with *Coventry* leading at 8 knots with both Tyne engines selected, and *Broadsword* about three cables fine on her starboard quarter as the two ships approached the eastern end of the patrol line. At this time *Coventry* also had control of two of *Hermes'* Sea Harriers on combat air patrol, which were fresh on task and joining from the east, heading for their station.[31]

Broadsword's 967 Doppler radar tracked two pairs of hostile aircraft some 10 miles and 1½ minutes apart, approaching to the south-west of Pebble Island on a heading of 080°. *Coventry* was satisfied with the warning provided on the data link and was fully ready for the raid. Instead of following the normal northerly track to the San Carlos amphibious operating area, these aircraft swung low over Pebble Island to attack *Coventry* and *Broadsword*. The Sea Harriers were fast approaching 25 miles to the east, but were too late to engage the first pair of aircraft without straying into *Broadsword*'s missile engagement zone, so they retired to the northeast, 10 miles off Cape Tamar, to await developments.

Coventry's 992 radar's moving target indication facility, a comparatively recent innovation, had nowhere near the performance of *Broadsword*'s 967 Doppler radar for indicating low targets over land. After persistent searching, *Coventry* only acquired the enemy aircraft on her 992 radar at about 10 miles' range as the first pair of aircraft came clear of the land, immediately to the north of Pebble Island. But they were not in sight visually and could not be acquired on the 909 fire control radars, probably because of an inaccurate target indication bearing, which needed to be quite precise since the 909 had a narrow beam.[32] *Broadsword* acquired them on her Sea Wolf's radar, but the computer system was confused by the two aircraft being wing-to-wing and refused to fire the missiles.[33]

At about 14.20 the ships reached the eastern end of their patrol line and decided to continue heading east as there was no immediate navigational danger and it was apparent that action was imminent. *Coventry* made a turn to starboard to keep her weapon arcs open and increased speed to 15 knots. Visual detection of the raid came when the aircraft were at about 8 miles, and they were identified as Skyhawks flying in close formation, very low (see Map 7). At the call 'Alarm Aircraft Visual', the target was engaged by the 4.5-inch gun at 6,000ft range, progressively reducing to 3,000ft. Some 18 to 20 rounds were fired in small groups: the missile/gun director and gun controller used the techniques developed as an anti-Exocet measure, which involved producing a water/shrapnel wall in front of the attack using surface-bursting shells.[34] Small arms and 20mm gun fire was also brought to bear by both ships and the attacking aircraft began a series of evasive weaving manoeuvres. Neither Sea Dart (*Coventry*) nor Sea Wolf (*Broadsword*) missiles were fired. Although they had been flying directly at *Coventry*, the gunfire and possibly the water/shrapnel

Map 7: The Skyhawk attacks on HMS *Coventry* and HMS *Broadsword*, 25 May

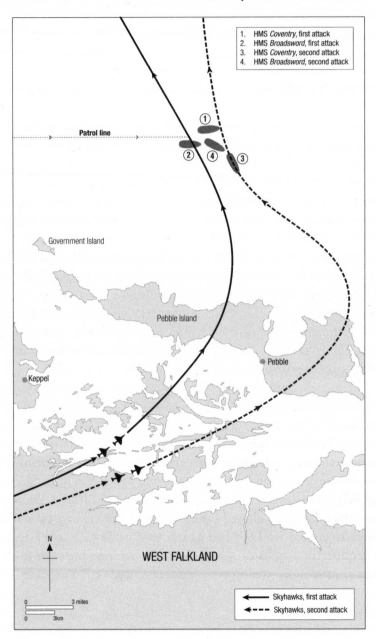

1. HMS *Coventry*, first attack
2. HMS *Broadsword*, first attack
3. HMS *Coventry*, second attack
4. HMS *Broadsword*, second attack

Patrol line

Government Island

Pebble Island

Pebble

Keppel

N

WEST FALKLAND

0   3 miles
0   3km

← Skyhawks, first attack
◄--- Skyhawks, second attack

barrier diverted the attacking aircraft towards *Broadsword*, who was engaged with their 30mm cannon and hit by one of four bombs dropped, which smashed through the starboard side aft, bouncing up through the flight-deck and destroying a Lynx helicopter that had been lent by *Brilliant*.

At about the time of the initial 992 radar detection, when the attacking aircraft were some 10 miles to the south, David Hart Dyke had ordered the officer of the watch to alter course to port, believing that he would be better placed to fight the action if he made ground to seaward. However, he was advised by the principal warfare officer that a turn to starboard would serve better to keep weapon arcs open, and thus before the port wheel had time to take effect the captain had given the order 'Come hard right 140' and ordered speed to be increased to 15 knots. Thus, by the time the first pair of aircraft overflew *Broadsword* their relative bearing from *Coventry* was about Green 150°,* although 4.5-inch gun fire was checked when they were on *Coventry's* starboard beam. Both 909s did eventually lock onto the targets, but at a short range of some 4½–5 miles, and Sea Dart was not fired: at this range it would have had minimal chance of a hit.[35] The 909s both observed 4.5-inch shells flying along the bearing but apparently falling short of the target, and the radar lock was broken at 1.4 miles.

The approach of the second pair of aircraft no more than 90 seconds later was detected on 992 radar by some positions in the ops room when they were over the north-east of Pebble Island, crossing fast from right to left at 8–10 miles, but, as they turned towards the ships, attention was still largely at the retreating first pair. In some positions their presence was not apparent until visual sighting was made at about 4–5 miles and broadcast.[36] At about this time, *Coventry* altered course to starboard using 35° on the wheel 'to ensure Sea Dart had a clear view of them',[37] and attempts to acquire the targets on 909 radar were being made with the Sea Dart controller switching between fore and aft radar repeatedly in

---

* This means that the aircraft were about 150° off Coventry's starboard bow, measured in a clockwise direction.

an unsuccessful attempt to acquire the target.[38] The Sea Harriers once again started to move towards the raid but were called off by Hart Dyke when only 4–5 miles away because Sea Dart was believed to have acquired the targets, and they were approaching *Broadsword*'s Sea Wolf engagement zone. The Sea Harriers retired into orbit some 10 miles north-east of Cape Tamar.[39]

Although *Coventry*'s 992 had picked up the intruders at 8–10 miles' range, the target indication operators were not alerted to their presence quickly enough to enable the 909 fire control radars to make a timely acquisition, and it is probable that the aft 909 was placed in blind arcs at a crucial moment by the ship's turn to starboard. The 4.5-inch gun was therefore put to follow the target automatically and both this gun and the close-range weapons opened fire almost simultaneously. However, the 4.5-inch fire was checked after only three rounds when it was reported that the gun was in depression. The gun elevation was wrong because the port visual sighting equipment was faulty and a pair of binoculars had been added as an improvisation, giving a false, depressed, angle of sight to the computer. Then the pressure of events may have caused the gun controller to use incorrect procedures in attempting to control his turret and bring it to bear on the target. He then ordered the gun to switch to emergency rifle mode to control the training motion, but the mounting eventually came to rest at about 5° elevation, facing broad on the port bow, well away from the target.[40]

Broadsword's aft Sea Wolf system was in blind arcs, but the ship had acquired the targets on her forward Sea Wolf system in low radar tracking mode. However, it suffered a multiple target indication problem, and the controller was not aware of *Coventry*'s alteration of course although it had been signalled on UHF. It was, in Bill Canning's view, an unnecessary alteration because on the original course of 090° targets from about 130° to 230° could be engaged by all systems in both ships, which were disposed at right angles to the threat. Experience in the amphibious operating area had indicated that aircraft had more difficulty in judging the time of bomb release than with the line of attack. Being beam on to an attack reduced the danger space; it also kept all weapon arcs open and was the position recommended by the Navy's warfare training analysts.[41] This experience does not appear to have been discussed with *Coventry*, who apparently favoured a fine (bow on) aspect to attacks, believing that it presented a smaller target. *Broadsword*'s officer of the watch, in the absence of other instructions from the ops room, followed *Coventry* round to starboard slightly inside the wake. This put *Broadsword* progressively down threat from the approaching aircraft.

Finally, as the incoming raid closed to less than 3 miles, possibly closer, a Sea Dart was fired by *Coventry*, but the launch angle and bearing of the missile appeared to be very wide of the approaching aircraft. In the frantic efforts to engage it at very short range it is possible that the 909 radar acquisition was on land or sea clutter, or that the radar's 'lock' on the aircraft was only very briefly obtained, and as a result nothing was achieved. Suddenly, springing out from over the land, the two enemy aircraft were sighted from the bridge coming straight for the ship at about 20° on the port bow, very fast and so low that water sprayed out behind them. In *Broadsword*, which was still recovering from the earlier attack and trying to cope with this one, the missile director experienced his worst dread, finding his view of the target blocked by *Coventry* and causing his system to lose its lock.[42]

Meanwhile in *Coventry*, in desperation, Petty Officer David Nuttall, the yeoman of signals, ordered Radio Operator Trev Trevarthen to try to blind the pilots' eyes by switching on the powerful signalling projector and pointing directly at them.[43] Just 16 seconds after the Sea Dart launching, *Coventry* was hit by 30mm cannon fire from the lead aircraft of the pair, and almost immediately afterwards three out of the four 1,000lb bombs dropped hit *Coventry* on the port side. A cannon shell sliced through the ship's side on the port side just above the waterline in the forward auxiliary machine room, passing aft into the forward engine room. Other cannon fire damage was sustained on the port side waterline aft, on the sonar winch aft, on the port side of the hangar, and apparently – from the first pair of aircraft – on the starboard side waterline.[44]

The first bomb pierced *Coventry's* hull, leaving a hole 6ft long and 2ft wide near the computer room, and exploded in the conversion machinery compartment, blowing up the deck of the computer room and rupturing a bulkhead and the ship's side. The fireball and bomb blast swept into the operations room from the computer room hatch. The computer room became a blazing inferno, trapping and killing seven men. The fire subsided but the generation of dense black smoke did not, thus forcing the evacuation of all 35 operations room personnel, with many suffering from burns and shock. This bomb put all weapon, sensor and communication systems out of action, except for the close-range guns.

The second bomb entered the naval store without exploding, and may have exited the ship outboard to sea. The third bomb entered the ship through the port Olympus gas turbine intake and exploded aft in the port side of the forward engine room and vented a small fireball and debris into the forward auxiliary machinery room. The machinery control room was put out of action by peripheral blast and smoke, but all the crew escaped. The junior ratings' dining hall amidships was devastated by the explosion below, killing all five occupants outright: they were ratings (including a petty officer) who made up a damage control and first aid team based in the dining room. Despite any take-cover position they may have adopted, they would have experienced severe upward and sideways blast from the deck and engine ductings.[45] One man in the technical office and four engineer ratings in the forward engine room were also killed.[46] There was large-scale underwater damage, and the forward auxiliary engine room and forward engine room subsequently flooded as the ship took a list to port, before finally capsizing and sinking some time later.

The men in the computer room probably died almost immediately. Hart Dyke recalled that in the operations room all was chaos following a vicious shockwave, a blinding flash and searing heat. The force of the impact had stunned him and knocked him out. When he came to he was still perched on the edge of his now broken chair. The radar screen into which he had been staring had disintegrated, his headset, microphone and anti-flash hood had been burnt off him without a trace, and little of his gloves remained. Men had been blown off their feet and thrown into corners of the room where they lay unconscious among the debris of wrecked equipment. Little could be seen in the thick black smoke except a few vague shapes of people with their clothes alight.[47]

Hart Dyke had been knocked senseless and after a time came to realize he was alone, semi-conscious and suffocating, and unable to find an escape from the room. He saw no alternative but to die. Somehow, he couldn't remember how, he made it to clearer air in the starboard passageway. Most of the ops room personnel, including the captain, suffered burns to their hands and faces, and some had much of their clothing burnt off and suffered from terrible burns.[48]

Petty Officer Sam MacFarlane, the radio office supervisor, had heard the Sea Dart launch, but then heard the ops officer announce, 'Missed target', and knew they were in trouble. He ordered everybody to lie down on the deck, but a young rating, Nobby Northeast, remained in his sitting position with his back against a panel. MacFarlane shouted at him to do as he was told, and he reluctantly got down. He had a lucky escape because in the ensuing explosion a huge chunk of metal flew against the panel where he had previously been sitting.[49]

But the youngest of the ratings was not so lucky. Seventeen-year-old Tug Wilson was badly hit on the back of the head by metal from a shattered door. The night before he had asked MacFarlane where he should lie if they did have to take cover. MacFarlane had pointed to a place between two strong bulkheads, not counting on the metal door being blown apart. As MacFarlane went to find out what was happening, a lieutenant told him, 'Get out. The ship's going down.' After evacuating the office, Sam MacFarlane saw his best friend, Petty Officer Chris Hill, with most of his clothes blown off, his flesh horrifically burnt (with 27 per cent burns). Sam helped Chris negotiate a maze of smoke-filled corridors and shattered ladders, manhandling and cajoling him up to the next deck. There was no fresh water from the taps so he was taken on deck and thrown into the sea, where he swam around, the cold water helping.[50]

It quickly become apparent that massive flooding was taking place in five main compartments; so rapidly did the heel develop that no serious attempts to contain flooding or repair damage could be made. The damage control headquarters had to be abandoned because of smoke: the three officers there, the first lieutenant and the marine engineer officer and his deputy, had also all been affected by the shock and blast of the explosion in the forward engine room and they moved via the starboard passageway to the aft damage control station, as did the personnel who evacuated the machinery control room and the mobile action repair team. In all, 27 men evacuated these areas on the orders of the marine engineer officer, Lieutenant Commander Rob Hamilton. With the damage control headquarters out of action, it was impossible to co-ordinate any damage limitation by establishing fire, smoke and flood boundaries in the way that the ship had rehearsed so often. All machinery and the ship's engines had stopped and there was no means of communication between damage control, firefighting and first-aid teams.[51]

The normal reactions and logic of the chief petty officer in charge of the aft damage control section and other senior rates were numbed by the shock of actually being hit and seeing casualties. They did carry out organized searches in their area and first reports were of no damage aft; a face-by-face check around the base, and reports received from shocked and distressed men, convinced the chief petty officer that all were accounted for. There was acute awareness of the angle of heel and the fear of being trapped below decks. However, the huge search and rescue potential of the aft damage control base was never used either to establish contact forward or check for survivors between the blast doors on 2 deck passageways. Thus, no patrol was sent forward along 2 deck passageways to check for stragglers from the machinery spaces or casualties in the forward extreme of the section in non-machinery spaces, even though personnel with breathing apparatus were available. By this time Lieutenant Commander Rob Hamilton had decided that the heel was serious and, fearing a capsize, he ordered the whole damage control party and nearby first aid team to make for the upper deck.[52]

However, two chief petty officers, Alan Fazackerly and David Rumsey, revisited smoke-filled compartments to check for survivors despite everyone else being on the upper deck, with the ship listing dangerously. Alan Fazackerly, searching the starboard passageway without breathing apparatus, found Chief Petty Officer Alan Estcourt unconscious, his clothes alight, slumped over the hatch coaming of the after-engine room and in imminent danger of falling back into the blazing compartment. He quenched the flames, took Estcourt to the first-aid post and thence to the upper deck, saving his life. David Rumsey saved the lives of two trapped and frightened young ratings in the transmitter equipment office close to the bomb hole and fire in the port passageway. He heard their agitated shouts for help, calmed them down and guided them past the damage to the upper deck.[53]

The forward damage control party was distracted from its primary task when faced with a flood of injured and shocked men evacuating the ops room. For it was only when facially burnt ratings evacuating that room burst through a watertight door that the chief petty officer in charge, Tom Sutton, and his men became aware that their section had been hit. The petty officer second-in-command switched role to first aider and took no further part in damage control attempts; he took the casualties into the forward bathrooms to have their burns doused in fresh water.[54]

Meanwhile, according to the board of inquiry report, the chief petty officer was organizing the firefighters and breathing apparatus team to go to the starboard access of the ops room. A leading hand and a rating wearing a fearnought fireproof suit (but not wearing breathing apparatus) approached the watertight door and were met by men evacuating the ops room who told them to 'get out as the ship was sinking'. They hesitated but continued to the door, where they were confronted with smoke

and debris and could not see inside, so they both returned to the
chief petty officer at the forward base, who was trying to organize
firefighting in the absence of fire-main pressure. Their report to
him was garbled but, having been re-equipped with lights, they
were told to return and assess the situation. They have admitted
that they were frightened at the thought of entering a smoke-
filled compartment, not knowing the state of the deck, and were
very disconcerted by seeing the injuries of evacuees, many of
them officers and senior rates.[55]

After re-visiting the ops room, the two ratings returned to the
base a second time, still with no information as to the state of the
ops room or the whereabouts of any trapped or injured personnel.
By this time the chief was becoming very irate over their hesitant
approach, so they were instructed to return to the ops room for
a third time and to hold the lantern in the doorway to guide any
survivors out. This they did and three ratings were led to safety by
their actions. On their final return to the forward damage control
base, the two ratings told the chief that they were going to leave
the section and join the queue to escape via the forecastle hatch.
They were very frightened as the heel was now approaching 20°
and they were surrounded by men, including some experienced
senior ratings, whose obvious intention was to escape before the
apparently imminent capsize.

The bewildered chief agreed that they should go as he was now
aware of the steadily increasing heel. He had never left the damage
control base control point to judge the conditions he was sending
the two young men into, or considered leading them himself.[56]
However, according to David Hart Dyke, Chief Petty Officer
Sutton was instrumental in guiding to safety many shocked and
injured men from the smoke-filled ops room, saving many lives.
When he eventually came to save himself and jump overboard,
Sutton immediately went to the aid of a badly burnt rating
struggling in the water without a life jacket and dragged him to a
life raft, thereby saving this man's life.[57]

The hopelessness of the situation led the ship's company very
rapidly to the conclusion that evacuation of the ship was the

only prudent course of action. No broadcast of a general order to abandon ship, or control it centrally, was possible because of the loss of power. The operation was therefore quite spontaneous, with groups of men being directed to make for the upper deck by their immediate superiors, in many cases doing so without specific orders, but it was nonetheless orderly in fashion. The centre of the ship at all deck levels was filled with smoke, many ladders were damaged, doors and hatches were buckled, and movement was difficult, not least because of the alarming list to port. Nevertheless, only minor difficulties were encountered, and no one perished as a result of problems in the evacuation to the upper deck.[58] Captain Hart Dyke later observed, 'I am still trying to discover who gave the order to abandon ship. Perhaps no one did. People just very sensibly got on and did it. It was the only thing to do.'[59]

As the ship steadily rolled over to port, men found it increasingly difficult to maintain their footing on the upper deck. The first men to jump did so when the list was less than 10° and were able to enter the water well clear of the ship's side. As the list developed it became progressively more risky, with a real danger of hitting underwater obstructions such as the stabilizer fins and bilge keels. As these obstructions broke surface (at about 25–30° list), men were able to slide, and then eventually to walk down the ship's side and then jump from the bilge. Various minor cuts and bruises were sustained during this phase, but unfortunately one man perished. Luckily it was clear, calm weather, although the water was cold (7°C); in other circumstances the risk of casualties would have been much greater.[60]

Lieutenant Commander Raymond Adams recalled that some people were reluctant to jump over the side. Some slid down the steep camber on the deck and into the water, whilst others used the scrambling nets. Fit and healthy, Adams jumped into the water and swam 30 yards to the furthest life raft. They used mugs to bail water out of the raft and their respirators as paddles to get clear of the ship. Several men were badly burned and were taken off in the first helicopter. After 1½ hours in the raft Adams was picked up by helicopter.[61]

In another life raft, Sam MacFarlane injected a seriously burned man, who was in agony, with morphine, which was carried by all senior rates round their necks. This worked. A Gemini assault craft with a powerful outboard engine attempted to tow his life raft away from the ship. They threw a rope, but the raft was too heavy and the Gemini was pulled under and sank.[62]

Of the 276 survivors who left the ship, two perished, one officer and one civilian laundryman. On average men spent about 15 minutes in the water and up to 90 minutes in life rafts. Even those wearing survival suits suffered discomfort from cold, although the duration of the rescue operation was such that this was not a serious factor. Life jackets, worn by 90 per cent of men, worked well and only a handful of men encountered problems with flotation, mainly because they lost their personal life jackets below decks and did not or could not find a spare before entering the water. Survival suits, however, posed different problems and attracted many adverse comments from survivors. Only 35 per cent of the 276 survivors managed to don the suit correctly; even amongst these men, many suffered ingress of water and later found difficulty with rescue when a 'Michelin Man' effect complicated the problems both of entering life rafts and then climbing scrambling nets on reaching *Broadsword*. Over half did not attempt to put on the suit or failed to do so properly before entering the water because of the list of the ship, loss of the suit below decks or reluctance to remove the life jacket.[63]

No general order to slip the life rafts could be given, and the launching of them was therefore undertaken on the initiative of individual officers and senior ratings when the ship was already listing to about 10° to port several minutes after the attack. No attempt was made to launch the port set of rafts, due to the apparent danger of capsizing. All eight starboard rafts were slipped, and all inflated correctly. Considerable difficulty was experienced in actually manhandling these rafts over the side of their stowages as the list to port increased. Men entered the rafts wherever they found them and, as a result, uneven loading took place. With only eight rafts in the water, some ended up very overcrowded, with as many as 47 men counted in one 25-man raft and some men outside in the water clinging to the grab ropes. There were problems when attempts were made to propel laden rafts away from the ship's side. Some of the forward rafts drifted around the bow and back close to the port side, becoming entangled with obstructions as the ship steadily rolled over. One raft was punctured by the antennae of an unfired Sea Dart missile still in the launcher and eventually sank, causing the occupants to take to the water again. None of the port side life rafts appeared on the surface when the ship capsized.[64]

Rescue was effected swiftly by *Broadsword*'s boats and helicopters from RFA *Fort Austin*. The majority of the men were placed in *Broadsword*, but some of the worst injured were flown directly ashore to a field hospital. By about 15.00 *Coventry* was lying on her port side, *Broadsword*'s Gemini was paddling clear with the last of the survivors and a Wessex helicopter was making a final search. The last survivors reached *Broadsword* at dusk, at about 16.00, some 1½ hours after entering the water, and *Coventry*'s upturned hull was still afloat. The search was called off at around the same time, when it was clear that no more survivors could be found. *Broadsword* transferred the fit survivors to other ships in the San Carlos area later that night, with RFA *Fort Austin* taking most, and sent the remainder of the wounded to the hospital ship *Uganda*. It was lucky that the circumstances for evacuation and abandonment had been largely favourable, with clear, calm weather, darkness had not fallen, the enemy did not make a further attack, and *Broadsword* and numerous large helicopters were close at hand. A winter battle in the South Atlantic might well have been unluckier, with serious consequences. The heroism of some men was also a factor, with several completely disregarding their own safety to assist others who were in difficulty both on board the ship and later in the water. The absence of panic and the cool manner in which the ship's company behaved was a credit to their underlying organization and discipline.[65]

* * *

Nineteen men had died. Most were killed instantly by the blast of bombs in the computer room, dining room, forward engine room and technical office. However, Kyu Ben Kwo, the laundryman from Hong Kong, died in the water on leaving the ship, and it was later learnt that he had a heart condition (with a pacemaker), which would probably have precipitated his death: sudden entry into the sea at 7° without a survival suit would be sufficient to cause his heart to fail due either to a sudden arrhythmia and/or coronary arterial spasm. He was later buried at San Carlos.

The first lieutenant, Lieutenant Commander Glen Robinson-Moltke, had been in the damage control headquarters when the second bomb exploded and was severely shaken and concussed by the blast. He had taken cover in the supine position with his head against a bulkhead. The marine engineer officer, Lieutenant Commander Rob Hamilton, thought Robinson-Moltke was dead, but a rating pulled him to his feet to find him alive if considerably confused due to concussion. He followed others out of the headquarters via the starboard passageway to the aft damage control base. Although several people spoke to him and received replies, he took no part in the organization of the activities going on at the time and was subsequently directed to the upper deck, where he was seen to be still very confused. He was helped into a survival suit and life jacket, and a rating in a life raft called a warning to him to mind the stabilizer, but when he slid over the side, barely conscious, he hit his head on the protruding stabilizer fin and almost certainly broke his neck. His life jacket was probably punctured as he was not seen afloat in the water and was never seen again. The only other officer killed was Lieutenant Rod Heath, the weapons engineer responsible for the Sea Dart system, who had died in the computer room.[66]

Thirty men were wounded; one of them, Marine Engineering Mechanic Paul Mills, suffered complications from a skull fracture he sustained and later died on 29 March 1983. Of the others, burns, bruising and lacerations were the most common injuries, whilst a few suffered from smoke inhalation, hypothermia or severe shock, and one man from near drowning.[67] On 26 May the fit survivors were transferred by RFA *Stromness* to South Georgia, where they boarded the requisitioned liner *Queen Elizabeth 2* for passage home, arriving in Southampton on 11 June. No member of *Coventry*'s ship's company received an award for bravery. However, Chief Petty Officer Aircrewman M. J. 'Alf' Tupper of 846 Naval Air Squadron, an aircrewman in one of the rescue helicopters, was awarded a Distinguished Service Medal for his bravery in rescuing men from life rafts (see Appendix).[68] After the war, a cross to commemorate crew members who lost their lives in *Coventry* was erected on Pebble Island.

* * *

A board of inquiry was convened at HMS *Nelson*, Portsmouth, on Monday 28 June 1982, and comprised Captain A. R. Barnden (president), Commander N. R. Essenhigh, Commander J. E. Bowns, Commander J. F. J. Simpson and Surgeon Commander H. A. Chandler. Their report was presented to the commander-in-chief, fleet, on 9 August 1982.[69]

The inquiry considered the tactical aspects of the events of 25 May. The Type 42/Type 22 combination, introduced after the loss of *Sheffield* and practised by *Coventry* and *Broadsword*, had shown initial promise. However, the inherent dangers were amply demonstrated when *Glasgow*, operating with *Brilliant*, was bombed on 12 May. *Coventry*'s manoeuvres during the successful Sea Dart engagements of 25 May appeared to be motivated by considerations of evasion. They complicated *Broadsword*'s up-threat manoeuvring, but the significance of the alterations of course did not seem to have registered with either ship. The manoeuvring methods failed, under great stress, because of the lack of guidance on evasive manoeuvring, the lack of anticipation of *Coventry*'s evasive action, the fact that the manoeuvring method was not positive enough, and the fact that the conning officer in *Broadsword* was not aware of the threat axis for the second attack.

In view of these shortcomings, the board concluded that the final engagement was not well handled: in hindsight it was possible to point to errors of judgement by both *Coventry* and *Broadsword*. But the situation had developed very quickly and every aspect would have had to have been handled faultlessly to have materially affected the outcome.[70] Admiral Woodward was later to put it this way: '*Coventry*'s swing to her right had not, in hindsight, been very clever, but equally *Broadsword* was supposed to be in charge. However, she had just been bombed, which ranks as a pretty serious distraction, and we have to put the loss of *Coventry* down to the fortunes of war.' He re-considered his earlier opinion that the Type 42/22 combination worked and decided that it probably didn't, not close to the shore anyway, not least because the disablement of *Glasgow* had happened in somewhat similar circumstances to those of *Coventry*.[71]

Regarding the patrol line, it potentially offered better Sea Dart opportunities than on previous days, but it placed the Sea Harriers down threat for incoming raids, and high frequency radio was needed for anti-air warfare co-ordination. The patrol location, 10 miles offshore – the minimum for a Type 42 to have any chance of engaging a direct attack – was a compromise between self-defence and the interception of enemy raids. Also, the Type 42 needed to be at least 2 miles clear of land and within 15 miles of the route of low-level approaching aircraft to have any chance of downing them.[72]

However, what had been needed was a defence umbrella for the amphibious operating area rather than a longer-range screen. Sea Dart was successful in two engagements, but neither the gun nor Sea Dart was used effectively in the final engagement. Regarding the final attack, where *Coventry* detected the first pair of aircraft on 992 radar as they crossed the coast at 10 miles, the fighter controller did well very nearly to complete a snap interception at very close range in confusing circumstances, but the 10-mile detection on 992 radar gave insufficient time for a reliable acquisition for Sea Dart on 909 radar. The action indication organization (the team of supervisors, reporters and compilers in the ops room) did not provide a clear picture to the captain in the latter stages of the attack; they had 90 seconds to do so. The turn to starboard, which put the final attack on the port bow, fouled Sea Dart arcs and complicated control and visual direction of the 4.5-inch gun. Visual gun direction, the report noted, was difficult in Type 42s and targets should be kept on one side of the ship if possible. Shifting to a target on the opposite side of a Type 42 was fraught with difficulty and, whenever possible, should be avoided by manoeuvring the ship.[73] *Coventry*'s Sea Dart team was very experienced, the gunners less so, and the command had no great confidence in the gun, following the problems during the naval gunfire support operations earlier in the month, despite the fact that the problems had been cleared by 14 May, since when many chaff shells had been fired.[74]

The deck 2 passageway in a Type 42 destroyer was divided into sections by doors for blast and smoke boundary protection, but there was no watertight integrity between sections due to the unsealed passage of pipework outboard of the door frames, so flooding could progressively be transmitted to at least five sections of the ship, as was the case in *Coventry*.

A long list of recommendations was made in the report, and some important ones are mentioned here. There was a requirement for Sea Dart to be able to engage low-level/pop-up targets at short range, and training for these situations should also be developed. The fitting of a close-range weapon system was considered necessary (after the conflict the other ships of the class were fitted with two twin 30mm guns and subsequently with two Phalanx close-in weapons).[75] On board, continuation training equipment for quick reaction situations needed to be developed. Fighting instructions should include recommended evasive manoeuvres against low-level bombing attacks. The need for the Type 42/22 combination should be validated, and suitable operating procedures and training established. Type 42s should all have non-watertight bulkheads made watertight by either self-help or support vessels (if on deployment) or by a shore-based fleet maintenance organization. More emphasis should be placed on sea survival and raftmanship courses as run by HMS *Daedalus*. Life-raft stowage and release arrangements should be improved.[76]

* * *

On the day of her sinking, *Coventry* was operating in the air defence role for which she had been designed and was in company with the new and effective *Broadsword* in what was thought to be a promising Type 22/42 combination for medium- and short-range defence against air attack. The ships were operating in relatively open waters where the shortcomings of the Type 42's fire control radar were less exposed and, given detection of aircraft at a range of 15 miles or more, Sea Dart could possibly be fired in automatic mode. The two ships therefore had a good chance of shooting down any intruding enemy aircraft, and indeed *Coventry* had succeeded in downing two Skyhawks in the morning. So what went wrong in the afternoon? *Coventry*'s loss was the result of two Skyhawk attacks in very quick succession on the ship and on *Broadsword*, which was damaged in the first. In the second attack, just 90 seconds later, the aircraft's emergence from over land to the south at only 10 miles' range meant that there was insufficient time for the Sea Dart fire control radar to lock onto them. In the panic that ensued after the first attack, the operator of *Coventry*'s 4.5-inch gun, which was in emergency mode, had problems training it onto the second pair of Skyhawks. Under great stress, in a rapidly developing situation, mistakes were made in manoeuvring the two ships, leading to *Coventry* increasing speed (in contravention of the agreement with *Broadsword*) and turning to starboard, placing *Broadsword* down threat (instead of up threat where she was supposed to be) and thereby blocking the latter's Sea Wolf. This was a critical error: the intruder got through and bombed *Coventry*, which had aggravated the situation by presenting bow on to the attack, a more dangerous angle than the preferred beam-on orientation. The damage to the ship was such that she quickly sank. With better manoeuvring, the damaged *Broadsword* might well have averted the disaster by shooting down the Skyhawks with Sea Wolf. As it was, the rapid onset of the second-wave attack allowed little time for recovery after the first wave and was fatal to *Coventry*.

7

The Loss of SS *Atlantic Conveyor*

One of the unsung but vital ships in the Falklands task force was the aircraft ferry *Atlantic Conveyor*. Converted from a combined container ship and car carrier, she was slated to take Harriers and helicopters down to the battle zone as the first reinforcements to the aircraft taken south aboard warships and RFAs. The Chinook helicopters would be particularly important for transporting troops and heavy equipment from the landing site to assault locations where the Argentinian troops would be engaged, and the Sea Harriers would replace any losses. On 25 May, whilst waiting to enter the total exclusion zone, she was part of a group of ships screening the aircraft carriers and was unlucky to suffer the impact of two Exocet missiles that had been deflected from their original target, the frigate *Ambuscade*. *Atlantic Conveyor*, 12 of her ship's company and her valuable cargo were lost when the ship had to be abandoned.

Atlantic Conveyor was a roll-on, roll-off container ship of 14,950 gross registered tons, owned by Cunard Line as part of the Atlantic Container Line consortium. A total of six ships of the class were ordered by the line to an innovative design, combining roll-on/roll-off and container storage in a single vessel. She had been built by Swan Hunter on the Tyne and completed in March 1970, and was powered by twin steam turbines, giving a top speed of 23 knots. The Atlantic Container Line (ACL) consortium was founded in 1965, comprising Wallenius Lines, Swedish America Line, The

Transatlantic Steamship Company Ltd and Holland America Line, for the Europe to North America trade. These four companies were later joined by the Cunard Steamship Company and the French Compagnie Générale Transatlantique. The Cunard-owned *Atlantic Causeway*, a sister ship of *Atlantic Conveyor*, was also taken up by the Ministry of Defence for the Falklands operation.[1]

Atlantic Conveyor was taken up from trade by the Ministry of Defence on 14 April 1982. She had been laid up in the West Canada Dock at Liverpool for nine months during which time considerable maintenance work was carried out in the engine rooms. Steam was raised with only minor problems that were soon overcome. A survey was carried out for the owners and the Ministry of Defence, which revealed only a number of very minor defects that would be rectified at Devonport during her conversion.

She sailed from Liverpool the following day and arrived at Devonport on Friday 16 April, entering the royal dockyard for modifications, with most of the work completed by 23 April. The dockyard project manager responsible for the conversion work commented on the generally good condition of the ship, which was considered to be well prepared for her role as an aircraft ferry and stores carrier. The ship was not fitted with any self-defence weapons or chaff launchers, although six locally mounted general purpose machine guns were later taken from embarked Wessex helicopters.[2] There was no access to the lower vehicle decks for the 24 aircraft and their associated equipment and fuel, which had to be stowed on the upper decks.

The modifications included covering the container hold with steel plates, fitting a replenishment at sea system, creating a system of shelters and equipment stores on the deck using standard shipping containers, and installing additional radio and satellite communications systems. The containers on the deck were used for storing fresh water and oxygen, accommodation for personnel of all three services, and workspaces for maintenance. Thirty-man life rafts were fitted on either side of the superstructure. A platform for Harrier jet operations was constructed forward and the stern container deck was extended at both after corners and modified for helicopter operations. The fan housings blocking the landing areas were removed. Folding guard rails were fitted beside both flight decks, aircraft lashing points were welded onto the upper deck area at about 10ft intervals, and a new upper deck hydrant system was installed. An aircraft guide path indicator was fitted aft and horizon bar lights were fitted on both decks.[3] All this work was completed in just eight days, a remarkable achievement for the royal dockyard.

Atlantic Conveyor carried a Merchant Navy crew of 32. This included 12 officers (master, chief officer, second officer, third officer, radio officer, chief engineer, second engineer, two third engineers, fourth engineer, chief electricial engineer and purser); seven petty officers (bosun, four mechanics, and two first cooks); two second cooks, a second steward and ten ratings (five seamen, three greasers and two assistant stewards). All were given the option not to sign on for the Falklands operation, but none took this option.[4] They were complemented by 126 armed forces' and RFA personnel for ship, squadron and flight deck duties, designated Naval Party 1840. The damage control teams, formed mainly of senior air ratings, lacked training and experience in below decks firefighting practices. The first lieutenant was not trained, nor had the background, for damage control – nevertheless he still performed well.[5]

Accommodation for the naval and military party of 126 men was obtained by boxing in upper deck areas of the superstructure to create two 24-man messes, installing two portacabins and converting a number of officers' cabins into messes for up to 12 men. Recreation and dining spaces were two-tiered: one for officers and chief petty officer equivalents and one for petty officers and junior ratings.[6]

Her master was Captain Ian North, of Cunard, and the naval party aboard for the Falklands operation was headed by Captain Mike Layard, RN. Captain North, aged 57, a bachelor whose home was in Doncaster, was 'a real old sea dog, a Yorkshireman who had been twice sunk in the Second World War', having first gone to sea in 1939. Charles Drought, senior third engineer in *Atlantic*

Conveyor, had sailed with Captain North before and described him as 'everyone's image of what a British captain should look like, with his neatly trimmed beard and commanding stature. He was a brilliant and fearless master who did not suffer fools gladly, but was scrupulously fair to all under his command.' On the passage south he became popular with both Royal Navy and Merchant Navy seamen, regaling them with stories of the sea, and occasionally, late at night, playing his trombone. When they 'crossed the line', the short, chunky North with his snowy beard played the part of King Neptune.[7] The board of inquiry was to comment that the excellent working relationship that developed between Captain North and Captain Layard permeated down to all levels. Royal Navy and Merchant Navy personnel worked well together and, with imaginative and sensible improvisation, produced a successful ship's company in a remarkably short time.[8]

Mike Layard, born in 1936 in Sri Lanka, had been educated at Pangbourne College and Dartmouth (joining the Royal Navy in 1954). Initially a seaman officer, he then became a fighter pilot in the Fleet Air Arm from 1960 to 1971, flying from *Eagle* and *Ark Royal*. He commanded 899 Squadron (flying Sea Vixens) in *Eagle* 1970–71 and the frigate *Lincoln* 1971–72. Following shore appointments he became the last commander (air) in *Ark Royal* 1977–78. In 1979 he was appointed as chief staff officer to the flag officer, Naval Air Command.[9]

The wide upper deck's edges were lined with a stack of three-deep containers and portakabins, the latter providing additional accommodation and workshop space, to make a sheltered pen for the helicopters and Harriers. Fuel cells were installed in adapted containers and provision was made for refuelling aircraft on deck, as well as providing liquid oxygen for the Harriers and fresh water for washing down all aircraft. *Atlantic Conveyor* was also to be an aircraft repair ship with a team of technicians from the Royal Navy's Mobile Aircraft Repair, Transport and Salvage Unit.[10]

Initially, when taken up from trade, it was intended that *Atlantic Conveyor* should be used only as an aircraft ferry, so no magazine arrangements were considered necessary. However, the need for further supplies of ordnance in the Falklands operation led to the late embarkation of 240 x 600lb RAF cluster bombs, AS12 and SS11 missiles, 7.62mm ball rounds in cases, and conventional and phosphor grenades. This ordnance was stored in both side pockets of C deck, lower forward, a location chosen to keep the explosives as deep as possible in the ship on steel decks and as far as possible from accommodation areas and superstructure. Stowage was controlled by the chief officer, assisted by an explosives representative from Royal Naval Armament Depot Ernesettle, near Plymouth. No sea transport officer from the Department of Trade (DoT) was available, but if one had been he 'would undoubtedly have found the stowages of ordnance to be in breach of all DoT regulations', according to the board of inquiry report. The other main concentration of hazardous cargo was 80 tons of kerosene, which was stowed on A deck forward with one complete steel deck division between it and the ordnance.[11]

A large amount of additional Royal Navy firefighting equipment, equivalent to that carried in a frigate, was embarked, both for flight deck emergencies and for normal ship's damage control purposes. At first, in the drills practised after leaving Plymouth, Merchant Navy procedures for firefighting and damage control were followed, but this soon changed to conform with Royal Navy procedures.[12]

The vehicle decks (originally designed for car stowage) were used for all manner of military stores including tentage and tent heaters for the entire military force in the Falklands, 11 Squadron Royal Engineers' stores, equipment and plant for the planned Harrier forward operating base ashore, stacker trucks, 12 combat support boats, specialist spares, dracones (floating rubber fuel tanks), fuel pumping equipment, water desalination equipment, generators, lighting sets and other non-aircraft munitions. The helicopters were flown to *Atlantic Conveyor* and the rotor blades were then removed and the airframes protected with Dri-Clad covers and corrosion inhibitors, since they were to be deck cargo, as would be the Harriers, which were to be embarked and similarly protected at Ascension Island.[13] The Harriers were to be embarked there to reduce exposure to salt-laden air on passage.

On Saturday 24 April the ship left her dock at 16.00 and anchored in Plymouth Sound. She was bunkered with oil, AVCAT aviation fuel and water, and embarked five Chinook helicopters of 18 Squadron RAF and six Wessex 5 helicopters of 848 Squadron Royal Navy. Sailing from Devonport late on Sunday 25 April, she then carried out a trial replenishment at sea with RFA *Grey Rover*, a new experience for her Merchant Navy crew. She proceeded south in company with the transport *Europic Ferry* and carried out initial damage control exercises to simulate action taken in the event of minor and major fires, as well as flying trials and emergency station drills.[14]

Built for the North Atlantic route, *Atlantic Conveyor* was not fitted with air conditioning, which made life uncomfortable as she sailed through the tropics.[15] She called at Freetown, Sierra Leone at 09.00 on 2 May for a brief refuelling stop and sailed from there independently at 06.00 the following day, to make a fast passage south, unhampered by the slower *Europic Ferry*, which left Freetown later.

At 06.00 on Wednesday 5 May the ship anchored off Ascension Island, where one Chinook was offloaded to assist with the Ascension Island stores lift and eight Sea Harriers of 809 Squadron Royal Navy and six GR3 Harriers of 1 Squadron RAF were embarked. Sidewinder missiles for the Harriers were also embarked and stowed in a container on the upper deck. These all-aspect infrared seeking air-to-air missiles, of the latest mark, had been specially provided for the Harriers by the USA, which had agreed to provide material support to Britain in the conflict. Most of the ship's victualling and general naval stores were transferred to RFA *Stromness* by helicopter, an operation which took 36 hours and was 80 per cent complete by the time the ship sailed. On 7 May *Atlantic Conveyor* left Ascension in company with the amphibious group, and further stores replenishment continued under way.

From 10 May one Sea Harrier armed with Sidewinder missiles and guns was on deck alert in *Atlantic Conveyor* at 20 minutes' notice in anti-shadower role.[16] The rules of engagement had been changed to allow it to shoot down any hostile shadowing aircraft that came within 40 miles. The chance came on the 15th when an Argentinian Boeing came overhead but, to the disappointment of the pilot and senior naval officers, the weather was too bad at sea level to launch vertically, and certainly to recover vertically.[17] *Atlantic Conveyor* proceeded ahead of the amphibious group, and the 14 Harriers were prepared by the Royal Navy and RAF maintenance teams aboard for transfer to the aircraft carriers. The Sea Harriers were to be integrated into 800 and 801 Squadrons in *Hermes* and *Invincible* respectively.[18]

When the ship crossed the line of 6° south, the pay of the Merchant Navy crew was increased by 50 per cent as a war bonus, which was appreciated by them if not by their envious naval and military colleagues on board.[19] On Wednesday 19 May *Atlantic Conveyor* arrived in the total exclusion zone and four Sea Harriers and four GR3 Harriers were disembarked to *Hermes*. On the next day she proceeded in company with *Ardent* to rendezvous with *Invincible* and disembarked four Sea Harriers to *Invincible* and one GR3 Harrier to *Hermes*, and then remained with the main battle group. On 21 May, the day of the first landings in San Carlos Water, the last GR3 Harrier was disembarked to *Hermes*. In the ensuing two days one Wessex 5 was transferred to *Stromness*, two Wessex 5s of 845 Squadron were embarked from other ships and a Lynx helicopter was embarked to be used as a 'hot spare' source for the remainder of the battle group's Lynx.[20] With the Harriers disembarked, there was room in *Atlantic Conveyor* for the long job of preparing the helicopters for their flight ashore after the landings at San Carlos.[21] The helicopters could not be flown off until a base was established for them, but one Chinook and the six Wessex helicopters of 848 Squadron were employed on load lifting between ships.[22]

Early on Tuesday 25 May, the ship received a signal from Rear Admiral Woodward ordering her to move from her holding station in the logistics area to the east to join the battle group, and then be ready in all respects to proceed, under cover of darkness, to San Carlos Water to disembark all helicopters and their associated personnel and stores at first light. The date, 25 May, was Argentina's national day and Admiral Woodward had warned that the enemy was likely to make a concerted effort against the task group. Captain Layard had already ordered the white superstructure of *Atlantic Conveyor* to be painted dark matt grey for the 100-mile voyage. During that day the helicopter stores were positioned on the aft flight deck and in C deck cathedral area ready for disembarkation, and this work was completed at 15.00 (Falklands Standard Time). At 15.10 a Wessex took off for a check test flight and a short vertical replenishment of *Hermes*.[23]

By the afternoon of 25 May *Atlantic Conveyor* had joined the carrier battle group about 75 miles west of the Falklands, and was on a 170° course at 12 knots in the north-west sector of the group. The wind was from 210° at 25 knots, and there was a swell of 2 metres from the north-west and a wave height of 1 metre. There was full cloud at 1,500ft and one-eighth cloud cover at 200ft, and visibility of 10–20km. The air and sea temperature were both 7°. It was known that Argentina still had an air-launched Exocet missile capability, and the main targets were thought to be the two aircraft carriers *Hermes* and *Invincible*.

The destroyer *Exeter* was being employed as a radar picket to the south-west of the battle group, with the frigates *Alacrity* and *Ambuscade* to the east of her. *Exeter*'s position 25–28 miles to the south-west of the carrier battle group reflected the view that air-launched Exocet attacks were likely to come from the base at Río Grande to the south-west. Close anti-air defence for the aircraft carriers was being provided by the destroyer *Glamorgan* and the frigate *Brilliant*, and Sea Harriers were on deck alert for combat air patrol duties. *Atlantic Conveyor*, RFA *Sir Percival*, the mercantile fresh water tanker *Fort Toronto*, and RFA *Regent* were forming a screen about 5 miles west of the two carriers, whilst RFA *Sir Tristram* was between the two groups (see Map 8).[24]

Unknown to the battle group, two Super Étendards of the 2nd Naval Fighter-Attack Squadron had taken off from Río Grande at about 13.30 and swept 450 miles north to refuel in flight from a tanker in a position 240 miles north of the Falklands, and then turned towards the south-east so that they might surprise the force by appearing from the north-west instead of the south-west.

Map 8: The strike on SS *Atlantic Conveyor*, 25 May

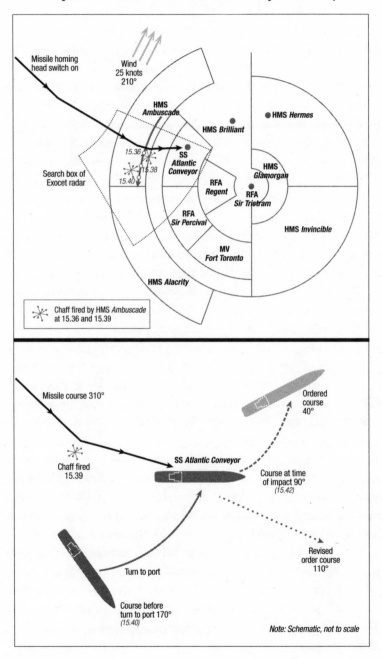

Piloted by Lieutenant Commander R. Curilovic and Lieutenant J. Barraza, they descended to low level when about 150 miles from the estimated position of the carrier battle group.[25]

At 15.36, half an hour before sunset, the first indication of an impending attack came as the frigate *Ambuscade*, further out in the north-west sector, detected the Agave radar emissions of Super Étendard jets on a bearing of 312° and fired chaff. *Exeter* also detected the radar emissions. Two aircraft were detected almost immediately by *Ambuscade*, some 28 miles to the north-west. One minute later, at 15.37, *Brilliant* detected the aircraft at 26 miles and at 15.38 *Ambuscade* detected that the Agave radar had locked on to a target. The missile release was detected by both *Brilliant* and *Ambuscade* at 15.39; *Ambuscade* fired a full pattern of chaff again, and an Air Raid Warning Red was broadcast on Tactical (task group tactical UHF radio, a tactical manoeuvring circuit) to all ships. It was evident that these aircraft had approached the group at low level and climbed to 200–250ft to start their attack.

At 15.40 the force was ordered to make an immediate downwind turn to port to 040°, which would have placed the ships broadside on to the missiles. Soon afterwards an immediate turn to starboard to 110° was ordered, also on Tactical, but this was not received by *Atlantic Conveyor,** which was still turning to port. The bearing of the missile release, although detected, was not broadcast on Tactical, and was thus not received by the RFAs and merchant ships, which were not equipped to monitor warfare voice circuits. The second turn (to 110°) would have presented the sterns of the ships to the missiles, the preferred orientation. *Atlantic Conveyor's* first lieutenant had piped emergency stations at 15.40 and the ship's siren was sounded as an additional alarm, but the threat direction was not known. Machine gun crews rushed to their action stations in the bridge wings, and the first aid and damage control teams hurried to their stations. Everyone was pulling on life jackets and anti-flash gear as they ran to their places of duty. *Invincible*

---

* This is stated in para 7, Annex A to the BOI report, but the reason why it was not received is not given.

launched her combat air patrol Sea Harriers, which were then held to the north to prevent a 'blue-on-blue' incident in which a missile fired by a British ship might have targeted the Sea Harriers.[26]

Having launched their missiles, the enemy aircraft broke to port and retired. The two missiles were tracked towards the task group by radar in *Brilliant* and visually by *Hermes* and *Ambuscade*. *Brilliant* and *Hermes* were about 3 and 5 nautical miles to the north-east of *Atlantic Conveyor* respectively, whilst *Ambuscade* was about 3 nautical miles to the south-west. The missiles appeared to be aimed at *Ambuscade*, but when 6–7 miles from her they veered left at an angle of about 20° from their original path. On the bridge of *Brilliant* Radio Operator Spence saw, through binoculars, two missiles flying low towards the force.

> They were very close together, I saw the first missile hit the side of *Atlantic Conveyor*, and it exploded almost immediately with a ball of fire. The second missile flew directly through the hole made by the first missile, but I did not see this second missile explode. Seconds later black smoke appeared from the hull of the ship.

The missile impact occurred at 15.42 on the port quarter of *Atlantic Conveyor*, which was in a port turn to 040°, the ship's head at impact being at about 090°. The hit in the port quarter was level with the end of the superstructure, some 10–12ft above the waterline, with the missiles entering C cargo deck in the vicinity of the lift shaft. In later analysis it was not clear whether the missile warheads had detonated.[27] At 15.41 Captain Layard had demanded to know the threat direction, but immediately afterwards the missiles struck.[28]

Eight people were known to have been between decks aft at this time. 'Hit the deck!' was called over the ship's broadcast, but the ship's internal telephone system was lost in the attack. At 15.42 *Invincible* had fired Sea Dart. Meanwhile, dense acrid smoke issued from all aft vents and the hole in the ship's side, so the ventilation fans were crash stopped from the bridge. The boilers went out and the shafts stopped turning. After a report of man overboard, Third Officer Martin Stenzel attempted to release the starboard bridge wing lifebuoy, but the release pin broke off in his hand. Radio Operator Borrill released the smoke-float only by cutting the line to the buoy, and it hit the water 1,000 yards from the man. At 15.44 a Wessex helicopter had been scrambled from *Hermes* and recovered the man overboard, Sergeant Hinchman, RAF, having been directed to the man by UHF radio from *Atlantic Conveyor*.[29]

Internal communications in the ship were rudimentary. The main broadcast system did not cover cargo deck areas, recreation areas or the bridge, and the alarm system only covered living spaces. The internal telephone system was lost at the outset. As a result, at least eight people who were below decks when the missile struck were completely unaware that the ship was at emergency stations.[30]

With the realization that the ship was on fire in the after cargo decks, Chief Officer John Brocklehurst had crash stopped all cargo hold ventilation fans from the bridge, but decided not to close the ventilation flaps in the hope that this would allow the dense black smoke now issuing from the after fan outlets to dissipate and thus assist the search and firefighting parties. He then went directly to the after section to assess the extent of the damage, but encountered dense smoke and intense heat on descending to A deck level. Realizing that a major fire was raging below decks, he returned to the bridge to close the ventilation flaps using the hydraulic system, but found that system to be inoperative.[31]

The lift shaft to the after engine room had collapsed, and smoke was reported as far forward as the forward damage control station. After donning their anti-flash gear and anti-gas respirators, Chief Engineer James Stewart and his staff managed to start the emergency diesel generators and the ship's main fire pump from the engine control room, where there was a lot of damage, and stopped all unnecessary machinery in the engine room, which itself was undamaged. By 15.50 the engine control room had become untenable due to smoke and was evacuated. Anti-gas respirators were in use on the after flight deck, where grenades and 7.62mm rounds were being ditched overboard.[32]

At 15.40 Petty Officer Mechanic Ernie Vickers had left the engine control room by the annexe workshop exit, intent on proceeding to his emergency station in the safety room. He became injured and trapped, and his cries for help were heard by Third Engineer Charles Drought. Wearing an anti-gas respirator, Drought crawled towards him and tried to free him, enduring the smoke and heat, but, realizing he couldn't, he had to seek help. Third Engineer Brian Williams and Petty Officers Frank Foulkes and Boleslaw 'Bill' Czarnecki, wearing breathing apparatus and asbestos gloves, twice braved the intense heat and smoke in attempts to rescue Vickers, but in their second visit they realized that he had perished. Williams had to be ordered to abandon ship when it was obvious nothing could be done. By 15.52 thick black smoke was reported on all of A deck and the forward damage control party moved to the upper deck. Second Officer Philip Bailey switched on the sprinklers in sections 1 and 2 of C deck.[33]

The ship's fire-main pressure was lost at 15.56 and the CO_2 firefighting system was activated by the chief engineer, but too little gas was released and the effect was negligible. The AVCAT fuel in the port and starboard containers was pumped over the side. The frigate *Alacrity* was standing by on *Atlantic Conveyor's* starboard quarter and attempted boundary cooling* from 50 yards, but this was ineffective. Meanwhile *Sir Percival*, standing by on the port quarter, reported flames through the hole in the ship's side, but was unable to assist because of dense smoke. Just after sunset, at 15.59, *Atlantic Conveyor's* fire-main pressure was restored. There were several explosions from aft on C deck.[34]

By 16.00 three men had succumbed to smoke and were being treated in the first aid clearing station. Amongst these was Chief Aircraft Engineering Artificer Richard Bentley, who led a damage control team that made several efforts to control the blaze. At 16.03 the ship's main broadcast system was lost. At 16.05 the fire was assessed as being out of control, with a risk of it spreading forward to the areas containing cluster bombs and kerosene. All non-involved personnel were told to muster on the starboard side of 1 deck and

---

* Boundary cooling involves cooling the adjacent sides of a compartment in order to reduce the heat, in an attempt to halt the spread of fire. In this case the sides of the hull were being hosed with water.

don their survival suits. Explosions below decks had become more frequent and pronounced, and shrapnel was seen coming through the ship's side. The aft flight deck was becoming untenable because of dense smoke. 'Abandon ship' was ordered by Captain North and Captain Layard, although fire parties were told to stand fast, and the ship was abandoned in a calm and orderly manner.[35] The presence of explosives, particularly cluster bombs, in the ship was a significant factor influencing the decision to abandon her.[36]

Four men jumped overboard and the rest either climbed down one of the ladders aft or were taken off by helicopter. Three ladders were put over the starboard side and four life rafts were launched over that side, the port side being untenable because of smoke. Some of the men who came down the ladders had to enter the sea to get to a life raft, where they caught hold of grab lines around the raft. Being wet, cold and exhausted, many found entry into the 25-man Royal Navy life rafts difficult. *Alacrity* was asked to look out for any survivors who had missed the rafts and drifted aft in the sea. A Wessex helicopter landed on the forward flight deck and picked up 15 members of the forward flight deck damage control party. A further seven were picked up immediately afterwards from the same spot by a Sea King helicopter, and both helicopters took their survivors to *Hermes*. By this time these men had been unable to get aft to the life rafts because of thick smoke.

Alacrity tried again to come alongside on the starboard quarter but had to pull away due to the difference in heights of the weather decks, and two ladders were destroyed in the process. At 16.15 'abandon ship' commenced in darkness. A life raft case was seen to strike Petty Officer Mechanic Frank Foulkes as he climbed down the ship's side, and he was not to survive. At 16.20 captains North and Layard and the fleet chief petty officer left the bridge. The first lieutenant ordered all life raft static lines to be cut, with the assistance of a diver from *Alacrity*, and *Alacrity* fired Coston gun lines over the life rafts and pulled the rafts clear, thus saving them from very real danger in their position close to *Atlantic Conveyor*. Six life rafts were pulled alongside *Alacrity* and the frigate went astern, with the rafts alongside, to clear *Atlantic Conveyor*'s area.

By 17.40 personnel from the six life rafts had been recovered to *Alacrity* using scrambling nets.

At 18.20 *Brilliant*'s sea boat was alongside a life raft and took two survivors aboard, before they were evacuated by a Sea King helicopter from *Invincible*. A Sea King from *Hermes* lifted a further five survivors from this life raft and recovered the body of Chief Petty Officer Edmund Flanagan from the sea. At 19.00 *Brilliant* recovered 24 survivors from the final life raft. Three men had died on the ship and nine more failed to survive after entering the water. A number of the latter were described as ageing and/or overweight and unfit.[37]

Captains Mike Layard and Ian North had jumped down the last 10 feet and splashed into the cold water, but North was floating too low in the water. Layard grabbed him by his life jacket, holding him up, but suction from the ship's movement in the swell dragged them both under the hull's overhang and they were forced under the water as the ship bore down on them. They resurfaced with Layard hanging on to North and getting a hand on a life raft. He shoved his fellow captain in the small of the back, straight at the raft, but the sea broke over them and North went under again. Layard dived after him but he was gone. Surfacing again, Layard grabbed another man who was in trouble and swam with him to the raft, where they were heaved aboard. Mike Layard passed out after that and it was several minutes before he could be revived. He sat with his head in his hands and wept for his friend Captain Ian North.[38]

Some control was established in two of the rafts. In one the ship's chief officer, John Brocklehurst, took charge of the internal affairs while Lieutenant Schwarz and Sergeant Barlow took charge of the outside and entrance to the raft. The latter two were seen assisting men aboard their raft for a considerable period of time. Some men in the life rafts became very stressed. A highly claustrophobic atmosphere developed with water swilling around in the bottom of the raft, an amorphous mass of people stacked just inside the entrance to the raft, more personnel being pulled into the raft and piled on top of others, and other personnel jumping around on the top of the raft's canopy. Chief Petty Officer Fowler came near to drowning in the water in the raft with people on top of him. But the only two men who failed to survive the raft trip, Leading Aircraft Mechanic Don Pryce and Laundryman Ng Por, were in dire straits, if not dead, on entry to the rafts.[39]

Getting out of the rafts was also exhausting for many who had to climb up the scrambling nets on ships' sides, often heavily weighed down by water within their survival suits. Those who suffered least were the men winched out of life rafts on helicopter strops or by swimmer davit into *Brilliant*.[40]

As the abandoned ship drifted, the bow section, which contained the kerosene and cluster bombs, was blown away by explosions late on 26 May or early on 27 May. On Thursday 27 May the burnt out midships and stern section of *Atlantic Conveyor* was taken in tow by the tug *Irishman* at 16.25 and headed east at 6 knots, but the tow parted after half an hour and the two men who had previously boarded the still smoking ship to connect the line, Able Seamen D. Betts and G. Bales, went across again to reconnect a line from *Irishman*. But the tow parted again in heavy fog at 23.50 and the ship sank. The fog had reduced visibility to less than the length of the tow line; *Irishman* turned back and swept through the area, but was able to find only three containers afloat at 50°40' south, 54°28' west. Both of the able seamen were awarded the British Empire Medal.[41] As well as tentage for 5,000 men, all the equipment to construct an airstrip for Harriers at the beachhead and many valuable stores, three Chinook and six Wessex helicopters went down with the ship. Without the Chinooks, most of the land forces would have to walk across East Falkland from San Carlos to Port Stanley. One Chinook and one Wessex were saved, the former having been airborne and the latter ashore at the time of the ship's loss.

Of the 12 men who died in the sinking of *Atlantic Conveyor*, six were from the Merchant Navy, three from the Royal Fleet Auxiliary and three from the Royal Navy. They were: Merchant Navy – Bosun (Petty Officer I) John Dobson, Mechanic (Petty Officer I) Frank Foulkes, Assistant Steward David Hawkins, Mechanic (Petty Officer II) James Hughes, Captain Ian H. North, and Mechanic

(Petty Officer II) Ernest Vickers; Royal Fleet Auxiliary – First Radio Officer Ronald Hoole, Laundryman Ng Por, and Laundryman Chan Chi Shing; Royal Navy – Chief Petty Officer Edmund Flanagan, Air Engineering Mechanic (R) Adrian Anslow and Leading Air Engineering Mechanic (L) Don Pryce.[42]

The use of an anti-gas respirator saved the life of Sergeant Hinchman, who was enveloped in smoke below deck. Five survivors reported that they were severely affected by smoke, and two others suffered from immersion hypothermia. Eleven men suffered cuts, bruises and burns, none of which were particularly serious.[43] The 133 uninjured survivors were taken back to Ascension in the chartered tankers *British Tay* and *British Tamar*. From Ascension they were flown home to RAF Brize Norton, where, on 7 June, they were greeted by their families, the news media and high-profile dignitaries including Cunard's chairman, Lord Matthews.

* * *

A board of inquiry was convened at Furse House, Queensgate Terrace, South Kensington, London, on 21 June 1982 with Commodore J. W. F. Briggs as president, plus Surgeon Commander J. W. Davies, Commander G. C. Mortimer, Commander P. D. Ambrose and Lieutenant Commander D. T. Grantham. Its report was sent to the commander-in-chief, fleet, on 21 July 1982.[44]

In the initial planning of *Atlantic Conveyor*'s operations, the report said, the prime task was seen as transporting Sea Harriers south as fast as possible, to compensate for an expected high loss rate of these aircraft during the conflict. When the expected high attrition rate did not materialize, it became clear, six days before sailing from Devonport for the South Atlantic, that the ship would be operating within the assault operations area, but no provision was made to fit any self-defence system or chaff launchers. At this time there was controversy in the Ministry of Defence over whether it would be legal to arm auxiliaries. However, chaff dispensers and probably close-range defensive weapons could have been fitted. It was said by the naval staff that fitting them might have delayed the departure date, though no assessment of this was made. Similarly, some damage control enhancements could have been made had this been considered.[45]

After the conflict Admiral Fieldhouse, the commander-in-chief, fleet, asserted that there had been time to fit self-defence weapons and chaff dispensers. He also said that no ship may, in the law of armed conflict, have simultaneously the status of a merchant ship and a warship. Thus, if a ship taken up from trade is assisting fighting forces or is in a convoy and protected by warships, in law that ship must be regarded as a warship, and she may then be armed for self-defence and for attacking the enemy.[46]

Rear Admiral Woodward had not regarded *Atlantic Conveyor* as a high-value unit after the Harrier disembarkation, despite the fact that it still had helicopters aboard including the very valuable Chinooks, which were needed for troop and equipment carrying in the forthcoming land operations. He saw her value as a 'helicopter delivery service platform', relieving the aircraft carriers of this task. If left to the carriers, it was said that this would have hampered and slowed down the combat air patrol and ground attack operations of the Harrier force. For this reason, the report said, *Atlantic Conveyor* was brought into the carrier battle group rather than staying in safer areas to the east until required to land her helicopters and stores. This was certainly a questionable decision, since helicopter deliveries were not being made within the carrier battle group on 25 May.

It seems that the real reason behind her positioning was that *Atlantic Conveyor* was being retained as a screening vessel for the carriers on that day. Rear Admiral Woodward, in command of the carrier battle group, had a problem immediately after the initial San Carlos landings on 21 May. Escorts were needed to protect the beachhead, to provide naval gunfire support on Port Stanley and other targets, and to protect the carrier battle group of auxiliaries and aircraft carriers to the east of the islands. On 25 May, only five escorts were available to protect the carrier battle group after other tasks had been allocated. The main airborne threat came from the west, and the loss of either aircraft carrier would have jeopardized the success of the whole Falklands operation. Woodward's plan, working from west to east, was to deploy the destroyer *Exeter* as a radar picket to the west of the whole group, with the frigates *Alacrity* and *Ambuscade* providing the next layer of defence, then the RFAs *Regent, Sir Percival* and *Sir Tristram* and the merchant ships *Atlantic Conveyor* and *Fort Toronto* screening the two carriers. The destroyer *Glamorgan* would provide close cover for both *Hermes* and *Invincible* whilst *Brilliant* would act as 'goalkeeper' (last resort defence) close to *Hermes*. The carrier battle group had to be positioned some 70–80 miles east of the Falklands in order to optimize Harrier missions, which put the ships within range of Exocet-armed Super Étendard jets.[47]

Visual and radar reports indicated that the missiles had initially been aimed at *Ambuscade*, but were deflected by the chaff fired from *Ambuscade* at 15.39 and had then homed in on *Atlantic Conveyor* (see Map 8). The wind was from 210° at 25 knots, and the chaff blooms drifted about 1½ miles to the north-east during the 3 to 3½ minutes that elapsed between firing them and the homing heads switching on in the Exocet missiles. When the homing heads switched on, they locked on to the chaff cloud and, not achieving impact, went into a wide search. In this mode, the head searches 18° either side of the centre line of the missile flight path out to 3½ miles. *Atlantic Conveyor* was unfortunately just inside this arc, and the nearest contact. The missiles acquired the ship's large radar echo and had approximately 2 miles to turn and steady on an interception course, which was within their capabilities.[48]

Captain Layard had, prior to the attack, considered that his best defence against Exocet was to turn the ship's stern directly towards the missile. The stern ramp had 1-inch-thick steel I-frames and 0.5-inch plating, and behind this (after a 3ft gap) was the stern door of 0.375-inch plating and more 1-inch-thick steel I-frames. It is not known whether the missiles would have penetrated such a barrier, or whether the stern ramp could have prevented major damage. As it was, the ship was executing a turn to port and at the time of impact was presenting her more vulnerable port quarter to the missile. The second signal, to turn to starboard to a 110° course, had not been received aboard *Atlantic Conveyor*, nor had the ship been advised of the main threat direction. Air Raid Warning Red had been received, but no threat direction was given.[49]

The turn to port that the ship was executing was presumably intended to present the stern to the supposed south-west threat. However, four minutes earlier *Ambuscade* had detected the threat from the north-west, so the signalled turn to 040° was inappropriate (something that the inquiry report failed to mention). The signal given shortly afterwards for a second turn, to 110°, was presumably ordered because it was realized that an error had been made. The new course would re-orientate the ships' sterns to the actual threat from the north-west (see lower diagram, Map 8). But *Atlantic Conveyor* continued to turn across the missiles' flight path, presenting the wrong aspect to the missiles, and their impact was made on the port quarter. This signalling blunder was not recognized by the board of inquiry, and put the ship in a much more vulnerable position than it might otherwise have been in. If the stern had been presented to the missiles, it is quite possible that major damage would have been avoided.

Lack of sufficient warning prevented any helicopter being launched from *Atlantic Conveyor* to lay chaff, although Wessex 5 helicopters that carried chaff were available on board. Overall, the report said, there was a need for better tactical communications when merchant ships were employed in company with warships in operational conditions.

During loading at Devonport, an explosives representative from RNAD Ernesettle had liaised with and advised the chief officer. The ship had been considered subject to Merchant Navy regulations governing the storage of explosives but no trained Royal Navy explosives officer was aboard. No information on the specific hazards presented by the various explosive stores was given to the ship. The board recommended that the commander-in-chief, fleet should co-ordinate all aspects of explosives information and magazine arrangements in ships taken up from trade, that they should be subject to Royal Navy explosives regulations, and that a trained explosives officer should be appointed to the ship's company, preferably as a dual appointment.[50]

The ship had no longitudinal or transverse bulkheads above the water line and the vast cavernous hold was sub-divided in the main only by light wooden vehicle decks. No fire curtains were fitted. Following the two missile hits, the lack of sub-division resulted in an inability to contain the fire and dense smoke.[51] When the ship was converted, the political situation was still one of 'talking' and active service was some way from declaration. It was by no means certain that ships like *Atlantic Conveyor* would be hazarded. As mentioned above, the commander-in-chief, fleet, in his submission to the board of inquiry questioned the legal objections to fitting self-defence weapons, and maintained that they could have been fitted.[52] Clearly, the addition of self-defence weapons and damage control enhancements would have been desirable, and their absence, as well as poor tactical communications, almost certainly contributed to the disaster.

There were errors of judgement, the board said, in not closing the ventilation flaps to cargo spaces immediately after the attack and failing to inject CO_2 early enough and in sufficient quantities, bearing in mind the hazardous nature of the cargo. However, given the design of the fixed firefighting system, it was considered highly unlikely that the rapid spread of fire caused by the two missiles impacting close to inflammable cargo could have been controlled.[53] The delay in operating the CO_2 system was because of the possibility that survivors were trapped below in the area of the missile entry, where a voice had been heard calling for help and the after fire party was attempting entry to determine the extent and exact location of the fire. When the CO_2 was released, the amount of gas introduced was far too little to have any effect at all. The discharge was of 57 cylinders of the gas, whereas it should have been of 336 cylinders. However, even if the correct amount had been released immediately after the impact, the CO_2 smothering would not have contained the spread of the intense fire to the wide range of combustible stores carried between decks. A later attempt to release greater quantities of CO_2 into the cargo areas was beaten back by a combination of dense smoke, intense heat and the difficulty experienced by the operator in gaining access through a manhole whilst wearing breathing apparatus.[54]

The board concluded that the loss of this valuable ship and her war cargo could mainly be attributed to the lack of airborne early warning, the shortage of suitable escorts and *Atlantic Conveyor*'s vulnerability in the absence of defensive armament. It was unfortunate that the order to turn directly down threat was not received by the ship, since a stern aspect might have resulted in controllable damage. Nevertheless, her loss was much to be preferred to serious damage to either of the aircraft carriers, and the board fully supported the stationing of merchant ships and RFAs up threat from the two carriers when necessarily within range of airborne Exocet attack.[55]

However, the report was less incisive on other steps which, if taken, would have greatly reduced the risk to the ship. Had the ship been fitted with chaff launchers, or been given sufficient warning of the immediate missile threat to allow a Wessex helicopter to be launched to deploy chaff, the loss might have been avoided. The risks to *Atlantic Conveyor* had been further increased by two other avoidable factors. The first was Woodward's decision to bring the ship forward early from the logistics area to the carrier battle group, rather than delaying by a few hours and giving her a direct transit to the amphibious area. This would have avoided lingering in daylight with the carrier battle group, where the threat of an attack on Argentina's national day was greatest. The second was the erroneous order given to the ship to turn too far to port, rather than presenting the ship's stern to the direction of the threat. This error was not acknowledged or analysed in the board's report. Yet had this error not been made, the ship might have been saved.

* * *

Afterwards, Captain Layard reflected that two things had left an indelible mark in his mind. 'Firstly, how brilliant the people were, in thought, strength of character and deed. Secondly, given willing hearts and when the need is imperative, there is no limit to what can be achieved. We astonished ourselves.'[56]

Captain Ian North was posthumously awarded the Distinguished Service Cross for gallantry and his enormous contribution to the campaign. Third Engineer Brian Williams was awarded the Queen's Gallantry Medal for his two attempts to free the trapped and injured mechanic Ernie Vickers when the engine room was filling with smoke. He showed exceptional bravery and leadership and a total disregard for his own safety (see Appendix).[57]

There were Mentions in Despatches (Gallantry) for Chief Air Engineering Artificer Richard Bentley for his role in the damage control team, Chief Engineer Officer John Brocklehurst for his leading part in damage control operations and in supervising the release of life rafts, Lieutenant Commander R. E. Wilkinson for his work as aviation officer, and Chief Petty Officer Nicholas Martin for his work as flight deck officer. Petty Officer Boleslaw Czarnecki was awarded the Queen's Commendation for Brave Conduct in assisting Third Engineer Brian Williams in his attempts to free Ernest Vickers.

Captain Mike Layard was made a Companion of the British Empire, whilst Lieutenant R. S. Collins and Fleet Chief Petty Officer M. J. Legg were made Members of the British Empire. Legg had helped to organize the mixed ship's company into a cohesive team and displayed great strength of character during the abandonment of the ship.

* * *

When a ship is lost, it is usually the result of a combination of factors, although one of these might be the most critical. In the case of *Atlantic Conveyor*, the loss resulted from a poor tactical decision and an unfortunate operational error. The decision to use unarmed auxiliaries as a screen for the two aircraft carriers was perhaps reasonable, but the inclusion of *Atlantic Conveyor* was a tactical mistake. She was carrying four Chinook and seven Wessex helicopters that were vital for the land assault on Stanley, and as such was a strategic asset that should not have been risked in the screen. Lacking many of the damage control features of a warship and unarmed, she was particularly vulnerable when targeted. When the threat from the Super Étendards was detected by the task group, an order was given instructing ships to turn onto what was a dangerous course, exposing their broadsides to the threat instead of their sterns. This critical mistake was quickly realized and a revised course was signalled, though not received in *Atlantic Conveyor* (which had also not received the threat direction), and it was too late for her to alter course again. Consequently, the Exocet missiles struck the side of the ship rather than the much stronger stern. Had the ship been fitted with chaff launchers or self-defence weapons, or been given enough warning of the immediate missile threat and its direction to launch a Wessex helicopter to deploy chaff, the missile hit might well have been avoided altogether.

8

The Loss of RFA *Sir Galahad*

In early June, as part of a build-up of troops in the southern flank of East Falkland, the landing ship *Sir Galahad* was tasked with taking soldiers of the Welsh Guards to Bluff Cove, an assignment that was to be plagued by poor communications, delays and questionable decisions, and to end fatefully with the largest British loss of life in a single incident during the Falklands conflict, and life-changing injuries for many. The burning *Sir Galahad* and the rescue of its survivors probably became the most enduring images of the Falklands conflict for the many people in the UK who saw the television pictures beamed into their homes.

Sir Galahad was a landing ship (logistics), or LSL, built by Alexander Stephen & Sons Ltd, Linthouse, and completed on 17 December 1966 to the order of the Ministry of Transport on behalf of the Army. One of six LSLs of the Sir Lancelot class, she was originally commercially managed by British India Line, and painted with a white hull and upperworks with a blue band around the hull and a buff-coloured funnel: this was the troopship livery of the day. She was transferred to the Royal Fleet Auxiliary on 7 March 1970 and repainted grey, but continued to be tasked by the Army. She had a full load displacement of 5,674 tons and a gross register tonnage of 4,400. Powered by two Mirrlees ten-cylinder diesels producing 9,400bhp, she had a top speed of 17 knots. Her crew consisted of 18 officers and 50 ratings, and she had accommodation for 340 soldiers (43 officers and warrant officers and 297 other ranks), and could carry 340 tons of stores and vehicles as well as two Mexeflote powered lighters. She had a flight deck aft for helicopters and, with bow and stern ramps, could deliver a full load of vehicles onto a beach. Like the others of her class, *Sir Galahad* had circular mountings on either bow for guns, and for the Falklands operation they were to be fitted with one 40mm Bofors gun on each side, though *Sir Galahad* only received one.[1]

Friday 2 April, when the order to send a task force south was given, found *Sir Galahad* on passage to Devonport following the major amphibious exercise in Norway. Arriving at Devonport the next day, the cargo was quickly offloaded and the weekend was spent hurriedly loading stores, vehicles, rigid raider boats, weapons, ammunition, and three Gazelle helicopters of 3 Commando Brigade Air Squadron, together with some 350 Royal Marines and crews of the Gazelles, ten Royal Corps of Transport soldiers to act as stevedores, and three Royal Navy signalmen. With the marines lining the ship's side, the three Gazelles ranged on the flight deck, and battle ensign flying, the ship sailed in company with *Sir Geraint* at 15.00 on Monday 6 April, and they met up in the Channel with their sister ships *Sir Lancelot* and *Sir Percival*, which had sailed from the military port of Marchwood near Southampton, and the frigates *Alacrity* and *Antelope*, which had also sailed from Devonport, to begin the long voyage south. *Antelope* was to escort the LSLs nearly as far as South Georgia. Another LSL, *Sir Tristram*, was in Belize and would catch up during the voyage south, whilst the sixth LSL, *Sir Bedivere*, was at Vancouver and would return to Marchwood to load before sailing for the Falklands on 27 April. All of the LSLs were manned by British officers and mainly Chinese ratings from Hong Kong.[2]

The LSLs reached Ascension on 19 April, where *Sir Galahad* spent ten days frantically cross-decking* Royal Marines and cargo. By then it had been decided which LSL would be doing what at the landings, which meant considerable reshuffling of the cargo

---

* Transferring men, supplies and equipment between ships.

which had been hurriedly loaded at Plymouth. The ship was fitted with a Bofors gun, and received six general purpose machine guns (GPMG) and a Blowpipe missile launcher, together with crews to fire them. Sandbags were also received, which were filled and placed on the upper bridge deck as protection for the GPMG crews.

The ship sailed from Ascension loaded with War Maintenance Reserve (emergency kit held in store by the Ministry of Defence) and a mixed array of vehicles, plus the Commando Logistic Regiment, HQ and Signals, and elements of the Field Dressing Station (for the initial treatment of casualties). During the cross-decking operation, the usually reliable Hong Kong Chinese crews in the LSLs apparently became uneasy about the role they might be called upon to play and a certain amount of unrest appears to have developed. A senior RFA officer was sent out from the UK to assess the situation, but by the time he arrived, the men had settled down to normal working, and the LSLs sailed from Ascension on 1 May.[3]

The LSLs had not been designed to carry so many troops for such a long period, and there were few facilities for relieving the boredom and making life easier in the cramped dormitories. There was very little upper deck space for physical training because of the amount of deck cargo embarked, and the flight deck was taken up by the three helicopters. However, Captain Phil Roberts, master of *Sir Galahad*, remarked, 'I have to admire the spirit of the Royal Marines. They remained unremittingly cheerful throughout the journey south. I received very few moans or complaints from them; they were all desperately keen to get down there and get on with the job.'[4]

As part of the amphibious task group, once they reached the Falklands latitudes the LSLs were held well away to the east of the total exclusion zone in the logistics area until a decision was made to run in to Falkland Sound and San Carlos Water on 20 May to start the amphibious landing operations. The group of five LSLs plus the requisitioned North Sea ferry *Europic Ferry* was carrying vast amounts of stores, provisions and munitions as well as various supporting units – the Commando Logistics Regiment, the 18

105mm guns of 29th Commando Regiment Royal Artillery, the Royal Engineers of 59 Independent Commando Squadron, the light helicopters of the 3 Commando Brigade Air Squadron and 656 Squadron Army Air Corps, 16 Field Ambulance Royal Army Medical Corps and the Rapier missile troops of T Battery, 12 Defence Regiment Royal Artillery – that would back up the first assault wave of troops from the assault ships *Fearless* and *Intrepid*, and the second wave of troops from the transports *Canberra*, *Norland* and RFA *Stromness*. Escorted by the frigates *Broadsword* and *Argonaut*, they would begin to pass through the narrow entrance to Falkland Sound four hours after the second wave. Thus, at 01.30 (Falklands Standard Time) on 21 May, the LSLs and *Europic Ferry* entered Falkland Sound under Fanning Head and, after loitering under the West Falkland cliffs, started to arrive off Ajax Bay in San Carlos Water at 03.00 to begin disembarking their troops and supplies.[5]

The Gazelles had been tasked with recce duties in support of 2 Para that day. One of them returned to *Sir Galahad* with the very sad news that the other two Gazelles had been shot down, with both pilots and a crewman killed.[6]

At 05.45 on 24 May, whilst still off Ajax Bay, *Sir Galahad* was attacked by A-4 Skyhawks of the Argentine Air Force's 4th Air Brigade and was hit by a 1,000lb bomb dropped by Lieutenant Luis Alberto "Tucu" Cervera's Skyhawk: the bomb did not detonate, but started fires. *Sir Lancelot* and the newly arrived *Sir Bedivere* were also hit 20 minutes later and, whilst still fighting a fire forward under her vehicle deck, *Sir Galahad* was strafed by Dagger fighter bombers, as was *Fearless*, whilst *Sir Lancelot* was hit by another bomb. The Chinese hands were evacuated by lifeboat to *Fearless*, and *Sir Galahad* was beached to extinguish the fire, the officers and remaining crew members being assisted by teams from other ships. The search also started on board for the unexploded bomb, which was found at 10.50, rolling around in the battery store among broken batteries and spilt acid. It had entered the hull on the port side, punched its way through several compartments, picking up an aluminium bulkhead on the way, and ended up in the battery charging room wrapped in torn steel and surrounded by smashed carboys of acid. After the bomb had been defused by Lieutenant N. A. Bruen, the commanding officer of Fleet Diving Clearance Team 3, *Sir Galahad* was re-floated in mid-afternoon. The bomb was removed and lowered over the side during the night and the ship was patched up to make her seaworthy to return to the logistics and loitering area to the east on 30 May, after ten days in San Carlos Water.[7]

Lieutenant Bruen was to be awarded the Distinguished Service Cross for his bravery in defusing the bomb. Chief Engineer Charles Adams, of *Sir Galahad*, received the Queen's Gallantry Medal for advising and assisting in the removal of the unexploded bomb; on the following day he went aboard *Sir Lancelot* to render similar services. Mentions in Despatches were awarded to Leading Seaman (Diver) A. S. Thompson, of Fleet Diving Clearance Team 3, for courage during removal of the bomb and to Driver Mark Brough, Royal Corps of Transport, who operated the crane during this operation.[8]

By 30 May *Sir Galahad* was ready to sail from San Carlos to join the carrier group and get back the Chinese crew (who were by then embarked in *Sir Tristram*). The ship had only discharged about 110 tons of ammunition by this time, plus all the vehicles stowed on the upper deck. Captain Roberts later commented:

> The ship by this time was like the proverbial tip. We felt rather relieved to sail out of San Carlos that evening and hopefully restore order if not some decent food, and above all get out of the firing line for a day or two. On 31 May our Chinese crew were returned by helicopter in atrocious weather conditions. They, surprisingly, were all very pleased to be back and straight away set-to to clean up the ship and within an hour had provided us all with a hot meal.[9]

Sir Galahad next carried out a supply run with back-loaded stores and ammunition from San Carlos Water to Teal Inlet, on the north coast of East Falkland, sailing at 21.00 on 2 June with *Sir Bedivere*, escorted by the frigates *Minerva* and *Yarmouth*, and making her entry through the Salvador Narrows in daylight on 4 June. Thankfully conditions were favourable, the low cloud and mist making air attacks unlikely, and unloading went on undisturbed, albeit slowly, throughout the daylight hours of 4 and 5 June, before the ship sailed for San Carlos at about midnight on 5/6 June, escorted by the frigate *Arrow*.[10]

By the beginning of June, 3 Commando operations were progressing well on the northern flank, with commandos established on Mounts Kent and Challenger. There were many pressures to move fast to capture Port Stanley: limited naval support due to losses and damage, and fatigue of aircrew; exposure and fatigue of troops in the mountains in atrocious weather; the political need for an early end to hostilities; and the onset of the southern winter. The commander of land forces decided to commit 5 Brigade, who had just landed in San Carlos, to operations in the south of the island to increase pressure on the Argentines and provide flexibility between axes of advance. An opportunity to accelerate came when part of 2 Para seized Fitzroy (some 25 miles west of Port Stanley) after being landed by the single Chinook helicopter, for which they had been given temporary tactical control. This decision, taken by Brigadier Tony Wilson, was considered by Commodore Mike Clapp, commander of the amphibious task group (COMAW*), to have been precipitate: neither he nor Major General Jeremy Moore, commander of land forces, knew anything of this move. It left a weak, unsupported battalion with no guns and no defence against attack by land, sea or air. It would be necessary to correct this unbalanced situation with some form of naval expedition to land men from ships, or to march them overland, supported by landing craft carrying their kit, weapons and ammunition.[11]

Mike Clapp was later to comment:

> What I did not appreciate, to begin with, was the lack of understanding of joint operations by the army brigade nor the near non-existent communications that were to dog that brigade... That they were to fight and not garrison in one of the most complicated of military roles in a sub-Antarctic winter must have been a disagreeable surprise to the army staff.[12]

* Commodore amphibious warfare.

Other elements of 2 Para and 1/7 Gurkhas were ferried forward by helicopter and the Falklands motor vessel *Monsunen* to help meet the need for support at Fitzroy to maintain let alone develop operations. However, the build-up in the south would also entail a bigger move of men and stores to Fitzroy and nearby Bluff Cove, and carried a risk of the fighting troops outstripping logistic resources. There were not enough helicopters because of those lost in *Atlantic Conveyor* and tasks in the north. Marching the troops was barely feasible, with no helicopters or snocats/tractors for cross country support and to lift their heavier fighting equipment, and anyway would be far too slow. Shipping men and stores was the only option if the southern operation was to proceed quickly. This had to be executed without over-riding risk, bearing in mind the unacceptability of losing either of the large assault ships (landing platform, docks or LPDs), *Fearless* and *Intrepid*, fully loaded at this stage, and the risks from land-based Exocet or air attack. The commanders of land forces, amphibious warfare and 5 Brigade all assumed that disembarkation from the ships would be at Fitzroy, with the troops then marching to Bluff Cove, the infantry assembly area, provided that their heavy equipment was transferred by sea.

Critical requirements were to move the Scots and Welsh Guards, the Field Ambulance, a Rapier missile squadron and large quantities of ammunition. Admiral Fieldhouse signalled Commodore Mike Clapp saying that no LPD was to be risked out of San Carlos in daylight – the loss of such a ship would be a political disaster. The plan involved *Intrepid* going as far as she could on the night of 5/6 June, bearing in mind the risk to her and her escorts if she was still in the area at daylight, and then despatching the Scots Guards to Bluff Cove on a long trip by the small landing craft utility that she carried, whilst *Intrepid* returned to San Carlos before daylight without her LCUs, thus avoiding the delay in waiting for them to return, to minimize the possibility of *Intrepid* being at sea during daylight.[13]

The Welsh Guards would follow the next night, to rendezvous with the LCUs and despatch them to Bluff Cove. The LSL *Sir Tristram* had been successfully used at Teal Inlet to the north and would be used to carry the weight of logistic needs, including Rapier missile systems and their ammunition, which would be set up at Bluff Cove. The plan was a modified version of an earlier plan which had entailed both the Scots Guards and some of the Welsh Guards being sent in *Intrepid*, in accordance with which the Welsh Guards had begun embarking in the LPD on 5 June. Amongst some confusion the Welsh Guards were eventually offloaded, and *Intrepid* sailed from San Carlos at 17.00 with the frigate *Penelope* as an escort and at 22.30 inserted four LCUs off Lively Island with the Scots Guards embarked.

The Argentines had already detected night amphibious helicopter operations in the Fitzroy/Bluff Cove area through radio signals. Suffering severely from exposure during the 50-mile trip by LCU, the Scots Guards came under fire from the mainland, and an aircraft flew close to them in the entrance to Choiseul Sound. They were also illuminated by starshell from the destroyer *Cardiff*, whose presence in the area was unknown to anyone directly involved in the operation: a horrendous 'blue-on-blue' attack by the friendly destroyer was only narrowly avoided. The LCUs completed their difficult and dangerous journey to Bluff Cove at 05.30. Surprisingly, Captain Peter Dingemans, in command of *Intrepid*, appears not to have given Major Ewen Southby-Tailyour, Royal Marines, the senior officer in the LCUs, a launch position from which he could start navigation: this necessitated a detour to get a firm position from the nearest point of land before heading to Bluff Cove without large-scale charts or depth sounder. Mike Clapp had expected *Intrepid* to drop the LCUs not more than about four hours' steaming away from Bluff Cove; in the event their journey had taken seven hours.[14]

Intrepid returned to San Carlos before daylight without her LCUs. The Scots Guards reached Bluff Cove at 05.30 on 6 June. The men had been cold and wet for four hours, and on arrival several were suffering from exhaustion and one had a damaged knee and had to be evacuated back to San Carlos. The men were not fit to fight when they disembarked, and their general state was such that the assembly area at Bluff Cove was altered so that houses in Bluff Cove Settlement could be used as a temporary hospital.[15]

On 6 June Captain Robin Green, the master of *Sir Tristram*, was briefed on the modified plan and after some confusion was clear that he was to proceed to Fitzroy. He was concerned about his lack of air defence and during the course of the day made arrangements with the destroyer *Exeter*, the air defence ship for the transport area, to receive air raid warnings via LAAWC (local anti-air warfare commander) radio, and he sailed at 19.00 for an uneventful passage. Unfortunately, the Rapier systems had not been loaded into the ship because low cloud had prevented them being lifted down from the mountains by helicopter. *Sir Tristram* had also been ordered to lift the Army's 16 Field Ambulance, but they were said to be disorganized ashore and failed to get there; nevertheless, *Sir Tristram* was well laden.[16] Meanwhile *Fearless* sailed from San Carlos with the 1st Battalion Welsh Guards embarked and steamed to a point that was considerably further inshore than *Intrepid* had achieved, apparently because she was achieving significantly faster speeds, and would still return under cover of darkness. *Intrepid*'s four LCUs were still supposed to be in the Bluff Cove area, but three of them had been 'hijacked' in Major Southby-Tailyour's absence by a Parachute Regiment major and sent to Fitzroy with 2 Para, whilst the other LCU was sheltering elsewhere because the weather was bad.[17]

Fearless waited at the rendezvous point whilst her escorts, the frigates *Penelope* and *Avenger*, went forward in a failed attempt to find the LCUs. Consequently, only half the Welsh Guards were sent ashore from the vicinity of Elephant Island, in *Fearless*' two LCUs under the command of Major Tony Todd, Royal Corps of Transport, and landed at Bluff Cove. This was despite Mike Clapp having agreed that they were only to be taken as far as Fitzroy, Major Todd having been briefed by Major Guy Yeoman (also of the Royal Corps of Transport) that his destination was Bluff Cove because Yeoman had not been informed of the new destination and had not had time to double check it.[18] *Fearless* made best speed for San Carlos, arriving there shortly after daybreak on 7 June, leaving her LCUs behind.

Sir Tristram had made the difficult navigational passage into Fitzroy under a bright moon and anchored there by daybreak on

7 June. She began unloading ammunition with *Intrepid*'s four and, later, *Fearless*' two LCUs and a 66ft Mexeflote pontoon.* However, *Intrepid*'s LCUs were recalled to San Carlos because of urgent tasks there unloading shipping, and were re-embarked in *Intrepid* on the following night (7/8 June) before sailing back to San Carlos. It had not been thought feasible for *Intrepid* to take the Welsh Guards with her on that night instead of just recovering the LCUs. This would have required a long delay in loading the LCUs whilst at sea and possibly prevented her from returning to San Carlos before daybreak. Also, the LCUs were badly needed for unloading shipping at San Carlos and another delay of 24 hours was unacceptable. Finally, 12th Field Ambulance and the Rapier battery, which was now released to provide air cover in Fitzroy, needed transportation, adding to the number of LCU trips which would be required. *Intrepid* was also concerned that a pattern had developed from which the enemy could recognize the amphibious build-up in the Fitzroy area. The task inshore at Fitzroy would involve risk in daylight hours, but it was preferred to risk an LSL and not such an important warship as an LPD like *Intrepid*.[19]

Given these considerations, it was decided by Commodore Clapp that *Sir Galahad* would take the rest of the Welsh Guards (352 men plus kit) to Bluff Cove, and 16 Field Ambulance (30 men plus kit and stores), G Company SAS (30 men) and four Rapier units to Fitzroy, at the request of General Moore, overnight on 7/8 June with offloading during daylight on 8 June. Clapp was not aware then that the first half of the Welsh Guards had been taken to Bluff Cove, not Fitzroy. In the morning of 7 June, at 09.18, Commodore Clapp signalled to Brigadier Wilson (5 Brigade) and *Sir Tristram* his intention to move a Rapier troop and the balance of the Welsh Guards to Bluff Cove. Later, in the afternoon, at 12.48, he signalled *Sir Galahad* to sail for Fitzroy, but did not repeat this to Wilson or *Sir Tristram*.[20]

---

* A powered raft with two diesel engines, used to move goods and vehicles between ship and shore when a pier is not available.

The risks of having two LSLs in the area were recognized, especially the lack of air defence. The possibility of sending a surface escort was considered and rejected because it was thought it would draw extra attention with little extra safety. The weather forecast predicted limited visibility and the risk was considered acceptable in view of the urgency. However, Admiral Woodward was said to be unaware that two LSLs would be together in this restricted water until late on 7 June or early 8 June, though he did speak of *Sir Tristram* being 'left to her own salvation'. Major Yeoman, Royal Corps of Transport, briefed *Sir Galahad*'s master, Captain Phil Roberts, on the assignment, saying that the plan was to sail from San Carlos at 17.00 on 7 May (after embarking the troops) and arrive at Bluff Cove at 03.00 on 8 May to offload the Welsh Guards and their kit. At 05.00 the ship would sail for Fitzroy, arriving there at 06.30 to offload 16 Field Ambulance and their kit and stores.[21]

Major Yeoman was advised by Captain Roberts that the ship's troop-carrying capacity had been reduced to 320 men after being hit by an unexploded bomb in the port troops' dormitories on 24 May, and was shown the damaged dormitory and the blocked escape route on the port forward side of the troops' alleyway. Major Yeoman then instructed Captain Roberts, in the presence of his chief officer, R. C. Ward, to place the Field Ambulance and SAS men in available troops' dormitories on the starboard side and accommodate the Welsh Guards in the tank deck. Details of the navigation plan were discussed and, in the view of the captain, entry into both Bluff Cove and Fitzroy at night presented very tricky navigational passages. The subject of air cover and air raid warnings was raised, and Major Yeoman assured Captain Roberts that combat air patrol cover would be provided and that HMS *Exeter* would provide air raid warnings in the normal manner. He further assured him that at no time would *Sir Galahad* be in 155mm artillery range from Port Stanley and that the risk in going to Bluff Cove was no higher than going to Teal Inlet, the ship's previous discharge point.[22]

Hearing of the master's concern about the blocked escape route from the port dormitories and the large number of troops being carried, Second Engineer Officer P. A. Henry immediately volunteered to go himself with the help of a Chinese fitter to physically cut out the buckled steelwork by hacksaw, no mean task. This was completed by 17.00 and the ship's carpenter erected temporary wooden steps, thus restoring the escape route from the port dormitories, allowing them to be used.[23]

Communications were established with *Exeter*, informing them that *Sir Galahad* would be in the Bluff Cove/Fitzroy areas on 8 June and that the ship would maintain constant watch on LAAWC radio. At about 13.00 the last of the Welsh Guards were embarked, as were the forward elements of 16 Field Ambulance. On talking to the latter, the chief officer discovered that their numbers would be 90, not the 30 indicated by Major Yeoman. Soon afterwards the chief officer was informed by Major Yeoman that the Air Defence Team (Rapier Batteries) consisting of 90 men and their equipment would also be joining shortly. He was told that this equipment would be loaded by a Sea King helicopter, which would remain with the ship for the passage round, with her aircrew and maintainers totalling about 12 men, to assist with off-loading. The Air Defence Team with five Rapier batteries and ancillary equipment arrived at 14.00 and were loaded onto the vehicle deck. The chief officer informed Captain Roberts that they would sail with approximately 595 embarked men, and the captain signalled Mike Clapp, COMAW, for permission to sail with this amount of men, given that existing lifesaving appliances would cover that number, which was approved.[24] As well as accommodation problems, these extra men put a great strain on the catering staff and other ship-board resources.[25]

The ship's gunnery instructor, Chief Petty Officer R. A. De La Haye, was tasked with briefing the embarked troops on safety, lifeboat stations, life jackets, etc, and was also responsible for allocating accommodation. The chief officer also spoke to Major G. Sayle, Welsh Guards, the officer commanding troops, and his senior NCOs, and pointed out the various exits and escape routes from the tank deck and told them where life jackets were stowed and where the life rafts were. By 19.59, when the last troops were embarked, it was considered that all troops had been fully briefed on safety and emergency matters. However, the Field Ambulance stores (on a Mexeflote) did not arrive until 19.45 and would take two hours to offload. Captain Roberts had been told by COMAW staff that his latest sailing time was 19.59, and he therefore decided not to sail until the following night. At 20.15 *Sir Galahad* signalled to Clapp, Moore and Wilson and the other task group and unit commanders (but not *Sir Tristram*) that the estimated time of completion of loading was 22.00, and that he would remain in San Carlos overnight, but at 21.30 he received a signal from COMAW instructing him to sail at 22.00 and proceed at best speed for Fitzroy settlement (which could still be reached by dawn). This signal was drafted and released by Commodore Clapp's duty staff officer, who had roused the staff officer operations to clear it with him. It was copied to General Moore and Admiral Woodward, but not to Brigadier Wilson or *Sir Tristram*, thereby missing an opportunity to keep these parties informed. Commodore Clapp himself did not see the signals until the next morning.[26]

Loading in San Carlos Water was completed at 21.45. There was considerable confusion over whether her destination was to be Fitzroy or Bluff Cove, but finally the former was confirmed and *Sir Galahad* sailed at 22.00 hours via Falkland Sound and Eagle Passage, her navigation track and estimated time of arrival being given to 'all concerned'. As the ship approached Fitzroy, the gun crews were closed up at action stations, and would remain so all day. The passage was made in total radar and radio silence so as not to alert the Argentines of the ship's movements. At 06.50 on 8 May *Sir Galahad* passed through the narrow dog-leg passage, 400ft wide, into Port Pleasant. The wind was gusting 25 knots on the starboard beam, but a full moon gave assistance in an extremely difficult navigational passage, the island on the port beam having an elevation of only 3 feet, and use was made of the radar on a short pulse and the bow thruster. The port anchor was let go at 07.15 on 8 June and the ship anchored some seven cables south-east of Fitzroy settlement and three cables east of *Sir Tristram*.[27]

Her arrival was unexpected for the troops offloading shipments onto the beach, partly because of a failure to receive the first signal from COMAW and the fact that they were not copied into the later signal from COMAW. So there was no co-ordinated plan for unloading both *Sir Galahad* and *Sir Tristram*, and considerable confusion in the use of assets for offloading onto the beach. The only good beach was unsuitable for beaching LSLs and was only usable for part of the day due to tides. Only one LCU and the Mexeflote were available for transhipment of men and stores to the beach (the other LCU having been sent to Darwin for stores), but they were already part-loaded with ammunition from *Sir Tristram*, and there was also a shortage of mechanical handling equipment on the beach.[28]

Unloading of the Rapier missile systems by the Sea King helicopter began at 07.40 and was completed by 10.00. By 11.00 two units were fully operational, whilst two other systems had defects. The Welsh Guards were mustered on the tank deck ready to disembark, but Major Sayle declined to land because they were expecting to move on to Bluff Cove and had been instructed not to be separated from their first-line supplies and kit. They had also been told, wrongly, that the bridge from Fitzroy to Bluff Cove was impassable, leaving them with a long march which would have reduced their capacity for immediate operations; in fact, the bridge had been blown up by the fleeing Argentines, but was now passable on foot following repairs by the Paras. Discussions became heated, but plans were made to land the Field Ambulance by Mexeflote and take the Welsh Guards to Bluff Cove by LCU in two trips. But first the LCU and Mexeflote had to unload their ammunition on the beach, and delays to this occurred due to beach problems.[29]

When the LCU returned at 10.45 Lieutenant Colonel Roberts, the commanding officer of the Field Ambulance and the senior ranking officer present, insisted that his advance party should go ashore in the LCU before it was committed to the long double trip to Bluff Cove. Accordingly, three Land Rovers and four trailers, plus some of the Field Ambulance team, were taken to Fitzroy settlement, and the LCU returned to *Sir Galahad* at 12.10. However, the LCU's bow ramp developed a hydraulic pump fault, making a stern discharge from *Sir Galahad* into it impossible, and a new plan was made to load the Welsh Guards' equipment into the LCU via the after ramp hatch. The LCU was secured to the port side and the hatch opened, whilst the ammunition was moved from the after end of the tank deck to No 2 hatch for discharge. The first load of bergens (packs) had been lifted by crane into the LCU, and men of Prince of Wales Company, 1st Battalion Welsh Guards were starting to board from the port shade deck. At 13.15 the second lift was about to commence when the air attack occurred.[30]

The enemy had learnt of activity in the Fitzroy/Bluff Cove area by detecting helicopter operations and from radio intercepts. At the time of the attack *Sir Tristram* still had some 102 tons of ammunition aboard in the tank deck, some of which had been streamed into the after trunk ready for loading into the next craft to arrive. There were also 200 jerricans of kerosene and 200 of diesel fuel stowed on the tank deck.[31]

The earlier mist and low cloud had cleared late morning; it was a bright sunny afternoon with two-eighths cloud cover and excellent visibility. In *Sir Tristram* the ship's defence teams were at defence stations on Blowpipe, machine guns and one of the Bofors guns, and were scanning the sky over the port side of the ship. Having heard that attacking aircraft had just approached San Carlos from the south, they presumed that the aircraft might also attack Fitzroy from the south, but in fact the four Skyhawks approached from the east. It is thought that they overflew Bluff Cove, rounded North East Point and flew due west along Port Pleasant at about 500ft above sea level. They were hidden from view from the ships by the high tussock grass of Pleasant Island (see Map 9). Sweeping round the eastern tip of Pleasant Island they dropped to an altitude of about 100ft, the leader being slightly higher. They flew in line ahead at an estimated 400 knots.

As the first aircraft approached *Sir Galahad*'s beam, it began to bank to port and released four 500lb bombs while banking

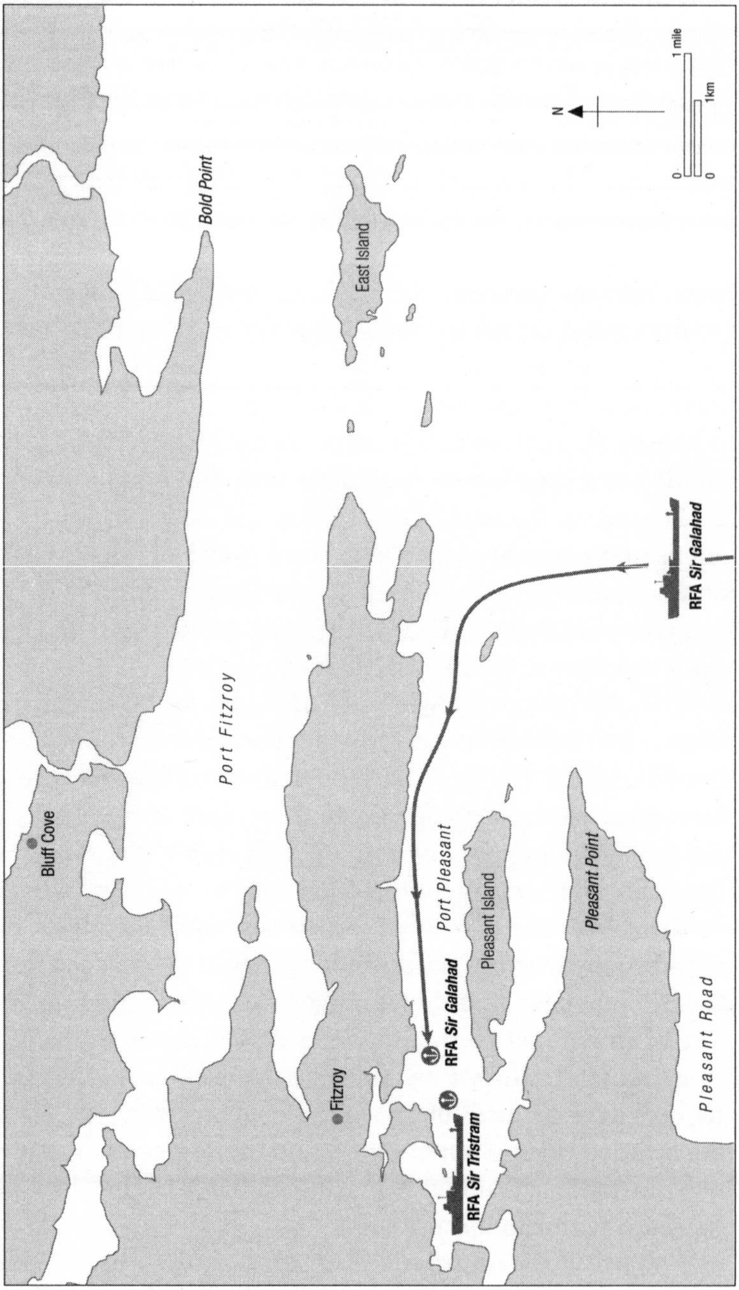

Map 9: Positions during the Skyhawk attack on RFA *Sir Galahad* and RFA *Sir Tristram*, 2 June

over the bridge superstructure of the ship. The leader continued to bank, passed over the flight deck of *Sir Tristram* and then climbed away towards the south. Because the aircraft was banking when it released its bombs, they tended to diverge. Two landed in the water between the ships, off *Sir Tristram's* starboard bow. Two passed over the forecastle of *Sir Tristram* and hit the water off her port bow. One of these ricocheted off the water and exploded on the land of Pleasant Point. The three bombs that landed in the water failed to explode.

The second aircraft followed about 200 metres behind the leader, and the third was about 100 metres behind it. These aircraft did not bank until they had overflown both ships. They approached the starboard beam of *Sir Galahad* in level flight at about 100ft altitude and released their bombs simultaneously, the second aircraft while passing over *Sir Galahad* amidships. The four bombs from this aircraft remained in a tight cluster and travelled towards the stern of *Sir Tristram* as the aircraft followed the flight path of the leader and climbed away to the south. Two of the bombs penetrated the starboard quarter of *Sir Tristram*, one passing through the tank deck, partly detonating in No 25 port ballast tank and killing the bosun, Yu Sik Chee, and crewman Yeung Shui Kam; the other passed through No 25 starboard ballast tank into the sea without exploding. Another bomb exploded beneath the transom, holing the ship and compounding the damage, whilst the fourth fell into the water off the starboard quarter.[32]

The third aircraft released a clutch of four bombs little more than 100 metres from the starboard beam of *Sir Galahad*. Three of these bombs entered the aft accommodation areas on the starboard side of the ship at poop and upper deck level. One transited the ship and made an exit on the port side of the poop deck in the region of the stewards' mess. The other two failed to explode, but big fires and thick black smoke developed immediately. The fate of the fourth bomb is unknown. The fourth and last aircraft attacked the ships with cannon fire only. It flew lower than the first three and trailed them by about 300 metres, strafing the flight deck of *Sir Tristram* and the starboard quarter of *Sir Galahad* with cannon fire. The aircraft climbed and banked to starboard after flying over the flight deck of *Sir Tristram* and followed the third aircraft to the south.[33]

Meanwhile, there was an air attack on ships at San Carlos, and the Sea Harriers in combat air patrol had been despatched to meet it. A warning of a second air raid was sent but was not received in *Sir Galahad*, probably due to listening on the wrong frequency. The warning was received in *Sir Tristram*, but the officer of the watch assumed it was for San Carlos only and took no action. His belief that an air attack going on 35 miles away could have no bearing on his own ship's safety was, in the opinion of the board of inquiry, extremely naïve. However, the radio operator told the Blowpipe missile launcher NCO (who happened to be on the bridge), who immediately alerted the air defence teams, but almost immediately afterwards the attack took place. Both ships were surprised by the direction and speed of the attack, neither Bofors gun nor Blowpipe was fired and machine guns claimed no hits. On shore, three Rapier units had systems defects (which was not entirely unexpected so soon after the move) and the fourth was masked by terrain. The Rapier unit assigned to protect the anchorage was one of the defective ones.[34]

In *Sir Tristram*, the captain immediately launched two lifeboats to help *Sir Galahad*, using two key deck officers. The absence of these two officers contributed to the inadequate reporting of the damage control position within *Sir Tristram*. There was dense acrid smoke in the tank deck of *Sir Tristram*, and reports were made of fire and an exploded bomb in the steering compartment, which was inaccessible through damage. Palletized ammunition immediately above the fire (100 tons of ammunition were still on board) and danger from 400 gallons of kerosene and diesel fuel added to the risks. Two men were dead, and the Chinese crew were said to be apathetic and bewildered. No significant firefighting was attempted and at about 13.50 hours the captain ordered abandon ship, which was done in an orderly fashion. 'We apparently had an unexploded bomb in the steering flat, which was on fire with the entrance blocked off by debris and the stern trunking above getting very warm, full of ammunition and cased diesel,' said Captain Green. 'I subsequently decided to abandon ship and leave it to the bomb disposal people to come and sort out the bomb.' On the next day the fire was still burning but controllable, and *Sir Tristram* was boarded to consider disembarkation of ammunition and stores.[35]

In *Sir Galahad* the approach of the fast, very low-flying aircraft was seen from the bridge by the officer of the watch, Second Officer R. H. Stanbrook, who immediately made the pipe 'Action Stations!' on the main broadcast at the same time that the captain entered the chartroom. They took cover behind the chart table, together with Major Tony Todd of COMAW staff, who had embarked during the afternoon. The ship shuddered with the impact of bombs, and seconds later a second aircraft flew low over the ship and again the vessel shook as bombs struck it. All ventilation was crash stopped, while fire alarm bells were ringing furiously on the bridge. Smoke immediately began to appear through the chartroom door, which had been blown open by the bomb, and the captain rushed to the bridge wing to assess the damage. The ship had not heard an air raid warning and was taken completely by surprise.

Black smoke was billowing from both sides of the ship and from the engine fan rooms, and there were fires on two or more deck levels. Flames were shooting forward out of No 2 ramp hatch, ammunition began exploding, and objects were flying in the air. The captain could get no reply from the engine room on the telephone and assumed that it had been hit. It was apparent to him that fires were out of control in many places in the after accommodation and in the tank deck, and that the ship could not be saved. Captain Roberts gave orders to abandon ship at about 13.20, later commenting, 'A well-ordered, happy and disciplined ship one moment and a burning inferno the next.' About this time he also noticed that *Sir Tristram* had been hit, and smoke was coming from her stern door and poop deck.[36]

In *Sir Galahad* the chief officer, second officer, and several others began launching life rafts from the flight deck: these were immediately filling up with Chinese crew, most of whom had been in the port side mess rooms and their only avenue of escape had been via the poop deck aft, from where they jumped into the water or climbed down ropes, most of them being in a shocked and distressed state. On the captain's instructions, Second Officer P. J. Snelson lowered No 4 lifeboat and began getting as many people into it as he could, in order to launch it as soon as possible before the whole of the after section of the ship burst into flames. Soon the lifeboat had to be lowered because it was being enveloped in smoke. Making his way forward, the captain opened a fire hydrant on the vehicle deck, but there was no pressure; he attempted to look down No 2 hatch but could only see flames and smoke. Several badly wounded men were being led forward from the entrance to the troops' cafeteria.

Chief Petty Officer De La Haye had by this time launched several life rafts on the starboard side and the life raft ladders were being lowered over the side. With a similar situation on the port side, the evacuation of troops to the life rafts was under way. There were many badly wounded, some with limbs blown off, others with very bad burns to face, hands and legs; others were shaking uncontrollably with fear. The captain helped get one casualty away in a Wessex helicopter just forward of No 2 hatch, but the pilot was not too keen to remain near the hatch, which by now was erupting with explosions and shrapnel. Captain Roberts asked some medical orderlies from 16 Field Ambulance to move all of the wounded from the forward hatch to the forecastle head where Sea King helicopters were already hovering over the bulwarks; he also took his survival suit off and helped a casualty into it. Royal Marines Sergeant D'Olivera was already evacuating the badly wounded by helicopter strops. 'It was very fortuitous that our foremast had been lowered in order to increase our arc of fire. This enabled the helicopters to hover four or five feet above the deck, so speeding up the evacuation of the very badly burned Welsh Guards,' said Captain Roberts. No 4 lifeboat had now been launched and Wessex helicopters were picking men out of the water aft. Soldiers were continuing to make their way down the port and starboard ladders to the life rafts, others were jumping from the port shade deck onto an upturned raft that had been placed on the Mexeflote, but all this was being done in an orderly fashion without panic.[37]

By this time, two lifeboats from *Sir Tristram* had been launched and joined in the rescue of survivors from *Sir Galahad* and in towing the life rafts clear of the ship's side. By about 13.50 all the soldiers and other personnel who were not seriously injured had been evacuated from the ship and the life rafts had been set adrift. Chief Petty Officer De La Haye, together with some of his naval ratings, checked that all dormitories, the shade deck and the accessible part of the tank deck had been fully evacuated. They then disembarked in the last life raft. The whole of the bridge front was on fire, and smoke and flames were billowing high in the air, whilst loud explosions, flames and shrapnel were erupting from No 2 hatch. All the remaining casualties were on the forecastle deck together with the chief engineer officer, Sergeant D'Olivera, Captain Roberts and several medical orderlies who were working with great patience and skill, providing first aid to the wounded, and where needed, drips had been put up and morphine administered.[38]

'They were in terrible pain, the smell of burning flesh was awful,' Captain Roberts later recalled. Among them was Simon Weston (a 20-year-old Welsh Guardsman), who became known for his public battle to recover from horrific burns. Captain Roberts added, 'I remember Simon particularly because he was huddled against the bulwarks of the ship groaning in agony. I tapped him gently on the head and said, "All right Taff, a helicopter'll be with you shortly", and his hair just fell out, which was horrifying.'[39]

Simon Weston, who sustained 46 per cent burns, was later to recall his experience as the giant fireball flashed through the tank deck, killing 22 men from his own platoon of 30 and leaving another seven badly burned, with only one man escaping unhurt:

A red alert went. We hit the deck and I saw this great orange and red streak. Trouble was, I watched, and didn't protect my face. Three lads next to me were in flames. I didn't feel a thing, just a rush of hot air in my throat. It took me about 15 seconds to get out, I moved so fast. A marine sergeant pushed me up the stairs and I kept on going till I got out. I saw a lot of bodies on fire, burning all over. I was put into a landing craft. Medics gave me some jabs. I was in a bad way. They cut the clothes off me, it didn't hurt much. You see, I was burned so bad that my nerve endings had gone, so I didn't feel it, though my legs, which weren't so bad, were a bit sore. When I got to the medical post I began to go into shock. I was seeing bodies all around me. There were a lot anyway. Some people were having tracheostomies on the spot. It was all operating tables and bodies and I started to panic. They knocked me out pretty quick as I was shouting and frightening the others.[40]

The ITN reporter Michael Nicholson was watching from the shore and saw hundreds of men rush forward along the decks pulling on their life jackets and orange survival suits. Many who were trapped on the wrong side of the ship jumped overboard as the flames spread. He saw men swim underwater away from the ship to avoid the burning oil and watched other men, who were safely forward of the flames, risk their lives to jump into the water with life jackets to save those men swimming below. The strong winds fanned the flames – enormous flames – and as the fuel tanks exploded the ship was half enveloped in thick black smoke. The casualties and survivors, many suffering from shock and burns, were picked up from the beach by soldiers who had run from their trenches to help. Dozens of soldiers waded out into the freezing water, some up to their chest, to pull men to safety.[41]

The evacuation of the badly wounded from the ship was a slow and painful operation, but Sergeant D'Olivera was carrying out this distressing work with great initiative and patience. The pilots of the Sea Kings showed great courage and determination in carrying out the evacuation, hovering as close to the deck as possible despite the loud explosions and debris that was being blown into the air. By 14.15 all the wounded and the medical orderlies had been evacuated by Sea King. Sergeant D'Olivera and the chief engineer were then winched up, followed by the captain, who was the last to leave the stricken ship. They were taken to Fitzroy settlement where a temporary dressing station had been set up for the injured, whilst the more seriously wounded were evacuated to the field dressing station at Ajax Bay, Port San Carlos. The purser, J. S. Hood, undertook a check of all ship's company survivors: he found that Second Engineer Officer Paul Henry, Third Engineer Officer Christopher Hailwood and Third Engineer Officer Andrew Morris were missing presumed dead. Some of the seriously injured Chinese crew had been taken to Ajax Bay and it was not possible to complete a check of the Chinese complement at this stage. The ship's air defence team, Royal Corps of Transport detachment, Bofors and Blowpipe crews and Royal Navy signallers were all accounted for.[42]

At about 14.30 the *Sir Galahad* survivors ashore were joined by the officers and crew of *Sir Tristram*, who had also abandoned ship. At 14.45 the ships were again attacked by Argentinian aircraft and all those ashore had to take cover. In the meantime, all the wounded were being evacuated by helicopter to *Fearless*, *Intrepid* and *Atlantic Causeway*. Conditions ashore at Fitzroy were pitiful. All pathways and tracks were a sea of mud. The medical post lacked any sort of facility and the medical teams were only able to administer elementary first aid. A lot of the cooks and stewards had been very badly burned, so much so that Captain Roberts had difficulty recognizing some of them. He gave assistance and reassured a lot of them, many of whom were shaking with shock, before they were eventually evacuated to Ajax Bay.

Some 150 wounded men arrived at the Ajax Bay field hospital, which was overwhelmed by the numbers. Realizing that he could not cope with them all, Surgeon Commander Rick Jolly, in command of the hospital, arranged for half of them – the less seriously burned – to be transferred by helicopters (which he unofficially requisitioned) to *Fearless*, *Intrepid* and *Atlantic Causeway*, each of which took about 25 men. After initial treatment, all the casualties were taken to the hospital ship *Uganda*.[43] The last of the *Sir Galahad* survivors, including the captain, left Fitzroy by Sea King at about 18.00 and were taken to *Intrepid*, where they were made most welcome and given every assistance.

* * *

Sir Galahad had been hit by three 500lb high explosive bombs on the starboard side aft, and was struck by a short burst of 30mm cannon fire in the area of the engineers' office and possibly the troops' cafeteria. No bombs exploded, but there were two fireballs/ fire-fronts. One was probably from a bomb that entered at upper poop deck level, passing downwards through the galley extension into the port engine room, smashing a 500-gallon header tank of diesel fuel that sprayed finely and ignited, causing burn casualties near the galley fire aft and dense black smoke. The butcher, Sung Yuk Fai, was killed instantly, and several other crew members in the galley were wounded; in the engine room and machinery control room Third Engineer Officer Andrew Morris, Second Engineer Officer Paul Henry, Third Engineer Officer Christopher Hailwood and electrical fitter Leung Chau were killed. The other fire-front was probably from a bomb, or possibly two, entering down No 2 ramp hatch and deflagrating (splitting open and burning of the explosive uncompressed). This created a fireball in the stern trunk, and 23 out of 35 in the Welsh Guards mortar platoon assembled there were killed. It flashed forward into the tank deck where the rest of the Welsh Guards were assembling, which is where the other casualties, mostly burns, mainly occurred.

A number of other small fires started as a result of these fierce blazes. Almost instantly the after accommodation at all levels had filled with black, acrid smoke, making it impossible for fire parties to muster at their allotted stations. The citadel, such as it was in an LSL with wooden entrance doors and aluminium superstructure, was breached in many places. The explosions caused havoc with the formica-faced asbestos-filled panelling that formed the majority of the internal divisions within the accommodation, and the majority collapsed like a pack of cards, some splitting and spilling asbestos dust and debris everywhere, others collapsing and

blocking alleyways, fire and repair posts, the engine room crash
stop ventilation panel and the engine room CO_2 smothering lever.
Light fittings, deckhead panels and other overhead fittings fell
down. Two breathing apparatus sets in the port forward dormitory
had been destroyed on 24 May when an unexploded bomb had
entered it. All other breathing apparatus sets were stowed inside
the aft accommodation, and they could not be retrieved because
of the smoke hazard, and therefore the search for personnel who
might be trapped in accommodation could not be thorough. It
was fortunate that only eight days earlier extra life rafts had been
fitted on the flight deck. Although they were difficult to launch
over the flight deck nets, they were invaluable to the majority of
the Chinese crew, who were trapped on the poop deck. There were
gallant attempts to get men out of the tank deck, where there
was dense smoke and fires. Abandoning the ship was orderly and
disciplined, and often heroic, evacuating 300 men in 30 minutes
using a lifeboat from *Sir Galahad* and life rafts, *Sir Tristram*'s boats,
the LCU alongside, the Mexeflote, four helicopters and a civilian
boat from Fitzroy.[44]

On the following day, Captain Roberts and Captain Robin Green
of *Sir Tristram* visited Commodore Mike Clapp in *Fearless* to discuss
their experience, and he expressed his deepest sorrow over the loss of
life and the injuries that had been sustained. All the survivors who
were not injured, except No 42 (Royal Marine) Commando (who
made up *Sir Galahad*'s air defence team and might be needed ashore
for the push on Port Stanley), were transferred to *Atlantic Causeway*
at 12.00 hours and she sailed for the total exclusion zone at 17.00.
Thence the survivors were transferred to the merchant tanker *British
Test* and taken to Ascension Island for repatriation by air to the UK,
where they received a warm but very sober welcome at Brize Norton.
Whilst on board *Atlantic Causeway*, a final list of dead and wounded
among the *Sir Galahad* ship's company was arrived at. In addition to
the known loss of the three officers, the fate of electrical fitter Leung
Chau and butcher Sung Yuk Fai was unknown and was recorded as
missing presumed dead.[45] The numbers of casualties amongst the
embarked troops were collated by the military authorities ashore,

bringing the total figures up to 48 men dead, with another 135 treated ashore for injuries, none of whom died.[46]

* * *

A board of inquiry into the loss of *Sir Galahad* and the abandonment of *Sir Tristram* was convened in Room 1325 at Express State Building, Ministry of Defence, Lillie Road, London, and its report was presented to the commander-in-chief, fleet, on 23 September 1982.[47]

The board investigated the factors influencing the decision to send troops by ship to the southern flank. The initial thrust of the land battle had been by 3 Commando on the northern flank. Whilst this had been successful, the appalling weather conditions were limiting the commandos' endurance and had hindered the supply by helicopter of food and ammunition to them in the mountains. These troops were heavily outnumbered by the Argentinian troops and needed to be augmented by the troops of 5 Brigade. Using the latter for an attack against Stanley on a southern flank would increase the pressure on the enemy and would also provide an option to swing the main thrust between two axes. The need for speed in the taking of Stanley was recognized because of the limitations on sustaining a force at sea and maintaining adequate air cover, and the climate could only be tolerated for a limited time.

From the earliest, it was envisaged that logistic support of the forward troops would be via helicopter, LCU or LSL and that this would be based on the Fitzroy/Bluff Cove area for the southern flank. This would be necessary to supply the troops not only with food and survival stores but also the heavy load of ammunition. The troops could be inserted at Fitzroy/Bluff Cove by marching, helicopters or shipping, or a combination of the three. 5 Brigade were confident that the advance could be made on foot from San Carlos, with some helicopter support to ferry equipment and ammunition forward. This was attempted and found to be too slow if not impossible. An early attempt by the Welsh Guards to march towards Darwin was thwarted by a lack of training, and an absence of either ground or air assets to assist in the moving of equipment. General Moore was concerned that an advance on foot would be too slow and would not leave troops ready for fighting in their optimal condition. An airlift of troops was impossible because of the loss of helicopters in *Atlantic Conveyor*, the remaining available helicopters being mostly committed to supplying 3 Commando in the mountains. The LSL supply route to Teal Inlet had been successful and had not been attacked by the enemy. Thus, shipping provided the only solution for the move to Fitzroy.[48]

With the rapid advances of 3 Commando in the north and 2 Para under 5 Brigade in the south, the need for troops and supplies in the Fitzroy area was paramount. The weather was causing survival problems for 3 Commando, with trench foot claiming 20 victims each day, whilst the troops were using stamina and ammunition just to maintain their position. Fitzroy and Bluff Cove had been taken without battle and there was an urgent requirement to take advantage of the advance and to reinforce troops and prepare for the next advance. Logistic support was needed even to maintain the position, and a field ambulance station was needed before any further direct battle could be considered. Any delay in establishing this support would hinder the advance on Port Stanley, with reflected adverse effects on the fighting efficiency of 3 Commando in the mountains. For all these reasons, the board concluded that the plan was justified.[49]

The board noted that an earlier plan to use an assault ship (LPD) to directly insert the troops in LCU and LCVP (landing craft vehicle and personnel) off Bluff Cove at first light was a good one, given that surprise, lowering cloud, and boldness were present, and would not give sufficient time for the Argentines to react with an air attack from the mainland. This plan was dropped on the instructions of Admiral Fieldhouse, who stated that politically a catastrophe at sea with large loss of life was unacceptable and that, in his view, some delay was acceptable. The plan to insert the LCUs from a stand-off distance was therefore the only practical alternative. The political and military pressures mounted rapidly in the period 3–7 June leading to much 'hot planning' and crisis management, with modification to plans becoming faster and more complex as time went by. All of these gave rise to the decision to send *Sir Galahad* and for her to be in Fitzroy on the same day as *Sir Tristram*. Rear Admiral Woodward's statement concerning *Sir Tristram* being 'left to her salvation' had been read in the LSLs, although not addressed to them, and did not engender a feeling of confidence or safety in the two ships.[50]

The inquiry identified a number of shortcomings in command and control that affected the Fitzroy/Bluff Cove operation. There was a blurring of responsibilities between Commodore Clapp and Rear Admiral Woodward, following a change on 1 June which re-designated the amphibious operating area as the transport area, with Clapp planning and conducting the amphibious support operations to Teal and Fitzroy in waters that until that time had been the exclusive preserve of Woodward. When the two LSLs were sent to Fitzroy they were under the control of Clapp (as they had been throughout the conflict), whilst the naval gunfire support units operating in the same area came under Woodward, and Clapp was not too sure where his responsibilities lay. Such a situation could lead to a 'blue-on-blue' encounter, as nearly occurred on the night of 5/6 June when *Intrepid*'s LCUs were on passage from Lively Island to Bluff Cove and then encountered *Cardiff*; both sides were unaware of the presence of the other, and the LCUs were illuminated by starshell.[51] No termination signal was issued at the end of the San Carlos assault phase, nor were any further instructions given by Admiral Fieldhouse or his staff: this resulted in the loose organization of command once the transport area was established.

Responsibility for the operational control of LCUs at Fitzroy was unclear, with the commander of the advanced element of 5 Brigade at Fitzroy apparently receiving no instruction that it was his responsibility. Brigadier Wilson was not entirely clear in his own mind about who was controlling the LCUs at Fitzroy and was relieved of tactical control of them after the events of 8 June which included the loss of one of *Fearless*' LCUs in Choiseul Sound.

The communications notifying those at Fitzroy of *Sir Galahad*'s imminent arrival were inadequate. This was a significant deficiency by COMAW staff, for it led to a failure to plan for her arrival and could have contributed to the delays in disembarking the Welsh Guards. The officer responsible for the deficiency was considered to be the staff officer for operations, Commander George Pearson. He had failed to grasp the significance of what the duty staff officer was telling him and should have instructed the duty staff officer to inform Commodore Clapp of the change of plan.[52]

Consideration of the air defence arrangements by the inquiry was comprehensive, given public concern over the loss of life through the air raid. The provision of a surface escort for the ships in Fitzroy had been considered but rejected because it was felt that additional attention would be drawn to their presence with little benefit to their safety. The navigational situation meant that, because of her draught, the closest a frigate could get was 8 nautical miles, and this defence would only have been of value if the attack developed in the direction of the frigate to the LSLs. It was felt that the very presence of this frigate (or Type 22/42 combination) would undoubtedly have provoked earlier enemy attention.

The absence of shore-based Rapier missile units at Fitzroy was felt to have been unavoidable: the four units available for loading in *Sir Galahad* on 7 June had been the first that could be made available. They had been almost immediately unloaded from the LSL on arrival at Fitzroy, but their reliability during the first 24 hours of their deployment had been poor, which was a cause for concern. With no air raid warning, three defective Rapier units and the remaining one masked by terrain, no shots were achieved. The Rapier units had no orders to protect shipping, showing a lack of co-ordination between staffs, though because of the system failures this may not have been a significant factor. Units of the shore-based Blowpipe team were not able to cope with the fast crossing targets at the close range of detection that occurred.

The standard combat air patrol had been on station to the south-east of the Fitzroy/Bluff Cove area when a raid developed on *Plymouth* in San Carlos. The aircraft were despatched to this raid before the raid on the LSLs had been sighted. A report (from a submarine operating off the Argentinian coast to provide early warning of air attack) concerning six aircraft leaving Argentina was received in *Exeter* at 12.47 with an estimated time of arrival of 12.50, but no destination could be derived from this report. The force anti-air warfare commander in *Invincible* apparently did not receive this report and consequently no strengthening of combat air patrols was attempted, though the board felt it was doubtful if much could have been achieved in the little time available. In this context, it is worth noting that Mike Clapp had been surprised to learn from Sandy Woodward just before the critical Fitzroy operation that he was withdrawing *Hermes* further to the east for a routine boiler clean, since Woodward must have appreciated how badly close air support and combat air patrols would be needed over the next few days if the cloud-base lifted.[53] As for Sandy Woodward, he was later to comment that he had feared the Fitzroy operation was trouble and should have stopped it, whatever the reactions of Mike Clapp and Jeremy Moore might have been.[54]

The air raid warning was heard in *Sir Tristram* on the LAAWC circuit but the officer of the watch expected to be called by their designated call sign, and therefore disregarded the warning as being irrelevant to the Fitzroy area. The board considered that it was extremely naïve of him to believe that an air attack going on only 35 miles away could have no bearing on his own ship's safety.[55] The naval rating monitoring this circuit persuaded the officer of the watch to inform the ship's Blowpipe team; minimal action took place in this ship apart from this weapon team. In *Sir Galahad*, although a specific call sign was not expected, there was evidence to suggest that an incorrect frequency was being monitored. The defence team in this LSL were taken by complete surprise. No Blowpipe was fired, and although general purpose machine guns were fired it was done in great haste and no hits were claimed. In *Sir Tristram* the attempt to fire Blowpipe was aborted because of the speed and level of the attack, and no machine gun crews claimed a hit. The misunderstanding over anti-air radio procedures in *Sir Tristram* contributed to the aircraft having a totally unopposed approach and effective delivery. A prompt response could have also warned *Sir Galahad*. However, the board recognized that no indication of the direction had been given and the aircraft approached from the east at very low level, thereby surprising even vigilant gun crews, but the failure of the officer of the watch to respond to an air raid warning may have contributed in a small way to the success of the enemy's attack. Surprisingly, the board felt that the decisions taken regarding the provision of Rapier missile units, frigate escort and combat air patrol had all been reasonable.[56]

The board found that exercises and drills in *Sir Tristram* had produced satisfactory results, but was critical of aspects of the ship's management. A much better standard of confidence and ability in the whole ship would have accrued if all departments had been briefed in regular top management meetings, where standards could also be monitored and mutual problems resolved. Fire damage to the ship could have been avoided had elementary damage control and fire procedures been followed. The captain became almost mesmerized by the sight of *Sir Galahad* burning and as a result his ability to react and influence decisions concerning the safety of his own ship were impaired. A better damage control organization for RFAs should be laid down and exercised during sea training at Portland. The board recommended better training in management leadership for RFA captains and heads of departments, and that captains should attend a tactical course at the Maritime Tactical School, HMS *Dryad*.[57]

The inquiry found that there was confusion over the destination of *Sir Galahad* and the differentiation between 'the Bluff Cove area', Bluff Cove and Fitzroy. The two sites are only 3½ miles apart by land, but for ships involve a sea passage of some 9 miles round a peninsula. Commodore Clapp always intended that Fitzroy should be the point of disembarkation. All the signals originating from Clapp's staff referred to Fitzroy, but those from General Moore's staff always referred to Bluff Cove. Moore was only concerned that the Welsh Guards should assemble in Bluff Cove. The point of disembarkation was not of particular interest as it was known that the bridge from Fitzroy to Bluff Cove was passable for foot soldiers. However, the Welsh Guards believed at all times that the disembarkation point would be Bluff Cove. Major Yeoman had briefed Captain Roberts that he would first disembark the Welsh Guards at Bluff Cove before proceeding to Fitzroy to disembark the other units. However, Commodore Clapp's later signal to Roberts, at 21.30 on 7 June, instructed him to proceed to Fitzroy, which he did. If the Welsh Guards had been made aware that they would be taken to Fitzroy at an earlier stage than 07.30 on 8 June, measures could have been taken to modify their instructions, and consequently (it was claimed) the Guardsmen could have landed within half an hour of arrival at Fitzroy. That this looseness of nomenclature crept in, and the significance of this was not apparent to staff officers and those in relevant command positions, was a contributory factor to the Welsh Guards being on board *Sir Galahad* at the time of the attack.[58]

In the opinion of the board, the decision by Major Sayle, officer commanding the Welsh Guards, not to proceed with a cross country march to Bluff Cove was reasonable. He was not aware that Fitzroy bridge was passable to infantrymen. His last orders were to land at Bluff Cove and to allow no separation of his men or equipment. He believed his route from Fitzroy would entail a 15-mile march, and that the landing craft would return relatively quickly.[59]

Commenting on COMAW's staff, the inquiry found there was a lack of amphibious training prior to officers taking up their appointments. The staff officer operations, Commander Pearson, had only just joined the staff at short notice on 5 April. He had been due to join *Fearless* as the executive officer. For either job he needed previous training in amphibious warfare, but had none (except classroom instruction on a course) and did not do the amphibious warfare planning course (AWPC) before joining. He tried to catch up on his knowledge during the passage south. During the conflict he became extremely tired and prone to 'nodding off for a second or two'. Commander-in-Chief Fleet Admiral Fieldhouse, commenting on the board of inquiry report, agreed that his actions, and finally inaction, were attributable to stress and fatigue: he was very new in post, with little, if any, experience of amphibious operations and only the scantiest of training to prepare him for the task; in the end, he could not cope with the pressures that were imposed by the situation.[60] Commodore Clapp (COMAW) had also not completed the AWPC, but had been in post for ten months, and had witnessed one, and commanded two, amphibious training exercises during that period.[61]

When the task force deployed to the Falklands, the officers appointed to Clapp's staff at short notice, increasing the numbers from five to nearly 20, had only a limited knowledge of amphibious operations for the most part. Two staff warfare officers who joined were air defence specialists but were also used for general warfare duties. One, Lieutenant Commander Mike Goodman, was said to be excellent, but the other was apparently barely satisfactory and he eventually left to join *Invincible*. For the LSL tasking and liaison, Clapp was fortunate to be able to keep the experienced Major Guy Yeoman as well as Major Tony Todd, who had joined as Yeoman's relief. Both were from the Royal Corps of Transport, but Clapp felt that a third RCT officer to work a proper watchkeeping system would have relieved the strain and fatigue on Yeoman and Todd. COMAW's staff undoubtedly became fatigued even by the time of the San Carlos landings, with some individuals suffering more than others. There was no evidence of major errors of judgement or ill-considered decisions occurring as a result, but performance did deteriorate generally, and some officers had to take on an extra burden to relieve their colleagues. Reduced mental activity in processing the data constantly arising from a fast-moving situation did become particularly apparent when newly arrived officers impressed with their relative speed and clarity of thought. In general the board believed that the staff did a first class job under very difficult and fast moving conditions, though they did not always get it right and, being very busy in their own particular tasks, did not liaise and cross-fertilize ideas or plans to the extent that might have been desirable.[62]

The inquiry found that the decision to abandon *Sir Galahad* at an early stage after the attack was a correct one. However, the decision to abandon *Sir Tristram* completely soon after the attack was unwarranted, and errors of judgement were involved.[63] Commodore Clapp disagreed with this finding, since the captain believed, on the advice of his chief officer, there was at least one unexploded bomb still on board. The ship, Clapp said, still had 120 tons of ammunition aboard, her position was known to the enemy, she had no communications, working machinery or firefighting capability and the officers' accommodation had been burnt out, indeed melted. In his view, the captain was absolutely right to abandon her until he could get proper teams on board. Mike Clapp heard that on his return to the UK Captain Green was castigated for leaving her, something that Clapp felt was grossly unfair and an example of how extraordinary some misconceptions and attitudes were back at home.[64]

However, with regard to the firefighting capability, a report on the damage sustained by *Sir Tristram* found that the fire main was available from the ship's plant to spaces forward of the bridge front, and firefighting equipment and hoses were intact and unused in their normal stowage positions.[65] The ammunition aboard was said by the inquiry to be needed for the vital final push on Port Stanley.[66] The Director General Stores and Transport (Navy), head of the organization that included the Royal Fleet Auxiliary, agreed that the total abandonment of the ship turned out to be unwarranted. However, he pointed out that as well as the belief that there was an unexploded bomb aboard, 'the Hong Kong Chinese were known to be incapable of fighting a fire' (they were said to have experienced a collapse of morale), and firefighting would therefore have to have been undertaken by officers only. He also pointed out that the master's training and experience were to place the saving of life as paramount.[67]

Admiral Fieldhouse was to comment that the master, as well as his chief officer and chief engineer, were all mentally stunned by events and took decisions that were out of character. Regarding the use of aluminium in superstructures, the board considered this was 'entirely acceptable', but Fieldhouse thought this was based on the premise that the substitution of aluminium in the existing LSL design would have severe operational penalties. He said that the use of aluminium to reduce topweight in warships, and hence increase payload, was an undesirable compromise that should be discouraged even at the penalty of increasing hull dimensions and total displacement.[68]

The board considered that Commodore Clapp was correct in making a timely and positive decision, in support of Major General Moore's request, to send *Sir Galahad* to Fitzroy. The consequences of delay could have led to an equal number of, or even more, casualties than occurred in the LSLs at Fitzroy, due to later enemy action and weather. This decision was one that had a considerable risk attached to it but was weighed carefully on the morning of 7 June, after the unsuccessful injection of all of the Welsh Guards battalion on the night before, and when the Rapier and Field Ambulance units became available to move forward: both were of prime importance to future operations. The level of need presented by Major General Moore justified the degree of risk involved. Having taken the decision, events turned against its successful attainment due to a number of factors, each of which on its own might not have caused a disaster; however, acting in concert they played their part in the eventual outcome. One of these factors was the change in weather that allowed the enemy to positively identify events at Fitzroy from an observation post on the morning of 8 June. This supported their previous intelligence derived from the insecure VHF circuits used by the British in the control of logistics, and led to an air strike being specifically tasked against the two LSLs. In planning the activities at Fitzroy, weather had not been considered a governing factor, although the presence of observation posts was strongly suspected.[69]

The time taken to offload *Sir Galahad* had affected the number of casualties. This delay was due to the limited assets available to offload and the state of the tide at the time of arrival. The limitation of the beach, which could only be used for 16 hours of any 24-hour period, was not communicated by the officer commanding the amphibious beach unit to anyone outside the Fitzroy area: commanders at the planning level were unaware of this limitation. If 5 Brigade Advanced HQ had known that *Sir Galahad* was to arrive on 8 June, they may well have reconsidered their decision to send one of *Fearless'* LCUs to Goose Green and kept her to assist in the offloading of both ships. Poor communications from Fitzroy to General Moore and Commodore Clapp prevented an adequate flow of information. The offloading was confused through the number of people involved in the decision making, but no negligence or slackness in its execution was apparent to the board.[70]

The vice-chief of naval staff commented that the underlying factor leading to this incident was the low priority that had been given to amphibious and joint warfare following the adoption of a defence policy which specifically excluded the need to cater for this type of operation, leading to a lack of resources to cover training and the development of expertise among most of the staff concerned.[71] Before the Falklands campaign it was considered unlikely that the UK would ever mount an opposed amphibious operation, and amphibious forces and training had been run down accordingly. So-called amphibious landings were actually administrative landings (i.e. into a non-hostile host country such as Norway), and NATO amphibious exercises were pre-planned and rehearsed in fine detail. 'Hot' planning, coping with fast-changing events, had fallen into disuse.[72] The dearth of expertise that resulted led both to a failure to fully appreciate the problems and risks of the operation at Bluff Cove, and to staff and communications failures in a fast-moving situation.[73]

The role of LSLs was also in the spotlight. They were originally commercially operated and manned by British India Line, and, unlike many RFAs, had retained many of their merchant ship characteristics. They had been almost totally dedicated to providing a secure line of communication and logistics to the British forces in Germany. Their precise task in a war situation had always been vague, and their relative priority in the prolonged period of tension of the Cold War even more unclear. Against this background it was scarcely surprising that the morale of the Chinese crew failed, or that the NBCD and medical organization of the ships were in some ways deficient. Mainly untrained and inexperienced in their new specialized employment in the Falklands, the gallantry of the officers in unprecedented circumstances was exceptional. The action of the captain of *Sir Tristram* in launching his lifeboats in an effort to save lives in *Sir Galahad* was entirely consistent with Merchant Navy training that safety of life at sea is paramount. For the future, it was essential to determine how LSLs should be protected and armed, and to define their true role in peace and war. Adequate tactical training, particularly in the amphibious role, should be provided for RFA staff, and LSLs should be manned by UK seamen as soon as possible.[74]

* * *

The gallantry displayed in the Fitzroy episode led to the award of five Military Medals to Army personnel. Sergeant Derrick Boultby of the Royal Corps of Transport, coxswain of the Mexeflote, had repeatedly returned to the area of the stricken ships to rescue survivors and, with complete disregard to his own safety, dived into the sea to rescue a Chinese crewman. Guardsman Stephen Chapman of the Welsh Guards ignored the danger of fire and exploding ammunition and the order to abandon ship, and rushed into a burning cabin to rescue a badly burned soldier. He returned time and again to the blazing interior of the ship to rescue his colleagues: his actions undoubtedly saved many lives. Lance Corporal Dale Loveridge of the Welsh Guards, with complete disregard to his own safety, and ignoring the order to abandon ship, repeatedly returned to the burning and smoke-filled areas of *Sir Galahad* to rescue his colleagues. Sergeant Peter Naya, Royal Army Medical Corps, despite injuries sustained from two explosions whilst standing in the ammunition-filled tank deck of *Sir Galahad*, continued to administer medical aid to many casualties, including several infusions to amputees. Well aware of the danger, he continued until evacuated as a casualty himself on the last helicopter. Warrant Officer Brian Neck, Welsh Guards, disregarded the order to abandon ship and immediately began to organize the evacuation of soldiers. He returned many times through smoke-filled areas, flames and continuing explosions to assist the hurt and injured.[75]

Amongst Navy and RFA personnel, Captain Phil Roberts of *Sir Galahad* was awarded the Distinguished Service Order for taking personal charge of the fighting and safety of the crew during repeated air attacks between 21 May and 8 June. Prior to the bombing of 8 June, he organized and controlled two abandonments of the vessel with considerable skill, despite the extreme danger, enabling many lives to be saved before her final loss. Second Engineer Paul Henry of *Sir Galahad* was posthumously awarded the George Medal: when the ship was bombed on 8 June, the engine room compartment quickly filled with smoke; Henry, stationed in the area, ordered Junior Engineer Officer N. Bagnall to take the only available breathing apparatus set and leave the engine room. He thus sacrificed his own life to save that of a subordinate.

The George Medal was also awarded to Chiu Yiu Nam, a Hong Kong crewman in *Sir Galahad*: realizing that soldiers were trapped inside the burning ship, Chiu donned a protective asbestos suit and fought his way time and again through smoke and flames into the bowels of the ship from where he led men to safety, only obeying the order to abandon ship when he was sure there was no one left alive. Of the Welsh guardsmen who survived, at least ten were said to owe their lives to the 'remarkably modest' Chiu. It was only later, after the commanding officer, 1st Battalion Welsh Guards, interviewed his guardsmen and heard about an unknown rescuer whose identity had been hidden behind a protective hood, that Chiu was identified and his extraordinary gallantry publicly and belatedly recognized.[76] His actions cast doubt on the slurs about the behaviour of the Chinese crew that were levelled in some official documents.

Two RFA personnel were awarded the Queen's Commendation for Brave Conduct: Second Officer Ian Povey rescued a badly injured soldier from a smoke-filled compartment and then displayed great presence of mind in supervising the lowering of injured men from the ship; Radio Operator David Sullivan of *Sir Galahad* risked his life on several occasions by guiding soldiers to the upper deck through smoke-filled compartments and then checked that nobody was left behind.

Third Officer Andrew Gudgeon, of *Sir Galahad*, was awarded the Queen's Gallantry Medal: he displayed great courage in an unsuccessful attempt to free a trapped man in a smoke-filled compartment; prior to this he also demonstrated a high level of bravery whilst he coxed a boat during the rescue of the crew of *Antelope*. Chief Engineer Officer Charles Adams also received the Queen's Gallantry Medal for his courage, determination and professionalism when giving valuable advice and assistance during the removal of the unexploded 1,000lb bomb from *Sir Galahad*. He spent a considerable time in the compartment where the bomb was lodged and made a significant contribution to the removal operation. At 02.00 on the following morning he volunteered to go to *Sir Lancelot* to advise on the removal route for an unexploded bomb, again working in close proximity to it.

Captain Robin Green of *Sir Tristram* received the Distinguished Service Cross, which must have alleviated any distress caused by his having been criticized for his actions. His ship came under repeated air attacks during the campaign; when she was bombed on 8 June, he showed great courage and set a fine example during the abandonment of the vessel. Colour Sergeant Michael Francis, Royal Marines, was awarded the Distinguished Service Medal: he brought his landing craft (LCU F1), which itself was narrowly missed by a bomb, alongside the blazing ship and rescued about 100 men, some badly injured. He returned to pick up others and to help life rafts to the shore; the award also recognized his actions during the rescue of the crew of *Antelope* (see Appendix).

Lieutenant Commander Hugh Clark, commanding officer of 825 Naval Air Squadron, was awarded the Distinguished Service Cross for his leadership and courage during the helicopter rescue on 8 June, and for his leadership of the squadron throughout the campaign. Lieutenants John Boughton and Philip Sheldon, 825 Squadron, were awarded the Queen's Gallantry Medal for their courage and great professionalism as helicopter captains during the rescue of men from the blazing ship, in an extremely dangerous situation. Mentions in Despatches were awarded to Lieutenant John Miller, 846 Naval Air Squadron, who hovered his Sea King helicopter above the blazing ship to rescue survivors, demonstrating great skill and courage; and Petty Officer Alan Ashdown, his crewman, who remained cool and calm whilst the helicopter collected survivors from the ship for over an hour, and operated the winch from an open position 100ft from exploding ammunition.[77]

* * *

On 21 June, the hulk of *Sir Galahad* was towed out to sea by the RMAS* tug *Typhoon* and sunk as a target by the submarine *Onyx*; it is now an official war grave. A replacement ship, with the same name, entered service in 1988.[78]

* * *

Sir Galahad was lost as a result of both tactical and operational errors. Despite the post-rationalizations of the board of inquiry, the decision to send the lightly armed *Sir Tristram* and *Sir Galahad* to Fitzroy virtually undefended, without escort or air cover, and without British command of the airspace, was a big mistake. Provision of dedicated combat air patrols to cover the operation was necessary, scarce though this resource was. If cover could not be provided, the operation was too risky and should have been vetoed (as Admiral Woodward, with hindsight, later acknowledged). The deployment to Fitzroy had not been well planned, having been forced upon the task group commanders because an advance party of 2 Para had seized Fitzroy without the knowledge of General Moore and needed back up. If the lost Chinooks had been available, they could have ferried troops there rather than using the landing ships. Communication failures bedevilled the operation, there having been five decision centres to co-ordinate: Admiral Fieldhouse at Northwood, Rear Admiral Woodward in *Hermes*, General Moore and Commodore Clapp in *Fearless*, 5 Brigade Headquarters at Darwin, and 2 Para and some elements of

---

* Royal Maritime Auxiliary Service.

5 Brigade Headquarters at Fitzroy and Bluff Cove.[79] These decision centres had to interact with the operational units, including two LSLs, the beach party, the LCUs, 16 Field Ambulance, the Rapier missile party, G Company SAS and the Welsh Guards. Resultant communication failures and misunderstandings contributed to the length of time it took to unload *Sir Galahad* at Fitzroy. Her planned arrival there was not signalled to the beach commander, so assets that would allow speedy unloading were not available. Other problems lengthened the delay before disembarkation of the Welsh Guards could begin: six hours after the ship had anchored at Fitzroy, they were still in the ship or the LCU alongside when the air attack began. The air raid warning was not heard in *Sir Galahad*, and in *Sir Tristram* it was largely disregarded, hence the LSLs were taken almost completely by surprise when the Skyhawks appeared. All these factors combined to result in the tragic loss of life and life-changing injuries sustained by the Welsh Guards and RFA ship's company.

9

Lessons from the Conflict

The Falklands campaign was the first since World War II in which modern weapon systems, employed by both sides in a conflict, were tested in combat. It saw the first use of modern cruise missiles against warships of a major navy; the first use of nuclear-powered submarines in combat; the first known use of vertical/short take-off and landing aircraft in combat; and was the first time since World War II that sustained air attacks were made against naval forces.[1]

As such, it attracted a lot of attention from military analysts and strategists. Given the scope of this book, the discussion of conclusions and lessons learned will not embrace all aspects of the wider campaign, on both sea and land, but will concentrate on those drawn from the analysis of the seven ship losses contained in the previous chapters.

The sudden emergency, following the invasion, was one that called for the rapid deployment of a seaborne task force to engage in an unexpected war. Since World War II the Royal Navy had suffered large reductions in size. In 1952 it had possessed 368 combatant warships of frigate/submarine size or larger;[*] by 1982 this number had been reduced to 94. The ships involved in the Falklands campaign represented some 40 per cent of the surface combatants of the Royal Navy, including virtually all

---

[*] At this time two cruisers and four frigates served on the South Atlantic station.

of its amphibious landing vessels. The main threat faced by the Navy had come from the Soviet Union, and the designs of ships and weapons supported the dominant strategy of working with NATO allies to oppose any Soviet threat, particularly in the North Atlantic. Thus, the Navy's anti-submarine role was uppermost in priorities, alongside the strategic nuclear deterrent in the shape of the Polaris submarines.

Further large cuts to the Navy's surface fleet were included in the 1981 Defence Review, with the withdrawal of the two assault ships, the ice patrol ship and four RFAs, the sale of the new carrier *Invincible*, and a reduction in the size of the destroyer and frigate force from 59 to 50. Fortunately, these cuts were only just beginning to be implemented when the Falklands crisis arose.

As the Navy had been reduced in size, it had been increasingly difficult to maintain a balanced fleet capable of fulfilling a variety of tasks and missions, although this had been the aim. Following the withdrawal of *Eagle* and *Ark Royal* in the seventies, the Navy lacked the large strike aircraft carriers needed to operate a multi-role mix of fixed-wing aircraft, which seriously impeded the task force in 1982, equipped as it was with only the two small aircraft carriers *Hermes* and *Invincible* carrying a very limited range of aircraft. Similarly, the amphibious force had been depleted by the withdrawal of the commando carriers *Albion* and *Bulwark*, a role partly and temporarily filled by *Hermes* until she was repurposed to carry Sea Harriers. The main amphibious capability remaining comprised the assault ships *Fearless* and *Intrepid*, backed up by six smaller landing ships that were intended for logistical support. It was not envisaged that the amphibious force would mount opposed landings; rather, its Cold War role would be to land troops in friendly Norway.

Because of the suddenness of the emergency, some of the ships and their ships' companies that were sent south, such as *Antelope*, had not been worked up to the required standard of combat readiness. Others, such as the landing ships (logistics), would find themselves in front-line roles that they had not been designed or trained for. The warships and auxiliaries were augmented by a variety of merchant ships taken up from trade, but these were not armed, and would find themselves incapable of self-defence when the need arose. The Falklands were some 8,000 miles from the UK naval bases, and the Royal Navy had no bases in the South Atlantic, so the logistical issues involved in sending and supplying the task force were huge.

As the task force sailed south, there was discussion of the main threats that it would face. The submarine threat was thought to be real, though the four Argentinian submarines were either old or small, and in the event did not play a significant role in the war other than as a 'force in being', presenting a constant threat which could not be ignored. Much greater was the threat from the air, to the task force at sea, the landings and the troops once ashore. How this would be dealt with would determine the outcome of the campaign. The Argentine Air Force and Navy aircraft were to carry out some 300 sorties against British ships and landings, mostly with 500lb or 1,000lb bombs, but also including five aircraft-launched Exocet and rocket and strafing attacks.[2]

Ideally the British air defence would be multi-layered, following the concept of 'defence in depth'. The outer rings of this would be airborne early warning conducted by surveillance aircraft, and long-range air defence fighters with multiple missile capability to intercept incoming enemy aircraft.[3] The inner rings would consist of escorts with air defence missiles to destroy any intruders that made it through the outer rings. Finally, ships would have effective 'last-ditch' close-in weapon systems for self-defence.

Lacking the large strike carriers, the Falklands task force had no airborne early warning and the outer defence ring rarely consisted of more than four Sea Harriers on combat air patrol, each with a short-range intercept radar and carrying only two air-to-air missiles.[4] Due to the distance of the air patrol stations from their carrier bases, the Sea Harriers were capable of maintaining station for only about 20 minutes. A large number of attackers penetrated this very thin outer air defence ring and had to be engaged by Sea Dart, Sea Wolf and Seacat missiles or 4.5-inch shells launched from escorts, with mixed success, as we have seen. When planes or missiles got through that defence the only resort was to deploy chaff or light guns, the latter being ineffective. The ships lacked the new anti-missile close-in weapon systems such as Vulcan Phalanx that had been installed in some US warships by this time. Also, the need for effective passive measures such as chaff and electronic threat warning systems was amply demonstrated in the British experience.

As we have seen, one destroyer and one aircraft transport were lost to Exocet strikes, whilst one destroyer, two frigates and one landing ship were lost to bombs. Another nine ships were hit by bombs which, had they detonated, could have caused their destruction; they were mostly saved by the incorrect fusing of the bombs. Seven anti-ship Exocet missiles were launched by the Argentines, five from aircraft and two from shore launchers. Three ships were hit by these missiles, causing two ships to be lost, but to fire, not to the explosions of the missiles (those that hit *Sheffield* and *Atlantic Conveyor* probably failed to explode). The destroyer *Glamorgan*, whose crew was at action stations, was hit by an Exocet missile that did detonate, and while a major fire and shrapnel caused casualties and 13 deaths, the ship was saved by effective damage control and firefighting.[5] This contrasted with the experience of *Sheffield*, whose crew was not at action stations and was inadequately prepared for the immediate tasks of self-defence, damage control and firefighting.

The low availability of Sea Harriers on combat air patrol led to the unescorted *Sir Galahad* and *Sir Tristram* conducting landing operations at Fitzroy without air cover, with disastrous results when Skyhawk bombers arrived on the scene. The lack of British air superiority throughout the conflict was of course a major factor in all of the sinkings, but was most critical during landing operations: the exposure of *Sir Galahad* and *Sir Tristram* was a bad mistake, leading to the largest British loss of life in a single incident. Nevertheless, taking the conflict as a whole, despite their paucity in numbers and the limitations of the aircraft, the performance of the Harriers and their aircrews was outstanding.

Aware of the British lack of airborne early warning, the skilful, determined and brave Argentinian pilots made their air attacks at low level, below ships' radar horizons, and flew over the land around the ships in San Carlos Water and Falkland Sound to sweep in largely undetected until the last seconds because of the clutter on ships' radar.

Of the ships' missile systems for close-range defence, Sea Wolf was particularly effective, but Seacat had a very poor record. The medium-range Sea Dart was fairly effective, although dogged by launching failures. In total at least 18 Sea Dart missiles were launched by Type 42 destroyers, as well as six by *Invincible*, and two by *Bristol*. Out of five missiles fired against helicopters or high-flying aircraft, four were successful, but only two (by *Exeter*) of 19 fired at low-level fixed-wing aircraft achieved hits, or just 11 per cent; however, a number of missiles were fired without guidance to deter low-level attacks. Success in the final stages of the campaign by the Type 42 destroyer *Exeter* can partly be attributed to being equipped with Type 1022 radar, which provided greater capability than the old Type 965 fitted to the earlier Type 42s.* The Type 965 was unable to cope with low-level targets as it suffered multiple path crossings and targets became lost in radar clutter from the surface of the South Atlantic (such as rain or snow) or from land. This resulted in Sea Dart being unable to lock onto targets at a distance when obscured by land, or fast-moving low-level targets obscured in ground clutter or sea-returns.[6]

This was a contributory factor in the loss of *Sheffield* because, due to the inadequacies of its 909 fire control radar, *Glasgow*'s Sea Dart was not able to lock onto the incoming aircraft: *Glasgow* found herself unable to fire Sea Dart missiles at the intruders because of a failure to acquire the small, fleeting targets on the 909 fire control radar in time.[7] Sea Dart's rather clunky electronics systems caused delays or failures to react, and its 909 fire control radar was designed to pick up long-range high-flying targets, not

---

* On 30 May 1982 *Exeter* shot down two Skyhawks (out of four attackers), despite them flying only 10–15 metres above the sea, which was below Sea Dart's theoretical minimum engagement altitude of 30 metres.

the low-level close-range targets that often presented themselves in the Falklands conflict. On 12 May, when *Glasgow* was under attack from Skyhawks, the Sea Dart loading system failed safe, with the launcher computer refusing to accept the two missiles, and *Glasgow* was hit by a 1,000lb bomb.[8] *Coventry* also experienced at least one Sea Dart system failure, when attempting to engage an Argentinian Boeing surveillance aircraft.[9]

Similar problems were experienced with the fire control system for the 4.5-inch gun and Seacat in the Type 21 frigates, where the emergency (visual or manual) mode had to be used in inshore environments, rather than the radar controlled automatic mode. This limitation contributed to the inability of *Ardent* and *Antelope* to ward off their attackers when they were bombed in the confined waters of Falkland Sound. The 4.5-inch Mk 8 gun itself had a history of unreliability, and this was persistent in *Antelope*.

During the conflict, Sea Wolf was the Royal Navy's only modern close-in (or point-defence) weapon. Amongst the task force ships it was fitted in the Type 22 frigates *Brilliant* and *Broadsword* and the Leander-class frigate *Andromeda*, which were assigned 'goalkeeper' duties to provide close anti-aircraft defence of the carrier task force. After the loss of *Sheffield*, a new tactic was devised, pairing each Type 22 frigate with a Type 42 destroyer. The two pairs were deployed some distance from the main fleet, covering likely attack routes, in an attempt to draw attacking aircraft into a 'missile trap', the intention being that, if the Type 42 was unable to engage targets at longer ranges with its Sea Dart missiles, the Type 22 would use its short-range Sea Wolf missiles to defend both ships and knock out the intruder.

When *Brilliant* and *Glasgow*, in combination, were attacked by a flight of four Skyhawk aircraft on 12 May 1982, *Brilliant* was able to shoot down two of these and cause a third to crash when trying to avoid a missile. A second wave of aircraft attacked during a failure of her Sea Wolf missile system, which led to *Glasgow* suffering heavy damage. However, *Broadsword* was unable to successfully defend *Coventry* when the pair were attacked on 25 May. *Coventry*, moving evasively, crossed in front of *Broadsword* and broke the Sea Wolf's lock on the attacking aircraft.

Sea Wolf suffered from problems with hardware failure causing launches to fail, and broken lock resulting from the extreme sea conditions and the Argentines' low-altitude hit-and-run tactics, and multiple targets and crossing targets – neither of which it was designed to intercept. Sea Wolf accounted for two confirmed 'kills' and three further possible successes from eight launches.[10]

Despite being obsolescent, Seacat was still widely used by the Royal Navy during the conflict, in which a hundred were shot in action. It was capable of sustained action, which compensated for its lack of speed, range and accuracy, but its effectiveness was poor.[11] Four aircraft shot down attracted claims from shipborne Seacat, but in each case there were competing claims from the launchers of Sea Wolf, Rapier or Blowpipe missiles. There was no clear-cut case of a Seacat 'kill'.[12] There was some evidence of a deterrent factor, for example on the morning of 21 May when Pucará aircraft turned back after Seacat missiles were fired from *Ardent*, and on 25 May when *Antelope* fired Seacat at an incoming Skyhawk, which turned back. In the first of the Skyhawk attacks on *Ardent* in the afternoon of 21 May Seacat failed to launch, which was a major setback for the ship.

The even more obsolete Sea Slug missile carried by County-class destroyers was only fired once in anti-air mode during the conflict, and on that occasion it missed. The low-level attacks experienced in the Falklands were outside the missile's operational capacity.[13]

The effectiveness of nuclear-powered submarines was demonstrated during the campaign, not least in the sinking of *General Belgrano*. It has been reported that the poor material condition of the 44-year-old ship, and limited damage control training of the crew, resulted in rapid, uncontrollable flooding of the cruiser. Following the sinking, the Argentinian surface navy effectively retired from action.[14]

* * *

The Royal Navy, particularly in its officer corps, has been described by Alastair Finlan as having a war culture that is essentially *offensive* rather than *defensive* in nature, and naturally emphasized winning (something the Navy had been conspicuously successful at since the time of the Spanish Armada). The culture has been inculcated through tradition (such as the hero worship of Nelson), artefacts such as battle paintings and the preserved HMS *Victory*, ship names and initial training (such as that for cadets at Dartmouth) over many generations, and reinforced by the strategies and tactics favoured in major wars, such as the two world wars of the 20th century. This culture will have influenced Sir Henry Leach when he advised Margaret Thatcher that a naval task force could recapture the Falklands. It also served the Navy well during the conflict that ensued. Within the Navy there are, however, sub-cultures that have been developed by the different branches of the service – aviation and aircraft carriers, submarines, surface escorts and amphibious warfare being obvious examples. It was significant that the task force commander, Admiral Fieldhouse, and the senior task group officer, Rear Admiral Woodward, were both submariners, with little experience of either aviation or amphibious warfare. This in turn affected how they used the naval power they had at their disposal, and drew criticism from some of the senior aviation and amphibious warfare experts within the Navy for some of their decisions.[15]

For example, Woodward's strategies for using Sea Harriers drew sharp criticism from Commander 'Sharkey' Ward, commanding officer of 801 Squadron, as seen in the case of *Ardent*'s loss, and the Fieldhouse/Woodward axis caused friction over amphibious warfare tactics with Commodore Mike Clapp and Brigadier Julian Thompson. Even Woodward was to comment in his memoirs that he was 'mildly astonished' when he was appointed task group commander rather than the obvious choice, Vice Admiral Sir Derek Reffell, flag officer of the aircraft carriers in the Third Flotilla, who also had significant amphibious warfare experience: '[H]e was very much better qualified than I, in just about every respect.' Reffell was also denied access to the decision making at Northwood, where his expertise could have been valuable.[16]

At operational level, the Navy's forces generally demonstrated high levels of skill and performance, reflecting high standards of training and preparedness, effective leadership, high morale and *esprit de corps*. But in the heat or fog of war mistakes are made, and sometimes these can be fatal. The preceding chapters have revealed some of these shortcomings and we have seen how they contributed to the loss of the ships.

Preservation of the war culture depended in part on conformance with standard operating procedures and desirable behavioural patterns. But the routines of combat readiness amongst personnel, which became ingrained in World War II, had weakened in post-war years. The most egregious illustration of this was in *Sheffield*, where there was an almost complete lack of war discipline, with a watch that was far from vigilant, key individuals missing from the operations room, the ship not being called to action stations, and the response to the missile threat negligible: chaff was not fired and point defence weapon crews were not alert. Although *Glasgow* had issued a warning, this was not broadcast by the anti-air warfare co-ordination team in *Invincible* because it was wrongly believed to be spurious. As a result, two Sea Harriers on combat air patrol, which had been told to investigate and set off west, were called back to their combat air patrol position by *Hermes*, and a second combat air patrol was diverted elsewhere. Whilst other ships were better prepared for action than *Sheffield*, her loss did provide a stark warning of what could go wrong and organizational routines were sharpened up in consequence.

In *Ardent*, the failings were of a different sort. After being bombed, the ship was abandoned prematurely and quite possibly unnecessarily because of exaggerated and inaccurate reports regarding the damage to the ship and its possible consequences. The wrong assessment of the probability that the ship might soon plunge was made by the marine engineering officer and the first lieutenant, and this was not adequately questioned by the captain. *Ardent* could probably have been saved by co-ordinated and determined damage control efforts and good leadership. Furthermore, in the haste to abandon ship a full search for survivors was not conducted, with ambiguous information transmitted to the captain, so there was no certainty that survivors were not left behind in the damaged areas.

Many failings contributed to the loss of *Antelope*. The captain and principal warfare officer (air) had been advised to station themselves on the bridge and the gun direction platform respectively when under attack in confined waters, where the 4.5-inch gun and Seacat would need to be used in emergency mode, but failed to do so. They remained in the operations room and as a result took little part in the action. In the operation to defuse the unexploded bombs, the captain and executive officer failed to seek external advice on the procedure and liaise adequately with the bomb disposal team (who also did not seek external advice on how to deal with a bomb with which they were unfamiliar). The captain and executive officer failed to prepare the ship for the eventuality of a bomb exploding, and as a result damage control organization was poor. Battle stress and competing priorities were amongst the mitigating factors when the question of negligence was considered.

The loss of *Coventry* came following two Skyhawk attacks in very quick succession on the ship and *Broadsword*, which was damaged in the first. In the ensuing panic, the operator of *Coventry*'s 4.5-inch gun, which was in emergency mode, had problems training it onto the second pair of Skyhawks. Under great stress, in a rapidly developing situation, mistakes were made in manoeuvring the two ships, leading to *Coventry* placing *Broadsword* down-threat (instead of up-threat where she was supposed to be) and thereby blocking the latter's Sea Wolf. So the intruder got through and bombed *Coventry*. Earlier that day *Coventry* had downed two Skyhawks, but her luck had now run out and she quickly sank.

The loss of *Atlantic Conveyor* resulted from a questionable tactical decision and an operational error. The decision to place unarmed auxiliaries in a screen for the two aircraft carriers may well have been a reasonable one, but the inclusion of *Atlantic Conveyor* was unfortunate. She was carrying four Chinook and seven Wessex helicopters that were vital for the land assault on Stanley. Arguably, therefore, she was a strategic asset that should not have been risked. Lacking many of the extensive damage control features of a warship, she was particularly vulnerable when attacked. When the incoming threat from the Super Étendards was detected by the task group, an order was given instructing ships to turn onto what was a dangerous course, exposing their broadsides to the threat instead of their sterns. The mistake was quickly realized and a revised course was signalled, though not received in *Atlantic Conveyor*. In any case, it was too late for *Atlantic Conveyor* to alter course again. Thus, the Exocet missiles hit the side of the ship rather than the much stronger stern. What is more, had the ship been fitted with chaff launchers or self-defence weapons, or been given sufficient warning of the immediate missile threat to allow a Wessex helicopter to be launched to deploy chaff, the missile hit might have been avoided altogether.

Sir Galahad was lost through a combination of tactical and operational mistakes. First and foremost, it was not prudent to send the two lightly armed landing ships to Fitzroy without either an anti-air escort or air cover, and preferably both. The operation at Fitzroy had not been properly planned; it had been forced upon Woodward and Moore because an advance party of 2 Para seized Fitzroy without the knowledge of Moore, and needed back up. Had the Chinooks been available they might have ferried troops there, but in their absence it was decided to send the two LSLs. A number of communication failures contributed to the length of time it took to unload *Sir Galahad*. Her planned arrival at Fitzroy was not signalled to the officer commanding the beach operation, so assets that would allow speedy unloading were not available. Other frustrations extended the delay in disembarking the Welsh Guards, so that six hours after the ship had anchored at Fitzroy they were still in the ship or the LCU alongside when the air attack began, with tragic consequences.

* * *

In the wake of the conflict there were many issues and lessons for the Royal Navy to consider. The survivability of the Type 21 and Type 42 escorts when damaged was in question. The older and larger County-class destroyer *Glamorgan* had survived an Exocet hit and her sister ship *Antrim* had survived bombing, as had the older frigates *Plymouth* and *Argonaut*, but the later classes had been less resilient when damaged, and had been particularly vulnerable to loss through the fires that broke out after being hit. The flammability of materials used in more recent designs, often to improve habitability, would have to be re-examined along with other design features, as would damage control and firefighting procedures and training.

Thus, important lessons were learned about the rapid spread of fire and smoke in ships, and about the use of materials that can prove hazardous in fires. Urgent studies were put in hand to address this. Examples of measures planned included improved fire zones; changes to the design of waterproof doors and hatches; the provision of more escape hatches; making bulkheads more smoke-tight; the re-siting of fuel tanks; reductions in inflammable materials; and additional fire pumps and breathing apparatus.[17]

The advisability of using ships built to mercantile, rather than warship, standards of damage tolerance (such as *Atlantic Conveyor* and *Sir Galahad*) was questioned. Such ships were especially vulnerable in combat zones, where their use for the carriage of troops or vital equipment was potentially very hazardous.[18] Furthermore, auxiliaries and transports deployed to combat zones needed to be equipped with close-in self-defence weapons and chaff launchers.

The Type 22 frigate lacked a main gun, meaning it could not be used for naval gunfire support operations (this was to be remedied in the last four of the class, which were ordered after the conflict and fitted with a 4.5-inch gun).

The escorts had performed quite well in their anti-air role, having protected the carriers and most of the amphibious force from damage. Nevertheless, there were glaring shortcomings which had to be addressed. The lack of good close-in weapon systems (CIWS) had been exposed. As an interim measure, the American

Vulcan Phalanx gun system was mounted in the carriers *Illustrious* and *Invincible*, and it was announced that CIWS would be fitted to the third new carrier, *Ark Royal*, the assault ships *Intrepid* and *Fearless*, *Bristol* and all the Type 42 destroyers. The Sea Wolf missile system was to be adapted to make it more effective when dealing with low-level attacks and to have all-weather capability, and improvements to Sea Dart would also be sought. Shipborne and airborne chaff and electronic countermeasures would be further developed to deal with sea-skimming missiles. There was a need for more realistic training in shipborne air defence, and all ships needed to be fitted with a wide range of on-board training systems. More realistic targets for the peacetime training of air defence weapon system operators were also needed.[19]

The deficiencies of shipborne radars in the Type 21 and Type 42 escorts would have to be addressed: the lack of a true moving target indication mode had been a serious problem. Argentinian aircraft could not be seen against the background clutter of the islands, and aircraft or missiles flying low over the sea could not be detected. The Type 1022 radar, first fitted operationally to *Exeter*, had shown itself to be more capable in these respects during the latter stages of the conflict. Similarly, the Type 967/968 fitted to Type 22s had performed better than the earlier types.

The lack of airborne early warning was a big problem, and was partly addressed by immediately equipping two Sea King helicopters with modified Searchwater radars for embarkation in the new carrier *Illustrious* that was being sent to the Falklands, and it was planned to include such provision in each of the operational carriers.[20]

* * *

A big boost for the Navy came after the conflict, with the reversal of many of the cuts announced in the 1981 Defence Review. *Invincible*'s sale to Australia was cancelled, and all three carriers of her class would be retained. The assault ships *Fearless* and *Intrepid* and the ice patrol ship *Endurance* would be retained and a replacement for *Sir Galahad* would be built. The cut to the number of escorts would be moderated, so that 55 ships would be in front-line service instead of the planned 50. Four new Type 22 frigates would be ordered to replace the four escorts lost in the conflict. All of the aircraft lost would be replaced, and a further seven more Sea Harriers and six more Sea King helicopters would be ordered. In addition to providing the monies for the replacement costs for all the ships, equipment and aircraft lost in the campaign, the defence budget would increase by 3 per cent per annum in real terms for the next three years.[21]

A sizeable garrison would be maintained in the Falkland Islands 'for the foreseeable future', including aircraft (Phantom, Harrier, Hercules, Chinook and Sea King) and an infantry battalion. Warships, with afloat support, would be deployed in the South Atlantic.[22] But the Navy might not have imagined how long the 'foreseeable future' might be. At the time of writing, nearly 40 years on, there is still a strong defence commitment to the islands, and in Argentina the 'Malvinas' issue remains a popular sentiment that rises up the country's political agenda every so often.[*] In consequence, a significant British military force is still maintained there. A new airfield, RAF Mount Pleasant, was opened in 1985 and is now home to the Typhoon fighter, Airbus Voyager and Atlas, and civilian-operated search and rescue helicopters, as well as the army garrison. A Royal Navy offshore patrol vessel is permanently based at East Cove Military Port, about 30 miles south-west of the Falklands' capital Stanley; the port has recently been upgraded so that it can berth the Point-class sealift ships. A larger warship, normally a frigate or destroyer, and an RFA replenishment ship are on station in the South Atlantic Patrol at all times, and the ice patrol ship still spends the southern summer in the Antarctic and Falklands region.

* * *

---

[*] When the author was in Ushuaia (the mainland Argentinian city on the Beagle Channel) in March 2020, large banners on the harbour front proclaimed, in English, 'Ushuaia Capital of the Malvinas'.

Sandy Woodward's last signal in the South Atlantic to all the forces under his command served as an epitaph for those lost in the combat, and read:

> As I haul my South Atlantic flag down, I reflect sadly on the brave lives lost, and the good ships gone, in the short time of our trial. I thank wholeheartedly each and every one of you for your gallant support, tough determination and fierce perseverance under bloody conditions. Let us all... as we return severally to enjoy the blessings of our land, resolve that those left behind for ever shall not be forgotten.[23]

Addendum

After the Conflict

Shortly after returning from the South Atlantic, *Conqueror*, with Chris Wreford-Brown still in command, carried out a successful clandestine sub-surface raid in the Barents Sea in July 1982, and captured Soviet Navy sonar towed array equipment from a Polish-flagged spy trawler for technical analysis by NATO. Wreford-Brown, born in 1945 and educated at Rugby School, had started his submariner training at HMS *Dolphin* at Gosport in 1968. He had also commanded the conventional submarine *Opossum* and, later, the nuclear-powered submarine *Valiant*. He was promoted to captain and commanded the frigate *Cornwall* as leader of the 8th Frigate Squadron. Not achieving flag rank, he retired from the Royal Navy in 1995 at the age of 50, and was employed as a director of Paignton Zoo until his retirement in 2010.

Conqueror was decommissioned in 1990. At the time of writing she is still held in storage by the Ministry of Defence at Devonport, awaiting final disposal. The periscopes, captain's cabin and main control panel from the submarine's control room are on display in the Royal Navy Submarine Museum in Gosport.

Following the conflict, Héctor Bonzo (ARA *General Belgrano*) took shore appointments as chief of naval superior personnel and later naval deputy secretary. In 1987 he founded the General Belgrano Cruiser Friends Association and was a member of the board during several periods. Captain Bonzo edited two books,

1093 Crewmembers and *323 Heroes of the Belgrano*. The first was written by him and released on the tenth anniversary of the Falklands conflict, revealing his experiences and paying homage to the crew. The second was written and edited in 2001 together with a group of *General Belgrano* survivors. He died in April 2009 in Buenos Aires at the age of 76. He was married and had three daughters.[1]

Clive Ponting, who had leaked secret information on the *Belgrano* sinking, resigned from the civil service in 1985. Shortly afterwards, *The Observer* newspaper began to serialize his book *The Right to Know: The Inside Story of the Belgrano Affair*. The Conservative government reacted by amending UK secrets legislation, revising the Official Secrets Act in 1989. Before his trial, a jury could take the view that if an action could be seen to be in the public interest, that might justify the right of the individual to take that action. As a result of the 1989 modification, that defence was removed. After this enactment, it was taken that 'public interest' is what the government of the day says it is. Ponting had also exposed the story of a Cold War cover-up – the 1952 attempt to develop bioweapons, during which a trawler off the Hebrides was accidentally doused with plague bacteria (the disclosure being published in *The Observer* newspaper in 1985). Following his resignation from the civil service, Ponting served as a reader in the Department of Politics and International Relations at the University of Wales, Swansea until his retirement in 2004. He died in August 2020.[2]

On his return from the Falklands, Captain Sam Salt (HMS *Sheffield*) was appointed in command of the destroyer *Southampton*. In the mid-1980s his seagoing career ended and he held the posts of Assistant Chief of Staff (Operations) at Fleet Command Headquarters, Northwood, and Director of Defence Intelligence (1986–87). He was promoted to flag rank despite his unimpressive performance in the Falklands. Subsequently he became senior naval representative at the Royal College of Defence Studies. As Assistant Chief of the Naval Staff he was responsible for the Royal Navy's planning for the Gulf War. After leaving the Navy in 1997, Salt worked in the private sector in a number of defence-related export, sales and marketing roles before retiring in 2005. He died of lung cancer, aged 69, on 3 December 2009.[3]

Surgeon Commander Rick Jolly (Senior Medical Officer of 3 Commando, Royal Marines) was later promoted to surgeon captain and after retirement continued to practise; he also enjoyed success as an author and cartoonist. Jolly's second book, *The Red and Green Life Machine*, was about his experiences in the Falklands War, and he subsequently wrote *Jackspeak: A Guide to British Naval Slang and Usage*. He died in 2018, aged 71.[4] The *Sir Galahad* survivor Simon Weston said: 'Without his organizational skills, the surgeons and medics would never have functioned. I can only thank him for saving my life and many others.'[5]

In 1986, while working on the Naval Staff at the Ministry of Defence, Commander Alan West (HMS *Ardent*) left documents detailing large cuts to the Navy on a canal towpath. These documents were found and then published in the national press. At a subsequent court martial West pleaded guilty to charges of negligence and breaching security and was issued with a severe reprimand. He went on to pursue a high-flying Royal Navy career, and the reprimand was time expired before he became eligible for promotion to flag rank. Promoted to captain in 1987, he was given command of HMS *Bristol* and the Dartmouth training squadron in March of that year. He led a study into employment of women at sea and then spent three years as head of naval intelligence, rewriting the NATO intelligence manual after the collapse of the Soviet Union. In 1993 he was promoted to commodore and became Director of Naval Staff Duties at the Ministry of Defence later that year. West became rear admiral on appointment as Naval Secretary in March 1994, responsible for officer appointments and also naval manning. In February 1996 he became Commander United Kingdom Task Group, deploying to the Gulf for the first UK fighter patrols over Iraq (conducted by Sea Harrier FA2) and to the South China Sea to cover the withdrawal from Hong Kong.[6]

The embarrassments and shortcomings of *Ardent's* loss and his later security breach did not impede West's rise to the top. In October 1997 he was promoted to vice admiral and Chief of Defence Intelligence. He became a full admiral in November 2000, taking up the posts of Commander-in-Chief Fleet, NATO Commander-in-Chief East Atlantic and NATO Commander Allied Naval Forces North. Finally, reaching the top of the Navy ladder, he was appointed as First Sea Lord and Chief of the Naval Staff in September 2002. In 2005 he championed Trafalgar 200, a celebration of the 200th anniversary of the Battle of Trafalgar. West led the demand by the Royal Navy for a major ceremony and is credited with persuading the government to include a large-scale international fleet review in the event, which was staged in the Solent and Portsmouth dockyard, for which he secured £4 million funding. During his time as First Sea Lord, West implemented the defence white paper entitled Delivering Security in a Changing World, which proposed cutting three Type 23 frigates, three Type 42 destroyers, four nuclear submarines, and six minehunters, and reducing the planned number of Type 45 destroyers from 12 to eight. In a message to the Royal Navy, West said, 'We must continue the shift in emphasis away from measuring strength in terms of hull numbers and towards the delivery of military effects... I am confident that these changes will leave the Navy better organized and equipped to face the challenges of the future.' He was successful in obtaining continued government backing for the construction of the two large aircraft carriers of the Queen Elizabeth class. Nevertheless, the cuts he and the Labour government had orchestrated were devastating blows to the Navy.[7]

West retired from the Royal Navy in February 2006. On 9 July 2007 he was created a life peer, Lord West of Spithead, and appointed as minister with responsibility for security, in the Home Office, during the Labour administration. West admitted during security vetting to an extramarital affair, and was forced to respond to rumours in 2007 about his friendship with Anni-Frid Lyngstad of pop group ABBA with the comment, 'I'm not having an affair with her.' Newspaper reports at the time said, 'He always had an eye for beautiful women' and that he was 'a bon viveur, fond of good wine, good food and good chat'. In May 2010 he left office when a Conservative government was elected. From 2014 to

2017 he was a member of parliament's National Security Strategy Joint Committee. In 2020 he became a member of parliament's Intelligence and Security Committee. From 2006 until 2018 he was the first chancellor of Southampton Solent University.[8]

After his return from the South Atlantic, a series of shore appointments followed for Commander Nick Tobin (HMS *Antelope*), who was not to have another seagoing appointment. He was promoted to captain in 1986, and in 1994 he was selected to set up and head the key directorate of naval manning in London and Portsmouth. Not achieving flag rank, he retired from the Royal Navy in 1996 aged 51 and worked as a bursar at Magdalene College, Cambridge. He became an operational director in the voluntary sector before taking legal training in 2004 to become a consultant with Steele Rose Ltd, a will writing and estate planning company. He had married Josephine Fisher in 1976. They live in Bath and have one daughter.[9]

Captain David Hart Dyke (HMS *Coventry*) received no further seagoing appointments. He served on the British Naval Staff in Washington, D.C., from 1982 to 1987. He then became Director of Naval Recruiting and was also appointed a naval aide-de-camp to the Queen. Unlike Sam Salt, he was not promoted to flag rank, despite having performed far better than him in the conflict. According to Sandy Woodward, an edict from the Ministry of Defence after the conflict was over stated that promotion boards should take no account of officers' service in the Falklands, because otherwise it would be unfair to those who had been unable to attend the action. This was, said Woodward, a complete disgrace and it was as well they hadn't been told this on the way south or the outcome might have been different.[10] On 1 January 1990 Hart Dyke was made a Commander of the Order of the British Empire (CBE), and retired from the Royal Navy a week later. He was appointed Clerk and Chief Executive of the Worshipful Company of Skinners, a livery company of the City of London. After retiring in 2003 he published *Four Weeks in May* (in 2007), his account of the loss of *Coventry*. He and Diana have two children: Miranda (the comedian and actor Miranda Hart) and Alice.[11]

Captain Mike Layard, senior officer of the naval party in *Atlantic Conveyor*, became commander of Royal Naval Air Station Culdrose on his return to the UK. From 1984 to 1985 he was captain of the destroyer *Cardiff*. He then became Deputy Director, Naval Warfare (Air) at the Ministry of Defence until 1988 when, promoted to rear admiral, he became flag officer, Naval Air Command. From 1990 to 1992 he was Director, Naval Manpower and Training. Finally, with the rank of full admiral, he was the first combined Second Sea Lord and Commander-in-Chief Naval Home Command from 1992. He retired from the Navy in 1995 and took up a number of voluntary roles in education, the health service and the Fleet Air Arm Museum. He is a keen sailor and artist. Married, with two married sons, he and his wife Elspeth live in Somerset.[12]

When the conflict ended, the landing ship *Sir Tristram* was towed to Port Stanley to be used as an accommodation ship. In 1983 she was brought back to the United Kingdom on a heavy lift ship and was rebuilt. She re-entered active service in 1985 and saw service in the Gulf War, the Balkan conflicts and the Iraq invasion of 2003. The ship was paid off in December 2005 but was then repurposed as a static training ship for special forces in Portland Harbour.[13]

Appendix

Honours and Awards

Citations from the *Supplement to the London Gazette* of 8 October 1982, published 11 October 1982.

DISTINGUISHED SERVICE ORDER

Captain Philip Jeremy George ROBERTS, Royal Fleet Auxiliary
From 21st May to 8th June 1982, RFA SIR GALAHAD suffered attacks by enemy aircraft. Throughout this period, Captain Roberts took personal charge of the fighting and safety of his ship, crew and embarked force passengers. On two occasions his ship suffered severe bomb damage and had to be abandoned, Captain Roberts organizing and controlling each operation. On the first occasion, a 1,000lb unexploded bomb remained in the ship, which was subsequently made safe and removed. Captain Roberts then returned with his crew, repaired the damage and continued operations in support of the Land Forces ashore. On the second occasion that SIR GALAHAD was hit, a large body of troops was still embarked, and evacuation of the ship was especially difficult and dangerous because of a fierce fire and the number of casualties sustained in the enemy's attack. The ship had been hit by a bomb which exploded in the recreation space, killing a number of soldiers, and also by rockets and possibly napalm. A fierce fire immediately took hold of the ship and small arms ammunition in the tank

deck started to explode. In this desperate, confused and hazardous situation, Captain Roberts organized his crew and the embarked troops with considerable skill. Their safe and timely evacuation was to a large extent due to his personal qualities of leadership and courage in the face of great danger.

Commander Christopher Louis WREFORD-BROWN, Royal Navy
In the early hours of 2nd May 1982 HMS CONQUEROR, with Commander Wreford-Brown in command, began surveillance of the Argentine cruiser GENERAL BELGRANO whilst assisting in the enforcement of the Total Exclusion Zone around the Falkland Islands. In total compliance with the authority given later in the day, Commander Wreford-Brown took HMS CONQUEROR into a classic attack, hitting the cruiser with two torpedoes from a range of 1,200 yards. HMS CONQUEROR then withdrew after successfully evading a depth charge attack by two escorting destroyers. The GENERAL BELGRANO subsequently sank. Following this action, HMS CONQUEROR continued to play a full part in the operation, including periods spent close inshore in shallow water. On one occasion, for example, she penetrated into Gulf San Matias in rough weather conditions in water only 27 fathoms deep. She was continuously at sea for longer than any other Royal Navy submarine. After the sinking of the GENERAL BELGRANO, the Argentine Navy withdrew to remain within their 12-mile limit for the remainder of the campaign. HMS CONQUEROR'S action was instrumental in proving the efficiency of the submarine blockade which, firmly deterring any action by enemy surface forces, allowed the Task Force Commander to concentrate his surface units against the air threat, thereby minimizing damage and casualties to our own forces.

DISTINGUISHED SERVICE CROSS

Lieutenant Commander John Stuart WOODHEAD, Royal Navy
On 4th May 1982, HMS SHEFFIELD was hit amidships by an Exocet missile launched from an Argentine aircraft and sustained major damage and casualties. Fire and thick acrid smoke spread

throughout the centre of the ship. After 4 hours' extensive effort, with fire approaching the forward missile and gun magazines, the order was given to abandon ship. At the time of the missile impact Lieutenant Commander Woodhead directed damage control action near the Operations Room. He then went below to the Computer Room and with the Computer Room crew began to assess the damage to his weapon systems. Smoke caused the Operations Room above and then the forward sections of the ship to be evacuated, but Lieutenant Commander Woodhead continued at his post and carefully and with extreme determination co-ordinated attempts to restore power to essential weapon equipment and succeeded in restoring the computer facility. By his exceptional qualities of leadership, dedication to duty and courage he inspired the Computer Room crew to follow his brilliant example. Later, overcome by smoke, Lieutenant Commander Woodhead and his team died at their posts. His praiseworthy actions were in the highest traditions of the Service.

Lieutenant Commander John Murray SEPHTON, Royal Navy
On 21st May 1982, HMS ARDENT on station in San Carlos Water came under heavy attack from the Argentine Air Force and sustained many bomb hits, causing great damage and loss of life. After the loss of the Seacat missile system, Lieutenant Commander Sephton, the Flight Commander, organized the use of small arms by the Flight as a last ditch defence against the concentrated and severe enemy attacks. In a dangerous and desperate situation he was last seen directing fire on the exposed Flight Deck, shooting a sub machine gun vertically up into an A4 Skyhawk the instant before it dropped the bombs that killed him. Three other Flight members were also killed. Lieutenant Commander Sephton's extreme valour and self-sacrifice was an example and inspiration to all the Ship's Company and undoubtedly deterred the enemy from making even more attacks.

Captain Ian Harry NORTH, Merchant Navy
On 14th April 1982 SS ATLANTIC CONVEYOR was laid up in Liverpool. On the 25th April she deployed to the South Atlantic

converted to operate fixed and rotary wing aircraft and loaded with stores and equipment for the Falklands Task Force. This astonishing feat was largely due to Captain North's innovation, leadership and inexhaustible energy. SS ATLANTIC CONVEYOR joined the Carrier Battle Group on 19th May 1982 and was immediately treated as a warship in most respects. Almost comparable in manoeuvrability, flexibility and response, Captain North and the ship came through with flying colours. When the ship was hit on 25th May Captain North was a tower of strength during the difficult period of damage assessment leading up to the decision to abandon ship. He left the ship last with enormous dignity and calm and his subsequent death was a blow to all. A brilliant seaman, brave in war, immensely revered and loved, his contribution to the Campaign was enormous and epitomized the great spirit of the Merchant Service.

Captain George Robert GREEN, Royal Fleet Auxiliary
RFA SIR TRISTRAM, commanded by Captain Green, joined the Amphibious Task Group at Ascension Island and rapidly took up the challenge. From the arrival of the amphibious ships at San Carlos Water on 21st May 1982 to June 1982, RFA SIR TRISTRAM was under constant threat of air attack. For a period of a week, repeated air attacks were pressed home on the anchorage when the very lightly armed ship had to protect herself while continuing to offload important Military equipment. She was the first Landing Ship Logistic to make the re-supply run to Fitzroy. The task had to be unescorted and meant lying at anchor by day off Fitzroy in an exposed position without benefit of adequate area air defence or warning. It was while there that the ship, still well loaded with ammunition, came under fierce surprise air attack and suffered the damage which caused her to be abandoned on fire. It is greatly to Captain Green's credit that he was successful in getting all his people off the ship safely with the exception of two crewmen killed by one of the bombs which hit his ship. Captain Green, by his personal example and courage, throughout the period, inspired his crew to do all that was asked of him and them, far beyond the normal call of duty.

Commander Nicholas John TOBIN, Royal Navy

On 24th May 1982, HMS ANTELOPE, commanded by Commander Tobin, entered San Carlos Water to provide anti-aircraft protection to Amphibious Forces. Air attacks during the previous two days had been extremely heavy, being mainly directed at the Frigates. HMS ARDENT had already been sunk with loss of life. During the day, HMS ANTELOPE had helped to fight off several air attacks and contributed significantly to the attrition of enemy aircraft in a series of spirited actions. One raid in particular singled out HMS ANTELOPE for *kamikaze*-like attention, in the course of which one enemy aircraft was shot down, probably by ANTELOPE, and another flew into the ship's foremast, knocking the top overboard and subsequently disintegrating. HMS ANTELOPE sustained hits which killed one rating, wounded others and left one unexploded bomb amidships. Commander Tobin anchored and calmly organized his Ship's Company before an unsuccessful attempt was made to defuse the bomb. The ensuing explosions ripped the ship apart, started uncontrollable fires and threatened further explosions from the ship's magazines. Commander Tobin correctly gave orders to abandon ship, without which great loss of life would have ensued. His firm direction during the brave and orderly evacuation of the ship into rescue craft and the quite extraordinary morale of her Company were remarked upon by the rescuers. Throughout the day Commander Tobin led his team in an exemplary manner with great courage and foresight.

Commander Alan William John WEST, Royal Navy

On 21st May 1982, HMS ARDENT, commanded by Commander West, was deployed to Grantham Sound to conduct Naval Gunfire Support during the amphibious landings in San Carlos Water; in particular, to cover the withdrawal of an SAS diversionary patrol. Isolated there, HMS ARDENT was subject to heavy air attack (at one stage 11 aircraft were involved). Despite these overwhelming odds, Commander West covered the SAS withdrawal and supported 2 Para establishing themselves on Sussex Mountain. He fought his ship bravely, shooting down one Pucará, and continued to bring fire to bear on enemy aircraft despite the progressive loss of the ship's propulsion, Seacat system and 4.5-inch gun. Eventually, after having been hit by no less than nine bombs and several rockets, and with no hope of saving the ship, he ordered her to be abandoned. The utmost credit should go to Commander West for continuing to fight his ship in the face of extreme adversity and in particular for the well organized manner in which she was abandoned. Without his calm courage and personal direction in the face of overwhelming odds, far greater loss of life might have occurred.

Lieutenant Commander Hugh Sinclair CLARK, Royal Navy
Lieutenant Commander Clark commanded 825 Naval Air Squadron during the assault on Port Stanley. His Unit had been hastily formed from an anti-submarine training squadron and arrived in the Falkland Islands with no military operational experience and little training in the support helicopter role. Short of equipment and expertise, they landed and set to work to form an effective and efficient organization. This Squadron was immediately used to support ground forces in the front line and, by wise direction, Lieutenant Commander Clark ensured that they rapidly learnt the necessary skills to produce creditable results. His exemplary leadership in the air in the face of ground and air attack by the enemy was reflected in the performance of his crews. Lieutenant Commander Clark showed total disregard for his own safety in rescuing survivors from the blazing wreck of RFA SIR GALAHAD, hovering in dense smoke amongst exploding ammunition. Responding to such an example, his Unit made a major contribution to the support of the troops engaged in the presence of the enemy which was in the highest traditions of the Service.

23675237 Warrant Officer Class 2 John Henry PHILLIPS, Corps of Royal Engineers
On 22nd May 1982 Warrant Officer Class 2 Phillips and another NCO of 49 Explosive Ordnance Disposal Squadron Royal Engineers were carrying out explosive ordnance disposal duties in the Falkland Islands. They were tasked to deal with an

unexploded bomb in the boiler room of HMS ARGONAUT. Another unexploded bomb lay in a flooded missile magazine nearby. Working in extraordinarily cramped conditions and in very unfamiliar surroundings, Phillips and a NCO successfully remotely rendered safe the bomb which was later removed from the ship. This action enabled the damage to the boiler room to be repaired, so that HMS ARGONAUT regained propulsion and was able to manoeuvre defensively in further air attacks. On 23rd May 1982, Warrant Office Class 2 Phillips and the same NCO were tasked to neutralize two unexploded bombs in HMS ANTELOPE. The first bomb examined could not be approached until extensive clearance of debris had taken place. They therefore set about rendering safe the second bomb, which was situated near the centre of the ship. The bomb had been slightly damaged and was assessed as being in a dangerous condition. They tried three times to render the bomb safe using a remote method, having to approach the bomb after each attempt to adjust the equipment, but on each occasion, the fuse could not be withdrawn. After a fourth attempt, which involved using a small charge, the bomb unexpectedly exploded. The blast was considerable. Despite a blast route of open doors and hatches up through the ship, the fully clipped steel door at the forward end of the passageway, where the bomb disposal team was standing, was completely blown off and nearly bent double. Warrant Officer Class 2 Phillips was seriously injured. Warrant Officer Class 2 Phillips displayed courage of the highest order and persevered with attempts to defuse the bomb in HMS ANTELOPE, fully aware that its condition was particularly dangerous.

GEORGE MEDAL

Second Engineer Officer Paul Anderson HENRY, Royal Fleet Auxiliary
On 8th June 1982, after RFA SIR GALAHAD had been bombed by Argentine aircraft during troop disembarkation in Fitzroy Creek, the Engine Room compartments quickly filled with thick

black smoke. Second Engineer Officer Henry and Third Engineer Officer Hailwood were present in the Main Control Room. A Junior Engineer Officer was at the after end of the Engine Room and had to fight his way back through thick smoke to the Main Control Room area. Second Engineer Officer Henry then told the Junior Engineer Officer to take the breathing apparatus and set and get out of the Engine Room, when they would follow. By this unselfish and courageous act, he saved the Junior Officer's life, at the same time sacrificing his own. The Junior Officer managed to reach safety, but both Second Engineer Officer Henry and Third Engineer Officer Hailwood perished. Second Engineer Officer Henry's act will stand proudly in the annals of the Royal Fleet Auxiliary Service.

Able Seaman (Radar) John Edward DILLON, D191232P
On 21st May 1982 Able Seaman (Radar) Dillon was in the After Damage Control Party on board HMS ARDENT in Falkland Sound. Following a bomb attack on the ship, he was assisting in the control of flooding in the Dining Hall when the area sustained further major bomb damage and he was rendered unconscious. On regaining consciousness, he found that he was pinned to the deck by heavy debris in the dimly lit devastated compartment. A fire was raging and the area was rapidly filling with thick smoke. He extricated himself and despite pain from a large shrapnel wound in his back attempted unsuccessfully to free a man pinned down by a girder across his neck. He then made his way through the smoke towards a further man calling for help, whom he found trapped under heavy metal girders, bleeding from head and face wounds and with his left hand severely damaged. After several attempts, between which he had to drop to the deck to get breathable air, AB(R) Dillon succeeded in raising the debris sufficiently to allow the man to drag himself free. AB(R) Dillon's antiflash hood had been ripped off in the explosion, so afforded him no protection from the heat, and his left ear was burned. In their search for an escape route, the man, who was heavily built, fell into a hole in the deck, but was dragged out by the much slighter AB(R) Dillon to a

hole in the ship's side where, although the man was able to inflate his own lifejacket, AB(R) Dillon was unable to follow suit, due to the pain in his throat caused by the smoke. Despite this, fearing that the weakened man would be dragged beneath the ship, AB(R) Dillon followed him into the water and pulled him away from the ship's side. By this time his exertions, pain and the cold of the sea had weakened AB(R) Dillon until he could do little to support himself in the water. Realizing that there was a danger of him pushing the man under the water if he continued to hold onto him, he moved away and appreciating that he could no longer swim or grasp the strop lowered to him from a helicopter, slipped beneath the surface. He and the man were then rescued by a helicopter crewman. There is little doubt that but for Able Seaman (Radar) Dillon's selfless acts with complete disregard for his personal safety the other man would not have escaped from the ship which was then being abandoned and sinking.

DISTINGUISHED SERVICE MEDAL

Petty Officer Marine Engineering Mechanic (M) David Richard
BRIGGS D13481S7
On 4th May 1982, HMS SHEFFIELD was struck by an Exocet missile fired by an Argentine aircraft. Petty Officer Marine Engineering Mechanic Briggs was in the vicinity of the After Section Base and set in motion the initial fire-fighting effort. He then moved forward to his action station at the Forward Section Base, but at this stage personnel were being evacuated from this area on to the forecastle. However, he led his team back to recover important equipment which was necessary to continue the fire-fighting operation. Unable to wear breathing equipment due to restricted access through a hatch, Petty Officer Marine Engineering Mechanic Briggs and his team re-entered the smoke filled forward section. In conditions of increasing smoke and almost no visibility Petty Officer Marine Engineering Mechanic Briggs made several journeys to the Forward Section Base to pass out much valuable equipment. Sadly, on the last attempt he was overcome by smoke

and rendered unconscious, subsequent attempts to revive him proving unsuccessful. Petty Officer Marine Engineering Mechanic Briggs demonstrated leadership, bravery and devotion to duty in trying to save his ship.

Colour Sergeant Michael James FRANCIS, Royal Marines P021992F
Colour Sergeant Francis, coxswain of LCU Fl, was working in the vicinity of HMS ANTELOPE when her unexploded bomb detonated, resulting in an immediate fire which caused her crew, already at emergency stations, to be ordered to abandon ship. Colour Sergeant Francis took his craft in to help with the close range fire fighting before being ordered to withdraw because of the considerable danger to his craft. In a later incident on 8th June he put his craft alongside RFA SIR GALAHAD to start offloading troops to Fitzroy. Whilst alongside there was a sudden and completely unexpected bombing raid on the vessel and her sister ship RFA SIR TRISTRAM by four enemy aircraft. RFA SIR GALAHAD was hit centrally, immediately bursting into flames and billowing black smoke. One bomb fell within 10 feet of LCU Fl. Despite the possibility of a second raid (which developed later), Colour Sergeant Francis stayed alongside and took off a craft load of about 100 survivors, including many very badly wounded. After landing this load Colour Sergeant Francis returned to the area of RFA SIR GALAHAD, by now an inferno, took off the few remaining survivors, helped RFA SIR GALAHAD's life rafts into the shore, and then checked the rest of the area and other life rafts for further survivors. These are two separate actions of calm and selfless bravery, one in the presence of the enemy.

Chief Petty Officer Aircrewman Malcolm John TUPPER, D083002W
From the initial landings at San Carlos until the surrender of the Argentine Forces Chief Petty Officer Tupper flew as aircrewman to the Commanding Officer of 846 Naval Air Squadron for 150 hours, carrying out a wide range of operational tasks. Amongst these were his participation in the rescue of the crew of HMS COVENTRY when he volunteered to be lowered into a life raft to give assistance

to hypothermic, shocked and wounded survivors, eventually becoming close to hypothermia himself. On another mission in the Mount Kent area he gave warnings of two hostile aircraft about to attack the helicopter and then calmly passed contact reports to the pilot enabling him to take evasive action. His performance as the Squadron Chief Aircrewman was exemplary and a particular inspiration to younger and less experienced crewmen.

Petty Officer John Steven LEAKE D197741A
Petty Officer Leake originally joined HMS ARDENT as a civilian NAAFI Canteen Manager. On the declaration of Active Service he volunteered to enrol as a petty officer on 15th May 1982. On 21st May 1982 HMS ARDENT came under heavy attack by Argentine aircraft. Using his previous Army training, Petty Officer Leake was stationed as a machine gunner. Throughout the air attacks he remained cool and calm even though the ship was being hit by bombs and cannon fire. He fired large quantities of accurate tracer at the attackers and inflicted damage on a Skyhawk. His courage, steadfastness and total disregard for his own safety undoubtedly saved the ship from many further attacks and was an inspiration to all those in the vicinity.

Acting Petty Officer (Sonar) (SM) Graham John Robert LIBBY,
Dl 52458V
Whilst on patrol north of the Falkland Islands on 25th May 1982 a floating wire aerial trapped round HMS CONQUEROR'S propeller, causing cavitation and noise to the detriment of her operational effectiveness. Acting Petty Officer (Sonar) (SM) Libby volunteered to carry out a dive to free the obstruction. With the submarine surfaced he knew full well that if she were detected by Argentine aircraft she would possibly have to dive without recovering him. He was also battered by heavy waves, threatening to part his lifeline and sweeping him away. Nonetheless he succeeded in clearing most of the obstruction, after 20 minutes in dark, freezing, and terrifying conditions, enabling HMS CONQUEROR to continue on her patrol unhindered. Acting Petty Officer (Sonar)

(SM) Libby demonstrated a degree of cold, calculated courage and willingness to risk his life for the benefit of his ship far beyond any call of duty.

Leading Seaman (Radar) Jeffrey David WARREN, D133771A
On 23rd May 1982 HMS ANTELOPE came under heavy attack by Argentine aircraft. Leading Seaman (Radar) Warren was at his action station as starboard 20mm gun aimer. He showed coolness and steadiness, shooting down one Skyhawk. Later, when a bomb detonated on board he joined a small team of fire fighters who attempted to extinguish the fires above the explosion area, although they had no protective gear available. He saved the life of another member of this team by pulling him clear when he was overcome by smoke and about to fall through a hole in the ship's side. Although he was affected by smoke himself, Leading Seaman (Radar) Warren joined another fire-fighting team until they were halted by a lack of fire main and equipment. He then assisted the Commanding Officer whenever possible until the ship was abandoned. He demonstrated noticeable bravery and disregard for personal safety while fighting to preserve his ship and the safety of his fellows.

QUEEN'S GALLANTRY MEDAL

Acting Colour Sergeant Brian JOHNSTON, Royal Marines, PO23116X
Colour Sergeant Johnston, coxswain of LCU F4, was working in the vicinity of HMS ANTELOPE when her unexploded bomb detonated, starting an immediate fire which caused her crew, already at emergency stations, to be ordered to abandon ship. Without hesitation Colour Sergeant Johnston laid his craft alongside the ANTELOPE and began to fight the fire and take off survivors. At approximately 2200Z he was ordered to stay clear of the ship because of the severity of the fire and the presence of a second unexploded bomb. Colour Sergeant Johnston remained alongside until his load was complete. In all LCU F4 rescued over 100 survivors from the ANTELOPE.

On 8 June, LCU F4 was attacked by enemy aircraft in Choiseul Sound. During this action Colour Sergeant Johnston and five of his crew were killed. Colour Sergeant Johnston's selfless bravery in the face of extreme danger was in the highest traditions of the Corps.

Chief Engineer Officer Charles Kenneth Arthur ADAMS, Royal Fleet Auxiliary
On 26 May 1982, Chief Engineer Officer Adams, RFA SIR GALAHAD, gave much valuable advice and assistance during the removal of an unexploded 1000lb bomb from his ship. During this operation, he spent a considerable time in the compartment where the bomb was lodged and made a significant contribution to the removal operation. At 0600 on the following morning he volunteered to go to RFA SIR LANCELOT to advise on the removal route for the unexploded bomb in that ship, again working in close proximity to an unexploded bomb. His courage, determination and professionalism, in difficult and dangerous circumstances, were of a high order.

Lieutenant John Kenneth BOUGHTON, Royal Navy
Lieutenant Philip James SHELDON, Royal Navy
On 8 June 1982, RFA SIR GALAHAD and RFA SIR TRISTRAM, carrying large numbers of troops, were attacked by aircraft of the Argentine Air Force. RFA SIR GALAHAD was left damaged and burning with a considerable number of casualties. Aircraft of 825 Naval Air Squadron were on the scene within minutes and were joined for a time by a Sea King IV and Wessex V. The helicopters captained by Lieutenant Boughton and Lieutenant Sheldon conducted pick-ups of troops and crew mustered in the extremely confined area of the LSL fore-deck. Many were injured or in shock. The rescues were conducted close to masts and rigging with little clearance for the aircraft and with no regard for personal safety. Ammunition and pyrotechnics were exploding and there was a threat of further attack by enemy aircraft. Evacuation and rescue continued until darkness and were in fact interrupted by a further

air attack. The professionalism and bravery demonstrated in these operations by Lieutenant Boughton and Lieutenant Sheldon is representative of the crews and their Squadron.

Third Officer Andrew GUDGEON, Royal Fleet Auxiliary
Third Officer Gudgeon had been relieved in RFA SIR GALAHAD at Plymouth on 4 April 1982 but volunteered to remain during the Falklands campaign. On two occasions during this time he showed great courage in risking his life in order to save others. When HMS ANTELOPE blew up and caught fire in San Carlos Water, he volunteered to cox the crash boat to pick up survivors. This he did knowing that HMS ANTELOPE had a second unexploded bomb on board. Despite the fire spreading rapidly and spent Seacat missiles landing nearby, he carried out the rescue of several survivors in a cool and determined manner. Later, when SIR GALAHAD was bombed by Argentine aircraft and set on fire at Fitzroy Creek, the accommodation aft was rapidly set on fire and quickly filled with acrid smoke. Third Officer Gudgeon, wearing breathing apparatus, entered the area to search for people trapped. On his way towards the Galley he found someone at the foot of the ladder, trapped by debris but still alive. He made an unsuccessful attempt to move him and then decided to seek assistance, but as there were no more sets of breathing apparatus, he returned to make another rescue attempt. Unfortunately the man died. Third Officer Gudgeon placed his concern for others above his own safety and carried out his tasks with great courage and determination.

Third Engineer Brian Robert WILLIAMS, Merchant Navy
At the time when ATLANTIC CONVEYOR was hit by Exocet missiles Mr Williams, the Engineer Officer, was stationed on watch in the Engine Control Room with the mechanic. Soon after the missiles hit, the mechanic left the room and shortly after this was heard calling for help. The room was filling with smoke and would shortly be abandoned. Nonetheless Mr Williams promptly put on breathing apparatus and set off to the rescue of the mechanic whom he found, following a further large explosion, seriously injured and

trapped in a way that assistance would be required to release him. Mr Williams went quickly to get help. Then, realizing that a further rescue mission was a forlorn hope and knowing that there was a grave risk of further explosions and the spread of fire, he armed himself with asbestos gloves and fresh breathing apparatus and accompanied by the Doctor and a PO Engineer again braved the appalling heat and smoke for a further attempt to rescue the mechanic. However, as they approached, the conditions became literally unbearable and the mission had to be abandoned. Mr Williams made his report calmly and then went to the Breathing Apparatus store where he began valiant efforts to recharge air breathing bottles. He was eventually ordered to the upper deck to abandon ship. Throughout the incident Mr Williams showed exceptional bravery and leadership and a total disregard for his own safety.

Marine Engineering Artificer (M) 1st Class Kenneth ENTICKNAPP, D113547S
On 21 May 1982, HMS ARDENT was on station in San Carlos Water, East Falkland Island providing a defensive cover against air attack from Argentine forces, as land forces' equipment and supplies were being put ashore. The ship was first straddled by 2 bombs with little damage caused, but a subsequent aircraft in the same wave hit the ship port aft, destroying the Seacat missile launcher. HMS ARDENT was then attacked by 8 aircraft resulting in 8 further hits and very severe damage. The Damage Control parties, working in exposed positions, suffered the most serious casualties. There was widespread flooding of major spaces and a list developed. MEA(M) 1 Enticknapp was in charge of the after damage control party. Although the area was wrecked by the first bomb hits and he was slightly injured, he led his team successfully in fire fighting and damage control. Then, in the second wave of attacks, further bombs hit his team, killing all except two of his men. Now seriously injured, MEA(M)1 Enticknapp continued to fight the fire with the remaining man until a further bomb felled him, trapping him in the wreckage. Despite his own serious injuries MEA(M)1 Enticknapp showed dedication to duty under constant

enemy attack in the best traditions of the Service in placing the safety of other lives above his own.

Petty Officer Medical Assistant Gerald Andrew MEAGER, D127245D

On 4 May 1982, HMS SHEFFIELD was engaged in air defence of the South Atlantic Task Group when she was hit amidships by an Exocet missile which caused major damage and casualties. After 4 hours, with fighting capability destroyed and fire approaching the forward missile and gun magazines, the order to abandon ship was given to prevent further loss of life. POMA Meager gave immediate first aid treatment to the more serious casualties then collecting together his first aid teams established a most effective casualty centre in the hangar. He provided excellent direction and considerate encouragement where it was needed, comforted those who were suffering from shock and organized the evacuation of casualties by helicopter. At one point, receiving a report that a man below decks had been overcome by smoke, Meager donned breathing apparatus and rescued an unconscious man in most difficult circumstances. He also retrieved the body of another apparently unconscious man to an area where he could attempt resuscitation, though his subsequent determined efforts to save this man's life were unsuccessful. Later, at the order to abandon ship, he supervised most efficiently the evacuation of the remaining wounded and continued his care for them whilst on board the rescue ship. POMA Meager's selfless dedication to duty and professionalism in difficult circumstances undoubtedly saved life and minimized many injuries.

CONSPICUOUS GALLANTRY MEDAL

23834301 Staff Sergeant James PRESCOTT, Corps of Royal Engineers

On 22nd May 1982 Staff Sergeant Prescott, under the command of another NCO of 49 Engineer Explosives Disposal Squadron Royal Engineers, was carrying out explosive ordnance disposal duties in the Falkland Islands. They were tasked to deal with an unexploded bomb in the boiler room of HMS ARGONAUT. Another unexploded bomb lay in a flooded missile magazine nearby. Working in extraordinarily cramped conditions and in very unfamiliar surroundings, Staff Sergeant Prescott and the other NCO successfully remotely rendered safe the bomb, which was later removed from the ship. This action enabled the damage to the boiler room to be repaired, so that HMS ARGONAUT regained propulsion and was able to manoeuvre defensively in further air attacks. On 23rd May 1982, Staff Sergeant Prescott and the NCO were tasked to neutralize two unexploded bombs in HMS ANTELOPE. The first bomb examined could not be approached until extensive clearance of debris had taken place. They therefore set about rendering safe the second bomb, which was situated near the centre of the ship. The bomb had been slightly damaged and was assessed as being in a dangerous condition. They tried three times to render the bomb safe using a remote method, having to approach the bomb after each attempt to adjust the equipment, but on each occasion, the fuse could not be withdrawn. After a fourth attempt, which involved using a small charge, the bomb unexpectedly exploded. The blast was considerable. Despite a blast route of open doors and hatches up through the ship, the fully clipped steel door at the forward end of the passageway, where the bomb disposal team was standing, was completely blown off and nearly bent double. Staff Sergeant Prescott died instantly. Staff Sergeant Prescott displayed courage of the highest order in persevering with attempts to defuse the bomb in HMS ANTELOPE, fully aware that the condition was particularly dangerous.

MILITARY MEDAL

24172118 Sergeant Derrick Sidney BOULTBY, Royal Corps of Transport
Sergeant Boultby of 17 Port Regiment, RCT, was the NCO in charge of MEXEFLOTE rafts throughout the Falkland Islands operations. At Ascension Island during a massive re-stow operation he worked

all hours under difficult conditions to move cargo quickly. In San Carlos Water, the MEXEFLOTE rafts played a major part in the logistic landing of equipment to ensure the success of the fighting troops. From the exposed position which such a raft offers, Sergeant Boultby worked continuously throughout daylight hours and in extreme weather conditions. The vulnerability of his position to constant enemy air attack did not deter him from his task and he was an inspiration to his crew and other RCT personnel. He was coxswain of the MEXEFLOTE present at Fitzroy during the bombing of RFA SIR GALAHAD and RFA SIR TRISTRAM, and repeatedly returned to the area of the stricken ships to rescue survivors and, with complete disregard for his own safety, dived into the sea to rescue a Chinese crewman. Sergeant Boultby's dedication to his tasks in dangerous conditions was outstanding.

23952578 Sergeant Peter Hurcliche Rene NAYA, Royal Army Medical Corps

On 8th June 1982, whilst at anchor in Fitzroy Sound, East Falkland, RFA SIR GALAHAD was bombed and set on fire by enemy aircraft. Embarked troops included two companies of infantry and the main body of 16 Field Ambulance, men and equipment. At the time of the attack, most of the troops were positioned in the tank deck, where substantial quantities of ammunition soon began to explode as the fire worked through the ship. Sergeant Naya, Royal Army Medical Corps, was standing in the tank deck when he was thrown against a bulkhead by an explosion and partially stunned. The lights went out and the tank deck began to fill with dense black smoke. A second explosion set his large pack alight and scorched the back of his head. Shrugging off the burning material, he managed to lead a soldier up two flights of stairs to daylight on the upper deck. He then helped to carry a man who had lost a leg up the forecastle, having first administered first aid. He treated many more casualties including another amputee, and set up several infusions until, with all casualties evacuated, he left the ship on the last helicopter later to be evacuated as a casualty himself. After three days only he returned to duty in the Advance Surgical

Centre of the field ambulance, where he worked through the most intense period of military activity and the passage of many battle casualties. Sergeant Naya, being a casualty himself, was well aware of the dangers he faced by remaining in the stricken vessel and yet, with no thought for his own safety, devoted himself to the care of his injured comrades until such care was no longer required. Sergeant Naya's conduct throughout showed immense personal courage. He acted in the highest tradition of the Royal Army Medical Corps.

23929678 Warrant Officer Class 2 Brian Thomas NECK, Welsh Guards

On 8th June 1982, the Royal Fleet Auxiliary Landing Ship, SIR GALAHAD, had begun landing operations at Fitzroy Settlement on the Island of East Falkland. Embarked, preparing to land, was 1st Battalion Welsh Guards. With only minimal warning, the ship was attacked and severely damaged by bombs from several enemy aircraft. Intense fire and smoke spread rapidly from the devastated deck areas. In the fire, confusion, and exploding ammunition many casualties were incurred. Disregarding the conditions and ignoring the order to abandon ship, Warrant Officer Neck immediately began to organize the evacuation of soldiers from amongst the wreckage. Many times, disregarding his own safety, he rushed back through smoke filled areas, flames and continuing explosions to assist the hurt and injured. His courageous example, encouragement and assistance to his colleagues undoubtedly saved many lives.

Select Bibliography

PRINCIPAL OFFICIAL SOURCES

Documents held at The National Archives:

DEFE 24/2837 Operation *Corporate* (Falklands Conflict), HMS *Conqueror* Report of Proceedings.

DEFE 25/555 Operation *Corporate* (Falklands Conflict), Board of Inquiry Report into the Loss of HMS *Sheffield*.

DEFE 69/920 Operation *Corporate* (Falklands Conflict), Report of the Board of Inquiry into the Loss of RFA *Sir Tristram* and RFA *Sir Galahad*.

DEFE 69/1043 Operation *Corporate* (Falklands Conflict), Board of Inquiry Report into the Loss of HMS *Antelope*.

DEFE 69/1056 Operation *Corporate* (Falklands Conflict), Board of Inquiry Report into the Loss of HMS *Antelope*, documentary evidence.

DEFE 69/1248 Operation *Corporate* (Falklands Conflict), Preliminary Report of the Circumstances of the Loss of HMS *Ardent*, 3 June 1982.

DEFE 69/1336 Operation *Corporate* (Falklands Conflict), Board of Inquiry Report into the Loss of HMS *Coventry*.

DEFE 69/1338 Operation *Corporate* (Falklands Conflict), Board of Inquiry Report into the Loss of SS *Atlantic Conveyor*.

FCO 7/6011 House of Commons Foreign Affairs Committee Investigation into the Sinking of the Argentine Cruiser *General Belgrano*, 2 May 1982 (1984).

FCO 7/6436 House of Commons Foreign Affairs Committee Report into the Sinking of the Argentine Cruiser *General Belgrano*, 2 May 1982 (1985).

Document held at the Ministry of Defence:
FOI 2019/00768 Board of Inquiry Report into the Loss of HMS *Ardent.*

BOOKS

Beaver, P., *Encyclopaedia of the Modern Royal Navy* (Wellingborough: Patrick Stephens, 1985).
Brown, D., *The Royal Navy and the Falklands War* (London: Leo Cooper, 1987).
Brown, D. K., *Rebuilding the Royal Navy* (London: Chatham, 2003).
Brown, P., *The Portsmouth Dockyard Story* (Stroud: History Press, 2018).
Clapp, M., and Southby-Tailyour, E., *Amphibious Assault Falklands* (Barnsley: Pen & Sword, 2012).
Dept of the Navy, *Lessons from the Falklands* (Washington, D.C.: United States Navy, 1983).
Drought, C., *The Loss of the Atlantic Conveyor* (Birkenhead: Countyvise, 2003).
Finlan, A., *The Royal Navy in the Falklands Conflict and the Gulf War: Culture and Strategy* (London: Frank Cass, 2004).
Freedman, L., *The Official History of the Falklands Campaign, Vol 2: War and Diplomacy* (London: Routledge, 2005).
Friedman, N., *British Destroyers and Frigates* (London: Chatham, 2006).
Hart Dyke, D., *Four Weeks in May* (London: Atlantic, 2007).
Higgitt, M., *Through Fire and Water* (Edinburgh: Mainstream, 2007).
Lippiett, J., *Type 21* (Shepperton: Ian Allan, 1990).
McManners, H., *Forgotten Voices of the Falklands* (London: Ebury, 2007).
Moore, J., *Jane's Fighting Ships 1981–82* (London: Jane's, 1981).
Prebble, S., *Secrets of the* Conqueror (London: Faber & Faber, 2013).
Puddefoot, G., *The Fourth Force* (Barnsley: Seaforth, 2009).
Pugh, P., 'The Empire Strikes Back: the Falklands/Malvinas Campaigns of 1982', *The Mariner's Mirror*, 93:3 (2007), pp.307–24.
Rossiter, M., *Sink the Belgrano* (London: Bantam, 2007).
Sciaroni, M., *A Carrier at Risk* (Warwick: Helion, 2019).
Secretary of State for Defence, *The Falklands Campaign: The Lessons* (London: HMSO, 1982).
Ward, S., *Sea Harrier over the Falklands* (Barnsley: Leo Cooper, 1992).
Winton, J., *Signals from the Falklands* (Barnsley: Leo Cooper, 1995).
Woodward, S., *One Hundred Days* (London: Harper, 2012).

References

1 GOING TO WAR

1 HMSO, *The United Kingdom Defence Programme: The Way Forward*, http://fc95d419f4478b3b6e5f-3f71d0fe2b653c4f00f32175760e96e7. r87.cf1.rackcdn.com/991284B4011C44C9AEB423DA04A7D54B. pdf (retrieved 8 Nov 2019).
2 P. Brown, *The Portsmouth Dockyard Story* (Stroud: History Press, 2018), p.170.
3 Falkland Islands Government, 'Our History', https://www.falklands. gov.fk/our-people/our-history/ (retrieved 18 Nov 2019).
4 D. Brown, *The Royal Navy and the Falklands War* (London: Leo Cooper, 1987), pp.50–54.
5 Royal Navy, 'Battles: The Falklands Conflict 1982', https://web. archive.org/web/20080409233735/http://www.royal-navy.mod.uk/ server/show/nav.3956 (retrieved 24 Nov 2019).

2 THE SINKING OF ARA *GENERAL BELGRANO*

1 Wikipedia, https://en.wikipedia.org/wiki/USS_Phoenix_(CL-46) and https://en.wikipedia.org/wiki/ARA_General_Belgrano (retrieved 1 Jan 2020).
2 J. Moore, *Jane's Fighting Ships 1981–82* (London: Jane's, 1981), p.26.
3 M. Rossiter, *Sink the Belgrano* (London: Bantam, 2007), p.54.
4 Ibid.
5 Ibid., p.89.
6 Brown, *The Royal Navy and the Falklands War*, p.84.

7 Rossiter, *Sink the Belgrano*, p.94, 98, 101; The Belgrano Inquiry, 'Thirty Years On: An Argentine View', belgranoinquiry.com/may-2nd-2012-mr-moro-replies (retrieved 1 Jan 2020).

8 FCO 7/6011, House of Commons Foreign Affairs Committee Investigation into the Sinking of the Argentine Cruiser *General Belgrano*, 2 May 1982 (1984).

9 Rossiter, *Sink the Belgrano*, p. 95, 97, 99–100, 102–03.

10 Brown, *The Royal Navy and the Falklands War*, p.130.

11 C. Wreford-Brown in J. Winton, *Signals from the Falklands* (Barnsley: Leo Cooper, 1995), p.46.

12 Rossiter, *Sink the Belgrano*, p.77, 140, 144–45.

13 FCO 7/6011; S. Prebble, *Secrets of the* Conqueror (London: Faber & Faber, 2013), p.102; Rossiter, *Sink the Belgrano*, p. 182; DEFE 24/2837, Operation *Corporate* (Falklands Conflict), HMS *Conqueror* Report of Proceedings.

14 FCO 7/6011; 'Argentine Aircraft Lost in the Falklands Conflict', Naval History, www.naval-history.net/F64-Falklands-Argentine_aircraft_lost.htm (retrieved 30 Sept 2019); Brown, *The Royal Navy and the Falklands War*, pp.125–26.

15 FCO 7/6436, House of Commons Foreign Affairs Committee Report into the Sinking of the Argentine Cruiser *General Belgrano*, 2 May 1982 (1985); Prebble, *Secrets of the* Conqueror, p.105; C. Wreford-Brown in Winton, *Signals from the Falklands*, pp.49–50; DEFE 24/2837, Report.

16 FCO 7/6011; FCO 7/6436; Prebble, *Secrets of the* Conqueror, p.106.

17 Rossiter, *Sink the Belgrano*, p.210

18 C. Wreford-Brown in Winton, *Signals from the Falklands*, pp. 50–51.

19 S. Woodward, *One Hundred Days* (London: Harper, 2012), pp.215–16.

20 FCO 7/6011.

21 FCO 7/6436; DEFE 24/2837, Report.

22 Ibid.; Prebble, *Secrets of the* Conqueror, p.107.

23 C. Madero in H. McManners, *Forgotten Voices of the Falklands* (London: Ebury, 2007), p.147, 149.

24 Belgrano Inquiry, 'Thirty Years On', belgranoinquiry.com/may-2nd-2012-mr-moro-replies (retrieved 1 Jan 2020).

25 FCO 7/6011.

26 Ibid.

27 FCO 7/6436; DEFE 24/2837, Report; Prebble, *Secrets of the Conqueror*, p.106; Woodward, *One Hundred Days*, p.221.

28 C. Wreford-Brown in Winton, *Signals from the Falklands*, p.50; Prebble, *Secrets of the* Conqueror, pp.110–11.

29 M Sciaroni, *A Carrier at Risk* (Warwick: Helion, 2019), p.32.

30 DEFE 24/2837, Report; Prebble, *Secrets of the* Conqueror, pp.115–16; C. Wreford-Brown in Winton, *Signals from the Falklands*, p.51.

31 DEFE 24/2837, Report; Prebble, *Secrets of the* Conqueror, p.118.

32 Ibid., p.120.

33 'My Part in the Sinking of the *Belgrano*', *The Scotsman*, 29 April 2007, https://www.scotsman.com/news/uk-news/my-part-in-sinking-of-the-belgrano-1-1418775 (retrieved 1 Jan 2020).

34 Woodward, *One Hundred Days*, p.223; C. Wreford-Brown in Winton, *Signals from the Falklands*, p.46 (from a lecture given at Cambridge University).

35 C. Wreford-Brown in Winton, *Signals from the Falklands*, p.52 (from a lecture given at Cambridge University).

36 Prebble, *Secrets of the* Conqueror, pp.116–17; Rossiter, *Sink the Belgrano*, pp.236–38; C. Madero in McManners, *Forgotten Voices*, pp.153–54.

37 C. Madero in McManners, *Forgotten Voices*, pp.151–53.

38 Rossiter, *Sink the Belgrano*, pp.238–39.

39 Ibid., pp.219–48; C. Madero in McManners, *Forgotten Voices*, p.153.

40 Rossiter, *Sink the Belgrano*, pp.249–54; C. Madero in McManners, *Forgotten Voices*, p.155.

41 Prebble, *Secrets of the* Conqueror, pp.122–23.

42 Ibid., pp.145–47.

43 FCO 7/6011.

44 FCO 7/6436.

45 Woodward, *One Hundred Days*, p.217.

46 George Allison, 'Britain was Right to Sink the *Belgrano*', *UK Defence Journal*, 27.1.2017, https://ukdefencejournal.org.uk/britain-was-right-to-sink-the-belgrano/ (retrieved 1 Jan 2020).

47 *Supplement to the London Gazette* of 8 October 1982, published 11 October 1982.

48 Brown, *The Royal Navy and the Falklands War*, p.371; Moore, *Jane's Fighting Ships 1981–82*, p.27.

49 Woodward, *One Hundred Days*, p.220.

3 THE LOSS OF HMS *SHEFFIELD*

1 DEFE 25/555, Operation *Corporate* (Falklands Conflict), Board of Inquiry Report into the Loss of HMS *Sheffield*.

2 D. K. Brown, *Rebuilding the Royal Navy* (London: Chatham, 2003), p.97

3 N. Friedman, *British Destroyers and Frigates* (London: Chatham, 2006), pp.286–87; Brown, *Rebuilding the Royal Navy*, p.94, 98; Moore, *Jane's Fighting Ships 1981–82*, p.566.

4 Woodward, *One Hundred Days*, pp.76–77.

5 DEFE 25/555, Report, Annex C.

6 DEFE 69/1336, Operation *Corporate* (Falklands Conflict), Board of Inquiry Report into the Loss of HMS *Coventry*, submission to Admiralty Board 22.10.82.

7 Moore, *Jane's Fighting Ships 1981–82*, p.566; Friedman, *British Destroyers and Frigates*, p.284, 286.

8 Sam Salt obituary, *The Guardian*, https://www.theguardian.com/theguardian/2009/dec/10/sam-salt-obituary; Rear Admiral Sam Salt, Obituaries, *Daily Telegraph*, https://www.telegraph.co.uk/news/obituaries/military-obituaries/naval-obituaries/6744685/Rear-Admiral-Sam-Salt.html (both retrieved 1 Sept 2019).

9 DEFE 25/555, Report, Annex C.

10 DEFE 25/555, Report, Annex D.

11 Ibid.

12 Woodward, *One Hundred Days*, p.95.

13 DEFE 25/555, Report, Annex D.

14 DEFE 25/555, Report, Annex H.

15 DEFE 25/555, Report and Annex H.

16 DEFE 25/555, Report, Annex G.

17 Moore, *Jane's Fighting Ships 1981–82*, p.25.

18 DEFE 25/555, Report, Annex G.

19 Woodward, *One Hundred Days*, pp.1–6.

20 Ibid., p.11.

21 Ibid., p.9.

22 S. Ward, *Sea Harrier over the Falklands* (Barnsley: Leo Cooper, 1992), p.172.

23 DEFE 25/555, Report.

24 Woodward, *One Hundred Days*, pp.16–17.

25 Brown, *The Royal Navy and the Falklands War*, pp.159–160.

26 D. Hart Dyke, *Four Weeks in May* (London: Atlantic, 2007), p.120.

27 DEFE 25/555, Report and Annex H.

28 P. Walpole in McManners, *Forgotten Voices*, p.161.

29 DEFE 25/555, Report and Annex H.

30 S. Salt in Winton, *Signals from the Falklands*, p.55.

31 'HMS *Sheffield* Survivor Recalls Horror of Sinking', BBC News, https://www.bbc.co.uk/news/uk-england-hampshire-17950566 (retrieved 1 Jan 2019).

32 Hart Dyke, *Four Weeks in May*, pp.91–93.

33 DEFE 25/555, Report and Annex K; P. Walpole in McManners, *Forgotten Voices*, pp.162–64.

34 D. Manley, 'The Loss of HMS Sheffield – A Technical Re-assessment', RINA Warship Conference, Bath, June 2015.

35 DEFE 25/555, Report.

36 DEFE 25/555, Report and Annex L.

37 *Supplement to the London Gazette* of 8 October 1982.

38 M. Collins in Winton, *Signals from the Falklands*, pp.61–62.

39 P. Walpole in McManners, *Forgotten Voices*, pp.164–67.

40 Woodward, *One Hundred Days*, p.22, 27.

41 DEFE 25/555, Report and Annex R; M. Chiplen and D. Ward in Winton, *Signals from the Falklands*, p.60.

42 DEFE 25/555, Report and Annex R.

43 *Supplement to the London Gazette* of 8 October 1982; Winton, *Signals from the Falklands*, pp.60–61.

44 'I Saw Comrade Die, Survivor Recalls Falklands Sinking', Forces Network, https://www.forces.net/news/i-saw-comrade-die-survivor-recalls-falklands-warship-sinking; 'A Sailor, A Survivor', YouTube, https://www.youtube.com/watch?v=68rPePPo5_k (both retrieved 2 Sept 2019).

45 Woodward, *One Hundred Days*, p.22, 25; P. Walpole in McManners, *Forgotten Voices*, p.167, 170.

46 S. Salt in Winton, *Signals from the Falklands*, pp.58–59.

47 Brown, *The Royal Navy and the Falklands War*, p.76, 120.

48 S. Salt in Winton, *Signals from the Falklands*, p.218.

49 DEFE 25/555, Report and Annexes K and N.

50 *Supplement to the London Gazette* of 8 October 1982.

51 Winton, *Signals from the Falklands*, p.61.

52 S. Salt in Winton, *Signals from the Falklands*, pp.218–19.

53 DEFE 25/555, Report.
54 Ibid.
55 DEFE 25/555, Report and Annex S.
56 Ian Cobain, 'Revealed: Catalogue of Failings that Sank Falklands Warship HMS *Sheffield*', *The Guardian*, 15 Oct 2017, https://www.theguardian.com/uk-news/2017/oct/15/revealed-full-story-behind-sinking-of-falklands-warship-hms-sheffield (retrieved 5 Sept 2019); L. Freedman, *The Official History of the Falklands Campaign, Vol 2: War and Diplomacy* (London: Routledge, 2005), p.305.
57 DEFE 25/555, Report and Annexes K and L.
58 Ibid.
59 DEFE 25/555, Report.
60 DEFE 25/555, Fieldhouse, letter to Deputy Under Secretary of State (Navy), 13 Sept 1982.

4 THE LOSS OF HMS *ARDENT*

1 J. Lippiett, *Type 21* (Shepperton: Ian Allan, 1990), pp.24–26.
2 Moore, *Jane's Fighting Ships 1981–82*, p.567; P. Beaver, *Encyclopaedia of the Modern Royal Navy* (Wellingborough: Patrick Stephens, 1985), p.93; FOI 2019/00768, Report of Board of Inquiry on the Loss of HMS *Ardent*, 6 August 1982, Appendix 1 to Annex G.
3 FOI 2019/00768, Appendix 1 to Annex D.
4 Lippiett, *Type 21*, pp.19–20.
5 RN Point Defence, Flight International, https://www.flightglobal.com/FlightPDFArchive/1973/1973%20-%202717.PDF (retrieved 29 Oct 2019); Lippiett, *Type 21*, pp.28–29.
6 Lippiett, *Type 21*, pp.24–25.
7 Brown, *Rebuilding the Royal Navy*, pp.103–04; Friedman, *British Destroyers and Frigates*, pp.295–96.
8 'Alan West, Baron West of Spithead', Wikipedia, https://en.wikipedia.org/wiki/Alan_West,_Baron_West_of_Spithead (retrieved 24 Sept 2019); Woodward, *One Hundred Days*, p.346.
9 FOI 2019/00768, Appendix 1 to Annex B.
10 Ibid.
11 FOI 2019/00768, Annex B.
12 Ibid; M. Higgitt, *Through Fire and Water* (Edinburgh: Mainstream, 2007), p.45.

13 FOI 2019/00768, Annex B.

14 FOI 2019/00768, Annexes B and Q.

15 FOI 2019/00768, Annexes C and E.

16 FOI 2019/00768, Annex C and Appendix 1 to Annex C; Brown, *The Royal Navy and the Falklands War*, pp.178–79.

17 FOI 2019/00768, Annex I.

18 FOI 2019/00768, Annex F; Brown, *The Royal Navy and the Falklands War*, p.184; M. Clapp and E. Southby-Tailyour, *Amphibious Assault Falklands* (Barnsley: Pen & Sword, 2012), p.143.

19 FOI 2019/00768, Annex F.

20 FOI 2019/00768, Appendix 2 to Annex F and Annex Q.

21 FOI 2019/00768, Report and Annex F.

22 FOI 2019/00768, Annex F; 'Argentine Aircraft Lost in the Falklands Conflict', Naval History, www.naval-history.net/F64-Falklands-Argentine_aircraft_lost.htm (retrieved 30 Sept 2019); Ward, *Sea Harrier*, pp.207–08.

23 FOI 2019/00768, Annex F; Brown, *The Royal Navy and the Falklands War*, p.191.

24 FOI 2019/00768, Annex F.

25 FOI 2019/00768, Appendix 2 to Annex F.

26 FOI 2019/00768, Annex F.

27 FOI 2019/00768, Map Appendix 9 to Annex F.

28 FOI 2019/00768, Annex F; Brown, *The Royal Navy and the Falklands War*, pp.193–94; Higgitt, *Through Fire and Water*, p.174, 176, 185.

29 FOI 2019/00768, Annexes F, G, H and Q; Higgitt, *Through Fire and Water*, p.403.

30 FOI 2019/00768, Annexes H and I; DEFE 69/1248 Operation *Corporate* (Falklands Conflict), Preliminary Report of the Circumstances of the Loss of HMS *Ardent*, 3 June 1982. ; Higgitt, *Through Fire and Water*, p.202, 205, 403.

31 FOI 2019/00768, Annex H; Higgitt, *Through Fire and Water*, p.208.

32 FOI 2019/00768, Annexes G and H.

33 FOI 2019/00768, Annexes F, G and H.

34 FOI 2019/00768, Annexes F and H; DEFE 69/1248; Brown, *The Royal Navy and the Falklands War*, pp.195–96; Woodward, *One Hundred Days*, p.371.

35 FOI 2019/00768, Annex H.

36 Ibid.

37 Ibid.

38 FOI 2019/00768, Annex I.

39 FOI 2019/00768, Annex Q; DEFE 69/1248.

40 FOI 2019/00768, Annex I.

41 FOI 2019/00768, Annex H.

42 Ibid.

43 Higgitt, *Through Fire and Water*, p.300; DEFE 69/1248.

44 FOI 2019/00768 , Annex D; Higgitt, *Through Fire and Water*, p.213.

45 FOI 2019/00768, Annex H.

46 FOI 2019/00768, Annexes F, G, H and J and Appendix 2 to Annex F.

47 FOI 2019/00768, Annex K.

48 Ibid.

49 Higgitt, *Through Fire and Water*, pp.241–42.

50 FOI 2019/00768, Annex H.

51 Higgitt, *Through Fire and Water*, pp.237–38.

52 FOI 2019/00768, Annexes K and Q; Higgitt, *Through Fire and Water*, p.220, 253, 255–57; K. Enticknapp in Winton, *Signals from the Falklands*, pp. 84–85.

53 Adapted from 'Falklands War Hero who Saved Lives of Hundreds of British and Argentine Forces Has Died Aged 71', *Plymouth Herald*, https://www.plymouthherald.co.uk/news/plymouth-news/falklands-war-hero-who-saved-1061956.amp (retrieved 27 Sept 2019).

54 FOI 2019/00768, Annexes K and Q.

55 FOI 2019/00768, Annex R.

56 FOI 2019/00768, Annex K.

57 McManners, *Forgotten Voices*, p.213; Ward, *Sea Harrier*, pp.210–11.

58 Brown, *The Royal Navy and the Falklands War*, p.246, 315.

59 FOI 2019/00768, Report.

60 FOI 2019/00768, Annex 1.

61 Ibid.

62 Ibid.

63 FOI 2019/00768, Report, Annex K; DEFE 69/1248.

64 FOI 2019/00768, Annex N.

65 FOI 2019/00768, Annexes F and G, Appendices 1 and 2 to Annex G.

66 FOI 2019/00768, Annex F and Appendix 14 to Annex F.

67 FOI 2019/00768, Annex H.

68 Ibid.

69 Ibid.

70 Ibid.

71 Ibid.

72 FOI 2019/00768, Report and Annex H.
73 FOI 2019/00768, Annexes H and J.
74 FOI 2019/00768, Report and Annex H.
75 Ibid.
76 FOI 2019/00768, Report.
77 FOI 2019/00768, Annex Q.
78 FOI 2019/00768, Annex H.
79 Higgitt, *Through Fire and Water*, p. 331; *Supplement to the London Gazette* of 8 October 1982.
80 Culture24, 'First Sea Lord Admiral Sir Alan West On Nelson and Trafalgar 2005', https://www.culture24.org.uk/history-and-heritage/military-history/pre-20th-century-conflict/art32693 (retrieved 25 Sept 2019).
81 Lippiett, *Type 21*, p.109.

5 THE LOSS OF HMS *ANTELOPE*

1 Brown, *Rebuilding the Royal Navy*, p.104.
2 Buckingham Covers, https://www.buckinghamcovers.com/celebrities/view/439-captain-n-tobin-dsc-ma-royal-navy.php (retrieved 23 July 2019).
3 DEFE 69/1043, Operation *Corporate* (Falklands Conflict), Board of Inquiry Report into the Loss of HMS *Antelope*, and Annexes D and S; DEFE 69/1056, Operation *Corporate* (Falklands Conflict), Board of Inquiry Report into the Loss of HMS *Antelope*, documentary evidence.
4 DEFE 69/1043, Report.
5 DEFE 69/1043, Annexes D and S.
6 DEFE 69/1056.
7 DEFE 69/1043, Annexes C and G; Brown, *The Royal Navy and the Falklands War*, pp.71–72; Clapp and Southby-Tailyour, *Amphibious Assault Falklands*, p.31.
8 DEFE 69/1043, Annexes H and S.
9 DEFE 69/1043, Annexes C, H and S; Brown, *The Royal Navy and the Falklands War*, p.92, 95, 149; Clapp and Southby-Tailyour, *Amphibious Assault Falklands*, p.82.
10 DEFE 69/1043, Annexes C and H.
11 DEFE 69/1043, Annex H.
12 DEFE 69/1043, Annexes J and S and Ship's Investigation.

13 Brown, *The Royal Navy and the Falklands War*, pp.205–07; Clapp and Southby-Tailyour, *Amphibious Assault Falklands*, p.153, 156; DEFE 69/1043, Ship's Investigation.

14 DEFE 69/1043, Annexes J and S and Ship's Investigation; Brown, *The Royal Navy and the Falklands War*, p.207; 'Argentine Aircraft Lost', Naval History, www.naval-history.net/F64-Falklands-Argentine_aircraft_lost.htm (retrieved 2 July 2019).

15 DEFE 69/1043, Annex X.

16 DEFE 69/1043, Annex J.

17 J. Warren in Winton, *Signals from the Falklands*, pp.98–99.

18 DEFE 69/1043, Annexes J and S; Brown, *The Royal Navy and the Falklands War*, p.207.

19 DEFE 69/1043, Annex S.

20 DEFE 69/1043, Annex J.

21 DEFE 69/1043, Annex X.

22 DEFE 69/1043, Annex K.

23 DEFE 69/1043, Annexes C, K and L, and Ship's Investigation.

24 DEFE 69/1043, Ship's Investigation.

25 DEFE 69/1043, Annex M; Brown, *The Royal Navy and the Falklands War*, pp.209–10.

26 DEFE 69/1043, Annex M.

27 DEFE 69/1043, Annexes M and X; Brown, *The Royal Navy and the Falklands War*, pp.209–10.

28 DEFE 69/1043, Annex M.

29 DEFE 69/1043, Report.

30 DEFE 69/1043, Report, Annex N and Ship's Investigation.

31 J. Warren in Winton, *Signals from the Falklands*, pp.100–01.

32 DEFE 69/1043, Annex N.

33 Ibid.

34 Ibid.

35 Ibid.

36 DEFE 69/1043, Annex N and Ship's Investigation; Woodward, *One Hundred Days*, p.390.

37 DEFE 69/1043, Annex P.

38 DEFE 69/1043, Report and Ship's Investigation.

39 DEFE 69/1043, Report and Annex P.

40 DEFE 69/1043, Ship's Investigation.

41 DEFE 69/1043, Annex B.

42 Clapp and Southby-Tailyour, *Amphibious Assault Falklands*, p.164.

43 DEFE 69/1043, Ship's Investigation.
44 *Supplement to the London Gazette* of 8 October 1982.
45 DEFE 69/1043, Report.
46 DEFE 69/1043, Annex H.
47 DEFE 69/1043, Annexes D and S.
48 DEFE 69/1043, Annexes J and S.
49 DEFE 69/1043, Annex L.
50 DEFE 69/1043, Annex M.
51 Ibid.
52 DEFE 69/1043, Annex M; Clapp and Southby-Tailyour, *Amphibious Assault Falklands*, p.165.
53 DEFE 69/1043, Annexes M and N.
54 DEFE 69/1043, Report.
55 Ibid.
56 DEFE 69/1043, Annex M.
57 DEFE 69/1043, Report.
58 DEFE 69/1043, Annex B.

6 THE SINKING OF HMS *COVENTRY*

1 Moore, *Jane's Fighting Ships 1981–82*, p.566; Friedman, *British Destroyers and Frigates*, p.284, 286.
2 Dyke, *Four Weeks in May*, p.15.
3 Beaver, *Encyclopaedia of the Modern Royal Navy*, p.252.
4 DEFE 69/1336; 'HMS *Coventry* (D118)', Wikipedia, https://en.wikipedia.org/wiki/HMS_Coventry_%28D118%29 (retrieved 28 July 2019).
5 'David Hart Dyke', Wikipedia, https://en.wikipedia.org/wiki/David_Hart_Dyke (retrieved 28 July 2019).
6 DEFE 69/1336 Report; 'HMS *Coventry* (D118)', Wikipedia, https://en.wikipedia.org/wiki/HMS_Coventry_%28D118%29 (retrieved 28 July 2019).
7 Moore, *Jane's Fighting Ships 1981–82*, p.566.
8 *Sea of Fire* DVD, Simply Home Entertainment (2007).
9 Woodward, *One Hundred Days*, pp.107–08.
10 *Sea of Fire.*
11 DEFE 69/1336 Report; Hart Dyke, *Four Weeks in May*, p.89.
12 DEFE 69/1336 Report.
13 Ibid.

14 Ibid.; Hart Dyke, *Four Weeks in May*, p.101; 'Argentine Aircraft Lost', Naval History, www.naval-history.net/F64-Falklands-Argentine_aircraft_lost.htm (retrieved 27 April 2020).

15 DEFE 69/1336 Report.

16 Ibid.

17 Woodward, *One Hundred Days*, p.268, 271; Hart Dyke, *Four Weeks in May*, p.101.

18 DEFE 69/1336, Report.

19 DEFE 69/1336, Report and Appendix 5 to Annex B.

20 DEFE 69/1336, Report and Appendix 6 to Annex B.

21 Hart Dyke, *Four Weeks in May*, p.120; DEFE 69/1336, Report.

22 DEFE 69/1336, Report.

23 Hart Dyke, *Four Weeks in May*, pp.132–33.

24 Woodward, *One Hundred Days*, pp.395–96; DEFE 69/1336, Report.

25 DEFE 69/1336, Report.

26 Ibid.

27 Ward, *Sea Harrier*, p.220.

28 DEFE 69/1336, Report.

29 Hart Dyke, *Four Weeks in May*, pp.145–46.

30 DEFE 69/1336, Report; Woodward, *One Hundred Days*, pp. 404–05.

31 DEFE 69/1336, Report.

32 DEFE 69/1336, Annex C.

33 Woodward, *One Hundred Days*, pp.405–06.

34 DEFE 69/1336, Report and Appendix 1 to Annex D.

35 Ibid.

36 Ibid.

37 Hart Dyke, *Four Weeks in May*, p.149.

38 DEFE 69/1336, Report and Appendix 1 to Annex D.

39 Ibid.

40 Ibid.

41 DEFE 69/1336, Annex C.

42 Woodward, *One Hundred Days*, pp.407–08; DEFE 69/1336, Appendix 1 to Annex D.

43 Hart Dyke, *Four Weeks in May*, pp.149–50.

44 DEFE 69/1336, Report.

45 Ibid.

46 Hart Dyke, *Four Weeks in May*, p.156.

47 Ibid., pp.150–52.

48 Ibid., p.153, 161; *Sea of Fire*.

49 S. MacFarlane in McManners, *Forgotten Voices*, pp.223–24.

50 Ibid., pp.224–26; L. Rumley, 'Surviving a Falklands Suicide Mission', http://news.bbc.co.uk/1/hi/uk/6705387.stm (retrieved 29 July 2019); S. MacFarlane in Winton, *Signals from the Falklands*, p.117.

51 Hart Dyke, *Four Weeks in May*, p.158; DEFE 69/1336, Annex F.

52 DEFE 69/1336, Annex F.

53 Hart Dyke, *Four Weeks in May*, pp.188–89; DEFE 69/1336, Annex F.

54 DEFE 69/1336, Annex F.

55 Ibid.

56 Ibid.

57 Hart Dyke, *Four Weeks in May*, p.159.

58 DEFE 69/1336, Report.

59 D. Hart Dyke in Winton, *Signals from the Falklands*, p.112.

60 Ibid.

61 R. Adams in McManners, *Forgotten Voices*, pp.228–30.

62 S. MacFarlane in McManners, *Forgotten Voices*, pp.229–32.

63 DEFE 69/1336, Report.

64 Ibid.

65 Ibid.

66 DEFE 69/1336, Annex H; Hart Dyke, *Four Weeks in May*, pp.192–93.

67 DEFE 69/1336, Annex G.

68 *Supplement to the London Gazette* of 8 Oct 1982.

69 DEFE 69/1336, Report.

70 Ibid.

71 Woodward, *One Hundred Days*, p.409.

72 DEFE 69/1336, Annex C.

73 Ibid.

74 DEFE 69/1336, Annex D.

75 Friedman, *British Destroyers and Frigates*, p.289.

76 DEFE 69/1336, Report.

7 THE LOSS OF SS *ATLANTIC CONVEYOR*

1 Think Defence, 'The Atlantic Conveyor', https://www.thinkdefence.co.uk/the-atlantic-conveyor/ (retrieved 26 Oct 2019); 'SS *Atlantic Conveyor*', Wikipedia, https://en.wikipedia.org/wiki/SS_Atlantic_Conveyor (retrieved 26 Oct 2019).

2 DEFE 69/1338, Operation *Corporate* (Falklands Conflict), Board of Inquiry Report into the Loss of SS *Atlantic Conveyor*, Annex D.

3 Think Defence, '*The Atlantic Conveyor*', https://www.thinkdefence. co.uk/the-atlantic-conveyor/ (retrieved 26 Oct 2019); M. Layard in Winton, *Signals from the Falklands*, p.72, 76.

4 C. Drought, *The Loss of the Atlantic Conveyor* (Birkenhead: Countyvise, 2003), p.19, 183–84.

5 DEFE 69/1338, Report.

6 M. Layard in Winton, *Signals from the Falklands*, p.73.

7 Woodward, *One Hundred Days*, p.416; Drought, *Loss of the Atlantic Conveyor*, p.30.

8 DEFE 69/1338, Report.

9 'Admiral Sir Michael Layard', Buckingham Covers, https://www. buckinghamcovers.com/celebrities/view/249-.php (retrieved 15 July 2020); 'Admiral Sir Michael Layard', Cranston Fine Arts, https://www. directart.co.uk/mall/profiles.php?SigID=1357 (retrieved 15 July 2020).

10 Brown, *The Royal Navy and the Falklands War*, p.94.

11 DEFE 69/1338, Annex D.

12 DEFE 69/1338, Annex I.

13 Think Defence, '*The Atlantic Conveyor*', https://www.thinkdefence. co.uk/the-atlantic-conveyor/ (retrieved 26 Oct 2019).

14 DEFE 69/1338, Report and Annexes A and B; Brown, *The Royal Navy and the Falklands War*, p.94.

15 Drought, *The Loss of the Atlantic Conveyor*, p.37.

16 DEFE 69/1338, Annexes A and D; Brown, *The Royal Navy and the Falklands War*, p.95.

17 Clapp and Southby-Tailyour, *Amphibious Assault Falklands*, pp.97–98.

18 Brown, *The Royal Navy and the Falklands War*, p.170.

19 Drought, *The Loss of the Atlantic Conveyor*, p.45.

20 DEFE 69/1338, Annex A.

21 Woodward, *One Hundred Days*, p.327.

22 Brown, *The Royal Navy and the Falklands War*, p. 205, 211.

23 DEFE 69/1338, Annex A; Woodward, *One Hundred Days*, p.417.

24 DEFE 69/1338, Annex A.

25 Brown, *The Royal Navy and the Falklands War*, p.227; Woodward, *One Hundred Days*, pp.417–18.

26 DEFE 69/1338, Annex A, Appendix 1 to Appendix 5; Woodward, *One Hundred Days*, pp.418–19.

27 DEFE 69/1338, Annex A.

28 Woodward, *One Hundred Days*, p.419.

29 Ibid.

30 DEFE 69/1338, Annex F.

31 DEFE 69/1338, Annex H.

32 DEFE 69/1338, Annex A; Drought, *The Loss of the Atlantic Conveyor*, pp.82–86.

33 DEFE 69/1338, Annex A; Drought, *The Loss of the Atlantic Conveyor*, pp.86–90.

34 DEFE 69/1338, Annex A.

35 DEFE 69/1338, Report and Annex A.

36 DEFE 69/1338, Annex B.

37 DEFE 69/1338, Report and Annex A; Drought, *The Loss of the Atlantic Conveyor*, pp.107–15.

38 Woodward, *One Hundred Days*, pp.420–21.

39 DEFE 69/1338, Annex L.

40 Ibid.

41 DEFE 69/1338, Annex A; Brown, *The Royal Navy and the Falklands War*, pp.239–40.

42 Think Defence, 'The Atlantic Conveyor', https://www.thinkdefence.co.uk/the-atlantic-conveyor/ (retrieved 26 Oct 2019).

43 DEFE 69/1338, Annex K.

44 DEFE 69/1338, Report.

45 DEFE 69/1338, Annexes A and M1.

46 DEFE 69/1338, Letter to DUS(N) at MOD, 13 Sept 82.

47 DEFE 69/1338, Annex A.

48 Ibid.

49 Ibid.

50 DEFE 69/1338, Annex B.

51 DEFE 69/1338, Annex F.

52 DEFE 69/1338, Annex M1.

53 DEFE 69/1338, Report.

54 DEFE 69/1338, Report and Annex E.

55 DEFE 69/1338, Report.

56 M. Layard in Winton, *Signals from the Falklands*, p.123.

57 *Supplement to the London Gazette* of 8 October 1982.

8 THE LOSS OF RFA *SIR GALAHAD*

1 Moore, *Jane's Fighting Ships 1981–82*, p.572; Clapp and Southby-Tailyour, *Amphibious Assault Falklands*, p.18, 23.

2 Brown, *The Royal Navy and the Falklands War*, p.68, 71–72, 92; P. Roberts in Winton, *Signals from the Falklands*, p.161.

3 G. Puddefoot, *The Fourth Force* (Barnsley: Seaforth, 2009), pp.108–09.

4 P. Roberts in Winton, *Signals from the Falklands*, p.162.

5 Brown, *The Royal Navy and the Falklands War*, pp.178–79, 181.

6 P. Roberts in Winton, *Signals from the Falklands*, p.163.

7 Brown, *The Royal Navy and the Falklands War*, pp.212–14, 216, 258; 'RFA *Sir Galahad*', Wikipedia, https://en.wikipedia.org/wiki/RFA_Sir_Galahad_(1966) (retrieved 24 April 2019); www.mcdoa.org.uk/The_Forgotten_Few_of_the_Falklands.htm (retrieved 24 April 2019).

8 DEFE 69/920, A. R. M. Jaffray, Deputy Under Secretary of State (Navy), letter to CinC Fleet, 8 Feb 1983.

9 Puddefoot, *Fourth Force*, p.120.

10 Brown, *The Royal Navy and the Falklands War*, p.276, 280, 286.

11 Clapp and Southby-Tailyour, *Amphibious Assault Falklands*, p.219.

12 Ibid., p.225.

13 Ibid., p.230.

14 Ibid., p.237, 240.

15 DEFE 69/920, Operation *Corporate* (Falklands Conflict), Report of the Board of Inquiry into the Loss of RFA *Sir Tristram* and RFA *Sir Galahad*, Narrative and Annex E5.

16 Clapp and Southby-Tailyour, *Amphibious Assault Falklands*, p.231, 239.

17 Ibid., p.243.

18 Ibid.

19 DEFE 69/920 Report, Narrative, and Annexes E4 and E5.

20 DEFE 69/920, Annex E2.

21 DEFE 69/920, Captain's Report.

22 Ibid.

23 Ibid.

24 DEFE 69/920, Captain's Report and Annex E2.

25 Puddefoot, *Fourth Force*, p.121.

26 DEFE 69/920, Captain's Report and Annex E2.

27 DEFE 69/920, Captain's Report and Annex E5.

28 DEFE 69/920, Narrative and Annex E5; Brown, *The Royal Navy and the Falklands War*, p.291; Puddefoot, *Fourth Force*, p.121.

29 DEFE 69/920, Captain's Report.

30 Ibid.

31 DEFE 69/920, Annex F2; Puddefoot, *Fourth Force*, p.122.

32 DEFE 69/920, Annexes E11 and F2; Puddefoot, *Fourth Force*, p.123.

33 DEFE 69/920, Annex E11.

34 DEFE 69/920, Annex F2 and Narrative.

35 DEFE 69/920, Captain's Report and Narrative; Puddefoot, *Fourth Force*, p.125.

36 DEFE 69/920, Captain's Report and Narrative; Puddefoot, *Fourth Force*, pp.124–25.

37 DEFE 69/920, Captain's Report; Puddefoot, *Fourth Force*, pp.124–25.

38 DEFE 69/920, Captain's Report.

39 'Falklands Hero's Courage Under Fire', *Bournemouth Echo*, https://www.bournemouthecho.co.uk/news/8413813.falklands-heros-courage-under-fire/ (retrieved 3 June 2019).

40 Polly Toynbee, '"I'm beautiful," said Simon Weston, a survivor from the Sir Galahad. "I was beautiful before and I'm beautiful now."' *The Guardian*, 11 Oct 1982, https://www.theguardian.com/uk/1982/oct/11/falklands.world (retrieved 25 Aug 2020).

41 M. Nicholson in McManners, *Forgotten Voices*, pp.327–28.

42 DEFE 69/920, Captain's Report.

43 R. Jolly in Winton, *Signals from the Falklands*, pp.169–71.

44 DEFE 69/920, Report, Captain's Report and Narrative; Puddefoot, *Fourth Force*, p.123.

45 Ibid.

46 DEFE 69/920, Narrative.

47 DEFE 69/920, Report.

48 DEFE 69/920, Annex E3.

49 Ibid.

50 DEFE 69/920, Annex E4.

51 DEFE 69/920, Annex E2.

52 Ibid.

53 Clapp and Southby-Tailyour, *Amphibious Assault Falklands*, pp.233–34.

54 Woodward, *One Hundred Days*, pp.456–57.

55 DEFE 69/920, Annex B1.

56 DEFE 69/920, Annex E6.

57 DEFE 69/920, Annex B1.

58 DEFE 69/920, Annex E8.

59 DEFE 69/920, Report.

60 DEFE 69/920, CinC Fleet's response, 26 Oct 1982.

61 Clapp and Southby-Tailyour, *Amphibious Assault Falklands*, p.23.

62 DEFE 69/920, Annex E13.

63 DEFE 69/920, Report.

64 Clapp and Southby-Tailyour, *Amphibious Assault Falklands*, p.295.

65 DEFE 69/920, Annex F3.

66 DEFE 69/920, Report.

67 DEFE 69/920, DGST(N)'s comments on Report, Annex A to D/ ST75/166/1/3, dated 25 Nov 1982.

68 DEFE 69/920, CinC Fleet's response, 26 Oct 1982.

69 DEFE 69/920, Report.

70 Ibid.

71 DEFE 69/920, VCNS comments on report, 22 Dec 1982.

72 DEFE 69/920, CinC Fleet's response, 26 Oct 1982.

73 DEFE 69/920, A. R. M. Jaffray to CinC Fleet, 8 Feb 1983.

74 Ibid.; DEFE 69/920, Memo from TMP Stevens, Head of NLC, 9 Dec 1982.

75 *Supplement* to the *London Gazette* of 8 October 1982.

76 'Chiu Yiu Nam's Medals Were Sold Last Year', The RFA Association, http://www.rfa-association.org.uk/?option=com_content&view=article&id=298%3Asds&Itemid=8 (retrieved 3 June 2019); Puddefoot, *Fourth Force*, p.123.

77 DEFE 69/920, Jaffray letter, 8 Feb 1983.

78 'RFA Sir Galahad', Wikipedia, https://en.wikipedia.org/wiki/RFA_Sir_Galahad_(1966) (retrieved 6 June 2019).

79 Freedman, *Official History*, p.604.

9 LESSONS FROM THE CONFLICT

1 Dept of the Navy, *Lessons from the Falklands* (Washington, D.C.: United States Navy, 1983), p.23.

2 Ibid., p.12.

3 Ibid., p.2

4 Ibid., p.3.

5 Ibid., p.3, 10.

6 'Sea Dart', Wikipedia, https://en.wikipedia.org/wiki/Sea_Dart (retrieved 14 April 2020).

7 Woodward, *One Hundred Days*, pp.16–17.

8 Brown, *The Royal Navy and the Falklands War*, pp.159–60.

9 Hart Dyke, *Four Weeks in May*, p.120.

10 'Sea Wolf (missile)', Wikipedia, https://en.wikipedia.org/wiki/Sea_Wolf_(missile) (retrieved 14 April 2020).

11 'Seacat (missile)', Wikipedia, https://en.wikipedia.org/wiki/Seacat_(missile) (retrieved 14 April 2020).

12 'Argentine Aircraft Lost', Naval History, www.naval-history.net/F64-Falklands-Argentine_aircraft_lost.htm (retrieved 2 July 2019).

13 'Sea Slug (missile)', Wikipedia, https://en.wikipedia.org/wiki/Seaslug_(missile) (retrieved 14 April 2020).

14 Dept of the Navy, *Lessons from the Falklands*, p.9.

15 A. Finlan, *The Royal Navy in the Falklands Conflict and the Gulf War: Culture and Strategy* (London: Frank Cass, 2004), pp.166–67.

16 Woodward, *One Hundred Days*, p.485; Finlan, *Royal Navy in the Falklands Conflict*, p.203, 208.

17 Secretary of State for Defence, *The Falklands Campaign: The Lessons* (London: HMSO, 1982), p.19.

18 P. Pugh, 'The Empire Strikes Back: The Falklands/Malvinas Campaigns of 1982', *The Mariner's Mirror*, 93:3 (2007), pp.307–24, and citing J. L. Hannah, 'Merchant Vessel Conversions: The Falklands Campaign', *Transactions of the Royal Institute of Naval Architects* (1985).

19 Ibid., p.22, 33, 35.

20 Ibid., p.21, 35.

21 Ibid., pp.32–35.

22 Ibid., p.34.

23 Woodward, *One Hundred Days*, pp.485–86.

ADDENDUM

1 'Merco Press, Captain of the Falklands War Cruiser Dies in Argentina', https://en.mercopress.com/2009/04/23/captain-of-falklands-war-cruiser-general-belgrano-dies-in-argentina; Peter Beaumont, 'Belgrano Crew "Trigger Happy"', *The Guardian*, 25 March 2003, https://www.theguardian.com/politics/2003/may/25/uk.world (both retrieved 1 Jan 2020).

2 'Clive Ponting', Wikipedia, https://en.wikipedia.org/wiki/Clive_Ponting (retrieved 2 Feb 2020); Obituary, Clive Ponting, *The Guardian*, 7 August 2020.

3 Sam Salt obituary, *The Guardian*, https://www.theguardian.com/theguardian/2009/dec/10/sam-salt-obituary; Rear Admiral Sam Salt, Obituaries, *Daily Telegraph*, https://www.telegraph.co.uk/

news/obituaries/military-obituaries/naval-obituaries/6744685/Rear-Admiral-Sam-Salt.html (both retrieved 1 Sept 2019).

4 'Rick Jolly', Wikipedia, https://en.wikipedia.org/wiki/Rick_Jolly (retrieved 27 Sept 2019).

5 'Falklands Hero Surgeon Dies Aged 71', *The Guardian*, https://www.theguardian.com/uk-news/2018/jan/14/falklands-hero-surgeon-rick-jolly-dies-aged-71 (retrieved 27 Sept 2019).

6 'Alan West, Baron West of Spithead', Wikipedia, https://en.wikipedia.org/wiki/Alan_West,_Baron_West_of_Spithead (retrieved 24 Sept 2019).

7 Ibid.

8 Ibid.

9 Buckingham Covers, https://www.buckinghamcovers.com/celebrities/view/439-captain-n-tobin-dsc-ma-royal-navy.php (retrieved 23 July 2019); Steele Rose Legal Services, https://steelerose.co.uk/team/nick-tobin/(retrieved 23 July 2019).

10 Woodward, *One Hundred Days*, p.494.

11 'David Hart Dyke', Wikipedia, https://en.wikipedia.org/wiki/David_Hart_Dyke (retrieved 28 July 2019).

12 'Admiral Sir Michael Layard', Buckingham Covers, https://www.buckinghamcovers.com/celebrities/view/249-.php (retrieved 15 July 2020); 'Admiral Sir Michael Layard', Cranston Fine Arts, https://www.directart.co.uk/mall/profiles.php?SigID=1357 (retrieved 15 July 2020).

13 'RFA *Sir Tristram*', Wikipedia, https://en.wikipedia.org/wiki/RFA_Sir_Tristram_(L3505) (retrieved 6 June 2019).

Index

Page numbers in **bold** refer to maps.